MW00583048

Other Resources

By Dr. Micheal Spencer:
The DisFactor
Truth: Rock Solid Faith
(4-Book Series)

By Pastor Rhonda Spencer:
No More Hurt
No More Hurt Workbook
God Cannot Lie
Living a WOW Life: 31 Day Devotional

All Other Resources are Available at:
Amazon.com

His Daily Word is printed by KDP Direct Publishing (an Amazon.com company) and is available at Amazon.com and other retail outlets.

HIS DAILY WORD

A Daily Devotional With:
Dr. Micheal Spencer &
Pastor Rhonda Spencer

January 1

Are you ready? This is the very first day of a new year and you have 365 days in front of you to make it the best ever.
Before we go into the new year, we want to take the successes and failures of the last year and evaluate them. Learn from the mistakes and use the successes to build a stronger foundation.
Many times we end up looking more at the failures than the victories. You and I cannot relive the year, we cannot change the past, we cannot allow those moments to stop us from moving forward to greatness. Paul believed this too.

Philippians 3:13 Brethren, I do not count myself to have apprehended; but one thing I do, forgetting those things which are behind and reaching forward to those things which are ahead, NKJV

We do want to evaluate the past, but we cannot allow it to define us.

~Dr Micheal Spencer

IN ORDER FOR THINGS TO CHANGE,
WE MUST CHANGE WHAT WE DO.
PUT HIS WORD INTO PRACTICE EVERYDAY.

January 2

THINK BIG. THINK, *AND BELIEVE BIG!!*

1 Corinthians 2:9, But as it is written: "Eye has not seen, nor ear heard, Nor have entered into the heart of man The things which God has prepared for those who love Him." NKJV

Ephesians 3:20-21, Now to Him who is able to do exceedingly abundantly above all that we ask or think, according to the power that works in us, to Him be glory in the church by Christ Jesus to all generations, forever and ever. Amen. NKJV

Now it is time to take from last years successes and think and believe BIG!
Today is the second day of the new year, and there is a decision to be made. Will I believe that God is BIG, or will I put God in a box and shackle His best for my life?

Challenge: If there were no limitations, no money constraints, no time constraints, no past constraints, how BIG would you pray and believe today?

There are no limitations to the King of Kings,
so pray HUGEMUNGOUS!!

~Dr Micheal Spencer

January 3

Creating a FAITH WALL with your family.

Habakkuk 2:2-3, Then the Lord answered me and said:"Write the vision And make it plain on tablets, That he may run who reads it. For the vision is yet for an appointed time; But at the end it will speak, and it will not lie. Though it tarries, wait for it; Because it will surely come, It will not tarry. NKJV

Take poster board and divide it into quarters. Each quarter will represent what you are believing for this year in faith. THINK BIG!
Spiritual Growth - Make the section red - write where you want to be by the end of the year.
Possessions - Make the section green - write the physical possessions you are believing for by the end of the year.
Educational Growth - Make this section yellow - write down how you want to grow intellectually by the end of the year.
Relationship Growth - Make this section blue - write down how you want your relationships to grow by the end of the year.

Speak over it everyday, and watch the
BIG GOD, do BIG THINGS.

~Dr Micheal Spencer

January 4

Getting Stronger

Isaiah 41:10 AMP
Fear not [there is nothing to fear], for I am with you; do not look around you in terror and be dismayed, for I am your God. I will strengthen and HARDEN YOU TO DIFFICULTIES, yes, I will help you; yes, I will hold you up and retain you with My [victorious] right hand of rightness and justice.

Don't be discouraged when you have to go through hard times, you are only getting stronger. Difficult times will become easier and easier as you successfully go through each one. So YES He is toughening us up to difficulties. I love it!

Challenge: The next difficulty you encounter, rejoice in it. Really, shout praise because you are being toughened up. Keep a soft heart and let only your skin get tough.

Bible Reading: I Peter 4:12-13; Job 4:3-5; Isaiah 58:11; Romans 4:20; 2 Timothy 4:17

~Pastor Rhonda Spencer

January 5

EXPECTANCY IS THE BREEDING GROUND FOR THE MIRACULOUS

The desire is the first spark in receiving.
What if my desires are not of the Lord?
Psalm 37:4 – Delight yourself also in the Lord, And He shall give you the desires of your heart. NKJV

The way to test them is to compare those desires with the Word of God. The desire sparks the hope and the hope lights the fire called faith.

Faith is – believing it is yours before you can see it in the natural realm.
Faith is not - "I will believe it when I see it",
it is , "I believe it before I see it done in the flesh."

God is not moved by hope (future), but He is moved by faith (now).
If you aim for nothing – you can be assured that you will hit nothing.

a. Luke 5:18-20 – Paralyzed man brought by his friends
b. Matt. 8:1-4 – Leprous man
c. Matt. 8:5-10 – Centurion – spoken word

~Dr Micheal Spencer

January 6

Experiment Day

A happy heart is good medicine and a cheerful mind works healing, but a broken spirit dries up the bones. Proverbs 17:22 AMP

A glad heart makes a cheerful countenance, but by sorrow of heart the spirit is broken. Proverbs 15:13 AMP

Recently, I have been walking around smiling at people, and realizing that MOST people do not smile! People need to experience a happy, joy-filled Christian, who, even in difficult times, refuses to allow anyone or anything to steal their joy.

Then [Ezra] told them, Go your way, eat the fat, drink the sweet drink, and send portions to him for whom nothing is prepared; for this day is holy to our Lord. And be not grieved and depressed, for the joy of the Lord is your strength and stronghold.

Nehemiah 8:10 AMP

HERE IS THE EXPERIMENT:

Be the first person at work that they see with a smile. Walk around all day with a smile! Walk into your workplace with a smile, and say, “good morning everyone, it is going to be a great day”.

You will start to see that joy and happiness are a lost reality to most people, but should be the normal for those who are bathed in the presence of Jesus.

Be the Jesus of joy today, wherever you are, and MESS PEOPLE UP WITH A SMILE!

~Dr Micheal Spencer

January 7

Experiment Day 2 -We did the smiling for a day! What was the thing that most shocked you about your experience?
It is sad to see so many people who walk like zombies around this earth with no purpose or direction. They have no eternal joy, just living moment to moment, hoping for a drop of happiness, or satisfaction.
Isn't it awesome that, as God's children, that is not our life experience?
We are just visitors here on this earth – our joy is not based on our human experience, our joy and happiness are based in our home country – HEAVEN with our DADDY!
Psalm 119:19 AMP I am a stranger and a temporary resident on the earth; hide not Your commandments from me.
Ephesians 2:6 AMP And He raised us up together with Him and made us sit down together [giving us joint seating with Him] in the heavenly sphere [by virtue of our being] in Christ Jesus (the Messiah, the Anointed One).
2 Corinthians 5:20 So we are Christ's ambassadors, God making His appeal as it were through us. We [as Christ's personal representatives] beg you for His sake to lay hold of the divine favor [now offered you] and be reconciled to God.
DAY 2 of the EXPERIMENT! Ok, walk your day with a smile on your face. Today, look people in the eyes, dead in the eyes, and smile, while looking in their eyes, ask the Holy Spirit if you are to stop and share Jesus with them.
Let's not make this hard, but simple, look in their eyes smiling and ask the Spirit if you should share Jesus with them.
CHANGE THE LITERAL ATMOSPHERE WHEREVER YOU ARE WITH A SMILE AND JESUS.
~Dr Micheal Spencer

January 8

The Happy Scientist Experiment

Don't you love doing experiments?
It does two things for you.

1). Gives you and I a purpose, a directive, an assignment.
2). It helps other people experience the love of Jesus through us.

but exhort one another daily, while it is called "Today," lest any of you be hardened through the deceitfulness of sin. Hebrews 3:13 NKJV
EXHORT – means to encourage, strengthen
We have been going around smiling at everyone (and seeing that most do not smile back), showing people that we live in joy, not the emotion called happiness.

TODAY……..
Continue the smiling, then within 30 seconds I want you to compliment them. It could be their attire, their car, their family, their teeth, their work ethic, the list is huge, but find something to build, and encourage them within 30 seconds of being near them.

This does multiple things for them and us. You have an assignment, a purpose, and they are being encouraged while today is called today. Watch and wait for the opportunity to share Jesus with them.

IT IS GOING TO BE A GREAT DAY!
BE A BUILDER, NOT A DESTROYER!

~Dr Micheal Spencer

January 9

NO FEAR

Psalm 56:3-4, 8, 10-11 NKJV Whenever I am afraid, I will trust in You. In God (I will praise His word), In God I have put my trust; I will not fear. What can flesh do to me? You number my wanderings; Put my tears into Your bottle; Are they not in Your book? In God (I will praise His word), In the Lord (I will praise His word), In God I have put my trust; I will not be afraid.

He sees every tear and promises to be with you, yes the King of Kings, the All Powerful, Creator of All Things is WITH YOU.

Bible Reading: 1John 4:18; Psalm 23:4; Genesis 26:24; Deuteronomy 31:5-9; 1 Chronicles 28:20

~Pastor Rhonda Spencer

January 10

Captivate Your Thoughts!

2 Corinthians 10:5 Casting down arguments and every high thing that exalts itself against the knowledge of God, bringing every thought into captivity to the obedience of Christ.

The great battle is not with Lucifer and his lair. The true battle that defeats or deters us from God's greatness is right between our ears. The battle of the flesh will not be completed until we see Jesus face to face, but we can win!

Before we were saved, we were run and driven by our soulish man. Our thoughts, decisions and emotions were controlling our entire life. The challenge is arresting the soul and commanding it to come into order.

Spirit first, soul second, and our physical body is nothing more than a slave to whomever we yield it to. The great news is that you have been freed from the control of the flesh, and sin, but we must TAKE the control.

Romans 6:6 knowing this, that our old man was crucified with Him, that the body of sin might be done away with, that we should no longer be slaves of sin.

Step one -make the decision to be aware of our thoughts

Step two –when (not if) the thoughts start going against the Word, you get aggressive

Step three –verbally tell your mind to *shut up* in Jesus name

Step four –how does the Word tell you to think concerning that situation

Step five –OBEY the WORD!!

~Dr Micheal Spencer

January 9

NO FEAR

Psalm 56:3-4, 8, 10-11 NKJV Whenever I am afraid, I will trust in You. In God (I will praise His word), In God I have put my trust; I will not fear. What can flesh do to me? You number my wanderings; Put my tears into Your bottle; Are they not in Your book? In God (I will praise His word), In the Lord (I will praise His word), In God I have put my trust; I will not be afraid.

He sees every tear and promises to be with you, yes the King of Kings, the All Powerful, Creator of All Things is WITH YOU.

Bible Reading: 1John 4:18; Psalm 23:4; Genesis 26:24; Deuteronomy 31:5-9; 1 Chronicles 28:20

~Pastor Rhonda Spencer

January 10

Captivate Your Thoughts!

2 Corinthians 10:5 Casting down arguments and every high thing that exalts itself against the knowledge of God, bringing every thought into captivity to the obedience of Christ.

The great battle is not with Lucifer and his lair. The true battle that defeats or deters us from God's greatness is right between our ears. The battle of the flesh will not be completed until we see Jesus face to face, but we can win!

Before we were saved, we were run and driven by our soulish man. Our thoughts, decisions and emotions were controlling our entire life. The challenge is arresting the soul and commanding it to come into order. Spirit first, soul second, and our physical body is nothing more than a slave to whomever we yield it to. The great news is that you have been freed from the control of the flesh, and sin, but we must TAKE the control.

Romans 6:6 knowing this, that our old man was crucified with Him, that the body of sin might be done away with, that we should no longer be slaves of sin.

Step one -make the decision to be aware of our thoughts

Step two –when (not if) the thoughts start going against the Word, you get aggressive

Step three –verbally tell your mind to *shut up* in Jesus name

Step four –how does the Word tell you to think concerning that situation

Step five –OBEY the WORD!!

~Dr Micheal Spencer

January 11

THOUGHTS.....Did you ever think about Adam and Eve, and that in the Garden they had everything they needed, and everything they wanted?
Did you ever think that they had unrestrained ability to be in the literal, physical, presence of God without dying. What changed all that?
God gave one edict – do not eat of the tree in the middle of the garden or you will surely die. This created the option for free will love or rejection. Then Satan came to Eve with a THOUGHT.
Genesis 3:1-7, Now the serpent was more cunning than any beast of the field which the Lord God had made. And he said to the woman, "Has God indeed said, 'You shall not eat of every tree of the garden (*Satan deposited a seed of truth, yet planted thoughts of doubt, wonder, questioning Fathers truth*)'?" And the woman said to the serpent, "We may eat the fruit of the trees of the garden; but of the fruit of the tree which is in the midst of the garden, God has said, 'You shall not eat it, nor shall you touch it, lest you die.'" Then the serpent said to the woman, "You will not surely die. For God knows that in the day you eat of it your eyes will be opened, and you will be like God, knowing good and evil (*Again a thought of questioning God at His Word and motives*)."- So when the woman saw (*thoughts change your entire landscape! Thoughts can totally change how you view life, Christ, and even yourself*) that the tree was good for food, that it was pleasant to the eyes, and a tree desirable to make one wise, she took of its fruit and ate. She also gave to her husband with her, and he ate. Then the eyes of both of them were opened, and they knew that they were naked; and they sewed fig leaves together and made themselves coverings.
Eyes were opened – not physical eyes – their thoughts were now corrupt, their minds were now messed up. They went from perfect thoughts – to now they can think evil.
Everything has changed – now who's thoughts will you choose?
GOD THOUGHTS-SELF THOUGHTS-DEVIL THOUGHTS

~*Dr. Micheal Spencer*

January 12

His Love Never Quits

Psalm 136:1-9, 23-26 MSG Thank God! He deserves your thanks. His love never quits. Thank the God of all gods, His love never quits. Thank the Lord of all lords. His love never quits. Thank the miracle-working God, His love never quits. The God whose skill formed the cosmos, His love never quits. The God who laid out earth on ocean foundations, His love never quits. The God who filled the skies with light, His love never quits. The sun to watch over the day, His love never quits. Moon and stars as guardians of the night, His love never quits. God remembered us when we were down, His love never quits. Rescued us from the trampling boot, His love never quits. Takes care of everyone in time of need. His love never quits. Thank God, who did it all! His love never quits!

You have never had an unloved moment, His love never quits.

Challenge: Remind yourself; others may have quit on you, but He isn't going anywhere. Say it out loud, "HIS LOVE NEVER QUITS".

Bible Reading: Romans 8:34-39; John 15:12-14; 1 Corinthians 13:8

~Pastor Rhonda Spencer

January 13

Spiritual Authority

Matthew 8:5-10, Now when Jesus had entered Capernaum, a centurion came to Him, pleading with Him, saying, "Lord, my servant is lying at home paralyzed, dreadfully tormented." And Jesus said to him, "I will come and heal him." The centurion answered and said, "Lord, I am not worthy that You should come under my roof. But only speak a word, and my servant will be healed. For I also am a man under authority, having soldiers under me. And I say to this one, 'Go,' and he goes; and to another, 'Come,' and he comes; and to my servant, 'Do this,' and he does it." When Jesus heard it, He marveled, and said to those who followed, "Assuredly, I say to you, I have not found such great faith, not even in Israel!

The onslaught against submitting to authority is a diabolical plot to divert God's church from its call and purpose. Where there is no submission to authority, there can be no order, or trusted release of authority and power.

Jesus was not just impressed by the Centurion, but marveled! What did he marvel at? The man understood authority, and the release of the power. He understood that Jesus was not working on His behalf, and that He was backed by a greater authority.

When we submit to authority, we can be trusted with authority.

Rebellion is the nature of Satan. There are two types of rebellion: 1. Outward – don't tell me what to do! 2. Passive rebellion – I sat down like you told me, but inside I'm still standing up.

Passive rebellion is the most dangerous because it is hidden to man, but not to the Father. Today ask the Spirit of God if there is any root of rebellion in your heart. Repent, realign, and watch the anointing increase in your life.

Those who submit to authority can be trusted with authority and power!

John 3:30 He must increase, but I must decrease.

~Dr Micheal Spencer

January 14

Healthy?

Proverbs 3:5-11 MSG Trust God from the bottom of your heart; don't try to figure out everything on your own. Listen for God's voice in everything you do, everywhere you go; he's the one who will keep you on track. Don't assume that you know it all. Run to God! Run from evil! Your body will glow with health, your very bones will vibrate with life! Honor God with everything you own; give him the first and the best. Your barns will burst, your wine vats will brim over. But don't, dear friend, resent God's discipline; don't sulk under his loving correction.

Run from anything that isn't in God's Word. Evil can disguise itself as light and good, beware that nothing creeps into your life to take your best away from God. Many times it's subtle and we wonder how we got where we are.

Challenge: Work on your health by walking in God's way and giving Him your first and best.

Bible Reading: 1 Timothy 4:7-9; Psalm 38:3; Psalm 3:7-9; Proverbs 15:30

~Pastor Rhonda Spencer

January 15

The SPIRITUAL LAW OF FAITH

FAITH- God called those things which were not as though they already are (Romans 4:17), without faith it is impossible to please Him (Hebrews 11:6), faith produces results (Matthew 21:21).
These are just a few.

Well I will believe it when I see it!
That does not make sense!
I don't understand!
No matter what you understand, it doesn't change the LAW!
It's just like electricity. You cannot see it (sometimes you see a shazaam expression), but majority of times, because of understanding, and laws, we are able to make it work on our behalf. We have lights, heat, water, so many evidences of the law of electricity, but when it is not understood, it can kill, or simply not produce. When there is a short in the electric line, the power is not working. When abused, people have died, when not activated people walk around in the dark.
The LAW OF FAITH needs to be understood, grown and matured so people know God, please God, and so they don't walk in the dark.

Grow in faith!!

~Dr Micheal Spencer

January 16

FAITH – Time.......

Mark 5:22-23
And behold, one of the rulers of the synagogue came, Jairus by name. And when he saw Him, he fell at His feet and begged Him earnestly, saying, "My little daughter lies at the point of death. Come and lay Your hands on her, that she may be healed, and she will live."
Mark 5:42 Immediately the girl arose and walked, for she was twelve years of age. And they were overcome with great amazement.
What an awesome example of FAITH, so much of an example that the Father made sure it was in His Word for us to learn from.
BUT...we forget easily that much happened between verse 22 & verse 42!
TIME, CIRCUMSTANCES, INTERRUPTIONS...
So many people give up between those two verses. They abandon their faith, their confession. They thwart their miracle on the threshold because of those three elements. Actually, what we do is cancel out our own supernatural manifestation of our desire by taking our eyes off Jesus.
Mark 5:36 As soon as Jesus heard the word that was spoken, He said to the ruler of the synagogue, "Do not be afraid; only believe."
At this moment Jairus could have given up, allowed the fact to disembark him from his miracle. Jairus chose instead to not allow fear, doubt, and even the truth to stop his faith in Jesus. He did not take his eyes or trust off of Christ, and because of that, his baby was raised from the dead.
Don't allow TIME, CIRCUMSTANCES, or INTERRUPTIONS to take your eyes or trust off Jesus.

~Dr Micheal Spencer

January 17

FAITH–Don't Let Others Steal Your Miracle

Mark 5:39-40 When He came in, He said to them, " Why make this commotion and weep? The child is not dead, but sleeping." And they ridiculed Him. But when He had put them all outside, He took the father and the mother of the child, and those who were with Him, and entered where the child was lying.

When Jairus and Jesus arrived at the house where the body of his daughter was located there were certain supernatural choices made.

1. Jairus made the decision to put his faith in Jesus.
2. He made the confession out of his mouth, that first came from his heart, "if you lay hands On my daughter, she will live."
3. When the situation did not get better, only worse, he chose to obey Jesus, "do not fear, only believe."
4. He chose to look to Jesus rather than look even at the facts. Jesus never told us to deny the facts,
but to declare the TRUTH!

Here is another key that Jesus taught when He got to Jairus house.

Jesus declared the TRUTH, "Why make this commotion and weep? The child is not dead, but sleeping."

When He did this people mocked Him, so what did He do? He kicked them out of the room.

When you are in faith and in a position of making a confession, do not just let anyone speak into your life.

Surround yourself with faith talkers, with faith walkers, not doubt casters.

Even if they are Christians, if they are doubt talkers, then subtract yourself from them and only surround yourself with people that live and walk the Word, and not the flesh.

~Dr Micheal Spencer

January 18

Faith – confession

Mark 5:22-24 And behold, one of the rulers of the synagogue came, Jairus by name. And when he saw Him, he fell at His feet and begged Him earnestly, saying, "My little daughter lies at the point of death. Come and lay Your hands on her, that she may be healed, and she will live." So Jesus went with him, and a great multitude followed Him and thronged Him.

This man came to Jesus with great desperation because girl his baby was dying, and there was no hope. He had heard about the miracles, the healing, and came to Jesus very focused and with clear direction. When he came to Jesus he did not mutter, or stutter, or hope, he came with his mind made up. Jairus declared his heart of faith, "Come and lay Your hands on her, that she may be healed, and she will live!"

His faith confession did not waiver, and Jesus went with him to raise his daughter. When faith turns Jesus, He will complete the miracle.

On the way, distractions came, and then the worst natural news came.

Mark 5:35, While He was still speaking, some came from the ruler of the synagogue's house who said, "Your daughter is dead. Why trouble the Teacher any further?"

I love Jesus! Jairus faith aimed Him, distractions did not change that fact. Circumstances, truth, negative news did not change Jesus direction!

He then looks at Jairus and said Mark 5:36, As soon as Jesus heard the word that was spoken, He said to the ruler of the synagogue, " Do not be afraid; only believe." Only believe what? The faith confession when he first came to Jesus! This is a key to the raising of his dead daughters life. He did not allow circumstances, truth, fear, distractions to change his confession of faith.

Faith changed Jesus direction to go heal her, and Jairus faith, and refusal to stop believing brought the completion of the miracle!

KEEP YOUR CONFESSION

~Dr Micheal Spencer

January 19

FAITH – YOUR SPIRITUAL MUSCLE

1. Our muscle can grow and lose strength, but rarely remains the same.
   a. Our faith also has the ability to grow and lose strength, but rarely stays the same.
2. Our faith muscle can be measured by our trust in our Dad & His Word.
3. He shows in the Word that there are different strengths.
   a. MEASURE OF FAITH
   Romans 12:3, For I say, through the grace given to me, to everyone who is among you, not to think of himself more highly than he ought to think, but to think soberly, as God has dealt to each one a measure of faith.
   b. LITTLE FAITH
   Matthew6:30-31, Now if God so clothes the grass of the field, which today is, and tomorrow is thrown into the oven, will He not much more clothe you, O you of little faith. "Therefore do not worry, saying, 'What shall we eat?' or 'What shall we drink?' or 'What shall we wear?'
      i. If you are always worried about the basics of life, then the Lord says you have little faith.
      Matthew14:31-32, And immediately Jesus stretched out His hand and caught him, and said to him, "O you of little faith, why did you doubt?" And when they got into the boat, the wind ceased.
   c. GREAT FAITH
   Matt. 8:10, When Jesus heard it, He marveled, & said to those who followed, "Assuredly, I say to you, I have not found such great faith, not even in Israel!
   Matthew 15:28, Then Jesus answered & said to her, "O woman, great is your faith! Let it be to you as you desire." & her daughter was healed from that very hour.
   d. INCREASE FAITH
   Luke 17:5-6, And the apostles said to the Lord, "Increase our faith." So the Lord said, "If you have faith as a mustard seed, you can say to this mulberry tree, 'Be pulled up by the roots and be planted in the sea,' and it would obey you
   From a weak, droopy muscle to a solid powerful muscle.

~Dr Micheal Spencer

January 20

HOW TO INCREASE YOUR FAITH MUSCLE

1. You must first FEED your muscles properly so that when you exercise them they will have the right fuel to increase in strength.
2. If you do not feed your muscles, they will deteriorate, not gain.
3. HOW DO YOU FEED YOUR SPIRITUAL MUSCLES?
   a. The Word of God
      i. Romans 10:17, So then faith comes by hearing, and hearing by the word of God.

      ii. Hearing the Word of God
         >Sunday's services
         Hebrews 10:23-25, Let us hold fast the confession of our hope without wavering, for He who promised is faithful. And let us consider one another in order to stir up love and good works, not forsaking the assembling of ourselves together, as is the manner of some, but exhorting one another, and so much the more as you see the Day approaching.
         >Daily Reading the Word
         >Teaching Classes
         >Bible Studies
         >Teaching on CD
         >Devour the Word

Those who choose not to FEED, will never increase, no increase, NO VICTORY

GET INTO THE WORD THIS WEEK!!!

~Dr Micheal Spencer

January 21

FAITH IS

NOW FAITH is the assurance (the confirmation, the title deed) of the things [we] hope for, being the proof of things [we] do not see and the conviction of their reality [faith perceiving as real fact what is not revealed to the senses]. For by [faith--trust and holy fervor born of faith] the men of old had divine testimony borne to them and obtained a good report. Hebrews 11:1, 2 AMP
Faith is
Faith is the NOW!
Possessing right now, what you cannot yet physically touch on this planet.
How do I do that?
When things are difficult, you have a need, or even a desire, the first thing is to make sure Daddy wants you to have it. How do you do that? Ask Him, the Holy Spirit will give you a red or green light. That feeling in your spirit that says, "all is good" or "that nasty feeling" that means no. You must also check it with the Word! The Word and God ALWAYS agree!!!!! God told me to rob a bank...lol. Does that agree with the Bible? NO! Then, no matter what you feel, it is NOT God's will.

Once you know it's Daddy's will, you are ready to grab it out of the eternal and make it manifest in the natural.

~Dr Micheal Spencer

January 22

FAITH IS THE CURRENCY OF HEAVEN

I am not saying you can buy your way to heaven, or that it is about money. Money is nothing more than an exchange to acquire what you desire.

Just like on earth there is a currency, so in heaven there are PRINCIPLES, to obtain what God has for us. Everything we have from God is by faith – understanding faith, and how to increase it means we can exchange the currency of heaven
Looking at it like a currency – you go to a place and do what has to be done to obtain currency to pay and acquire what you want to purchase.
God is not moved by:
Need OR Hope
God is moved by faith
Hebrews 11:6, But without faith it is impossible to please Him, for he who comes to God must believe that He is, and that He is a rewarder of those who diligently seek Him.

FAITH MOVES GOD, AND PLEASES GOD

EVERYTHING WE HAVE IS BY FAITH:
Salvation is by faith
The Baptism in the Holy Ghost is by faith
Healing is by faith
Faith is the currency of heaven to acquire from the hand of God
We must have MORE faith in God!
We must learn and grow to trust Him more!
IF HE SAYS IT, I BELIEVE IT, AND THAT'S SO!

~Dr Micheal Spencer

January 23

Faith is....What Next?

Now that we know that faith is the currency of heaven, and that we need to trust the truth of the Word. We need to know if what we are asking for is the will of God.
1 John 5:14-15 Now this is the confidence that we have in Him, that if we ask anything according to His will, He hears us. And if we know that He hears us, whatever we ask, we know that we have the petitions that we have asked of Him.
When we know that what we are asking for is the will of God, then we take the Word of God and use it. You can trust the Word of God!
You must be convinced in your spirit that it is the desire of God to give you your desire or need or faith cannot be released. When you are convinced through the Word and through prayer that the green light is on, then you can release your faith to obtain from the eternal.
HOW DO I RELEASE MY FAITH TO RECEIVE?
And Jesus answered them, Truly I say to you, if you have faith (a firm relying trust) and do not doubt, you will not only do what has been done to the fig tree, but even if you say to this mountain, Be taken up and cast into the sea, it will be done. And whatever you ask for in prayer, having faith and [really] believing, you will receive. (Matthew 21:21, 22 AMP)
And God said, Let there be light; and there was light. (Genesis 1:3 AMP) Words are the release of your faith. It is like an oil well, until it is released from the well, the wealth cannot come forth.
We release faith by speaking, declaring, decreeing with confidence in prayer, what we are wanting from heaven.
Matthew 7:7 Ask, and it will be given to you; seek, and you will find; knock, and it will be opened to you.

~Dr Micheal Spencer

January 24

Faith- It's Time To Grow Up

1 John 5:4 For whatever is born of God overcomes the world. And this is the victory that has overcome the world—our faith.

OUR FAITH IS THE VICTORY THAT OVERCOMES!
I have seen where some people put their faith in faith.

I have seen where some people put their faith in a confession.

Our faith that overcomes the world and its system is our faith in what God, our Daddy can do.
Faith is not a magic word – Faith is TRUST.
Faith is the action word for TRUSTING that someone will do what they say they will do.
So our faith is what gives us the ability to look at the obstacles of the world, and in our lives and OVERCOME (succeed, prevail, defeat) those obstacles.
So understanding faith is a mandatory to be able to live a consistent life of VICTORY.

~Dr Micheal Spencer

January 25

THEY HAVE NO SAY IN IT...

Nehemiah 2:20 MSG I shot back, "The God-of-Heaven will make sure we succeed. We're his servants and we're going to work, rebuilding. You can keep your nose out of it. You get no say in this.

Christians, be strong and courageous. Look at those who have gone before us and how they were strong and courageous even in the all out attacks around them.

Daniel, a man that followed God's ordinances...people hated him for it, his peers even. People planned how they could trap him, trick him and cause his destruction. Their plans against him went all the way up to the king...yet he was not moved, he was fixed....not on what they did against him....he was fixed on the Word of God and obedience to it.... THEREFORE THEY HAD NO SAY IN IT!

Nehemiah, a man on a mission for God to rebuild; as if it wasn't enough to inspire people to work with him and keep them all focused, he had a constant onslaught against him trying to stop him. Nehemiah was mocked, taunted and their desire was to kill him....yet, he wouldn't even come away from his work for a moment to give their threats attention. THEREFORE THEY HAD NO SAY IN IT!

And our best example yet JESUS, he only did good....yet even his closest friends betrayed Him when he needed them the most, he was beaten and mocked....BUT STILL He was willing to die for those very same people....
THEREFORE THEY HAD NO SAY IN IT!

CHRISTIANS....No one in this world can take your love, joy, peace or stop you from your destiny if you don't allow them to have a say in it...If they are not the source of those things and JESUS is then don't miss a beat,
THEY HAVE NO SAY IN IT!

Challenge: Don't allow what anyone says about you; other than the Word of God, direct your day.

~Pastor Rhonda Spencer

January 26

Words determine Your Result

A word out of your mouth may seem of no account, but it can accomplish nearly anything-or destroy it!

James 3:5-6 MSG A careless or wrongly placed word out of your mouth can do that. By our speech we can ruin the world, turn harmony to chaos, throw mud on a reputation, send the whole world up in smoke and go up in smoke with it, smoke right from the pit of hell.

We are the only created things that were made in God's image and His likeness. We are the only creation that speaks like our Creator.
God used the spoken words to fashion the planet!
Romans 4:17b, God, who gives life to the dead and calls those things which do not exist as though they did;

Words activate or cancel our faith. How is that possible? Matthew 12:34B, For out of the abundance of the heart the mouth speaks.

The words spoken are the capsule containing the release of faith, or the cancellation with doubt.
Watch your mouth, feed your faith, and speak the Word of Faith!

~Dr Micheal Spencer

January 27

Demonic or Just Life

How do you know if the bad stuff happening is demonic or just life happening?
This question is simply revealed.
2 Corinthians 2:11 lest Satan should take advantage of us; for we are not ignorant of his devices.

We know that by nature Father will NEVER use what was paid for on the cross against us in our lives.
WHAT WAS ACCOMPLISHED ON THE CROSS?
1). Freedom from sin (Jesus will never tempt you with sin, James 1:12-15) THE BLOOD
2). Jesus will never put sickness or disease on your body (1 Peter 2:24). THE BODY
3). Freedom from poverty (2 Corinthians 8:9). Poverty is part of the curse, and not for the saints.

We know the basic tactics, devices of Satan.
1). Offense 2). Division 3). Separation 4). Seclusion
Our flesh (mind, emotions, and will) are the enemy of God.
Romans 8:6 AMP "Now the mind of the flesh [which is sense and reason without the Holy Spirit] is death [death that comprises all the miseries arising from sin, both here and hereafter]. But the mind of the [Holy] Spirit is life and [soul] peace [both now and forever]."

~Dr Micheal Spencer

January 28

Demonic, or Just Life. Pt 2

How do you know if the bad stuff happening is demonic or just life happening? We answered this question yesterday. We know the basic tactics, devices of Satan.
1). Offense 2). Division 3). Separation 4). Seclusion
THIS IS HOW YOU KNOW IF IT IS DEMONIC.
When one of the blessings of the Christ is being attacked in your life you need to take immediate action in the spirit. If it is drawing you away from Jesus, His house, or your anointed purpose, it is demonic!
Ephesians 6:11-13 AMP Put on God's whole armor [the armor of a heavy-armed soldier which God supplies], that you may be able successfully to stand up against [all] the strategies and the deceits of the devil. For we are not wrestling with flesh and blood [contending only with physical opponents], but against the despotisms, against the powers, against [the master spirits who are] the world rulers of this present darkness, against the spirit forces of wickedness in the heavenly (supernatural) sphere. Therefore put on God's complete armor, that you may be able to resist and stand your ground on the evil day [of danger], and, having done all [the crisis demands], to stand [firmly in your place].

Because we know Jesus will NEVER use what He delivered us from to tempt or kill us, we know it has to come from the diabolical world.
Take an aggressive posture and REBUKE THE DEVIL, AND HE WILL FLEE FROM YOU!
Be aggressive against the thief!
John 10:10 AMP The thief comes only in order to steal and kill and destroy. I came that they may have and enjoy life, and have it in abundance (to the full, till it overflows).
~Dr Micheal Spencer

January 29

A WAY OUT

1 Corinthians 10:13 NKJV No temptation has overtaken you except such as is common to man; but God is faithful, who will not allow you to be tempted beyond what you are able, but with the temptation will also make the way of escape, that you may be able to bear it.

...There is hope, He always provides a way out.

Challenge: Don't fall into temptation, look for the way out that God WILL provide. Pray, stand still, don't give in, you will find the way of escape. It's His Word and He holds His Word above His name.

Bible Reading: Deuteronomy 30:18-20; Deuteronomy 28:25; Matthew 7:12-14

~Pastor Rhonda Spencer

January 30

Be A World Changer!

The other day I was with a family and the child said, "Caring is sharing".
Getting that into them at a young age creates a person who is God-like. God loves to share, God loves to give, God loves to bless.
We live in a world today where God has become of very little importance. He has become a religious icon, instead of a living King. This is evidenced by how our world is so intensely hostile, and loaded with greed. In the Kingdom of God we have slid into the same mindset. We give our lives to Jesus, He makes a difference, He is alive to us, BUT, we do not share the greatest message ever given.
We need to become like the Samaritan woman who met Jesus at the well. She had such a life change that she ran back to her city and started telling everyone that she met Jesus. The city had a transformation because of one person. Read this, her testimony changed a city!!!!!

John 4:39-42 And many of the Samaritans of that city believed in Him because of the word of the woman who testified, "He told me all that I ever did." So when the Samaritans had come to Him, they urged Him to stay with them; and He stayed there two days. And many more believed because of His own word.
Then they said to the woman, "Now we believe, not because of what you said, for we ourselves have heard Him and we know that this is indeed the Christ, the Savior of the world."

Would your testimony change a house, a street, work, city, county, region, state?

~Dr Micheal Spencer

January 31

A GREAT DAY TO LAUGH!

Life can get really serious! INTENSE! EXTREME!

Proverbs 15:13 NLT A glad heart makes a happy face; a broken heart crushes the spirit.

The problem is when we allow life to get so intense for so long that we lose our joy and our smile.

"You do not understand, Pastor, how hard life is right now!"

"Pastor, everything is collapsing around me. I have nothing to smile about!"

I'm not talking laugh like LOL...
I mean laugh like you might pee yourself!
HONESTLY! There are times you have to make a decision to simply LAUGH.
If you are going through difficult times, then take a second and LAUGH in the devil's face right now! Tell him he will never win because Jesus already defeated him.

If you have not laughed because of life, then it is time to get your smile on!

Proverbs 17:22 MSG A cheerful disposition is good for your health; gloom and doom leave you bone-tired.

CHOOSE TO LAUGH TODAY!
LAUGH AT THE DEVIL! LAUGH AT YOURSELF!
LAUGH AT A SITUATION! LAUGH, LAUGH, LAUGH, IT HAS BEEN TOO LONG!

~Dr Micheal Spencer

February 1

Bursting a Button

Deuteronomy 32:9-10 For the LORD's portion is His people; Jacob is the place of His inheritance.10 "He found him in a desert land And in the wasteland, a howling wilderness; He encircled him, He instructed him, He kept him as the apple of His eye.
WE ARE HIS KIDS. It is so easy to forget that we have an amazing DAD!
We are the APPLE OF HIS EYE.
Deuteronomy 32:9-10 The original Hebrew for this idiom was 'iyshown 'ayin, and can be literally translated as "Little Man of the Eye." This is a reference to the tiny reflection of yourself that you can see in other people's pupils.
Matthew 7:9-11, Or what man is there among you who, if his son asks for bread, will give him a stone? Or if he asks for a fish, will he give him a serpent? If you then, being evil, know how to give good gifts to your children, how much more will your Father who is in heaven give good things to those who ask Him!
DADDY IS FOR YOU. Father is not out to beat you down and rip you up. He is not here to use you and abuse you. We have the Greatest cheering section out of this world! FATHER GOD IS SHOUTING OVER YOU!
"For the Lord your God is a mighty Savior. He will give you victory. He will rejoice over you in great gladness; He will love you and not accuse you. Is that a joyous choir I hear? No, it is the Lord Himself exulting over you, in happy song." Zephaniah 3:17
Jeremiah 32:41, Oh how I'll rejoice in them! Oh how I'll delight in doing good things for them! Heart and soul!'
Psalm 35:27, Let them shout for joy and be glad, Who favor my righteous cause; And let them say continually, "Let the LORD be magnified, Who has pleasure in the prosperity of His servant."
Today if you feel alone, or that you are just getting tired......
LISTEN...He is shouting for you!

~Dr Micheal Spencer

February 2

Don't know what to do?

Proverbs 2:6, 8-9, 11-12, 20-21 MSG
God gives out Wisdom free, is plainspoken in Knowledge and Understanding. He keeps his eye on all who live honestly, and pays special attention to his loyally committed ones. So now you can pick out what's true and fair, find all the good trails! Good Sense will scout ahead for danger, Insight will keep an eye out for you. They'll keep you from making wrong turns, or following the bad directions So-join the company of good men and women, keep your feet on the tried and true paths. It's the men who walk straight who will settle this land, the women with integrity who will last here.

LORD HELP ME TO WALK STRAIGHT ACCORDING TO YOUR WORD, WITH INTEGRITY. GIVE ME INSIGHT AND KEEP ME FROM WRONG TURNS.

Bible Reading: Psalm 1:1, Psalm 26:1, Proverbs 25:6

~Pastor Rhonda Spencer

February 3

Do you feel the squeeze?

So don't lose a minute in building on what you've been given, complementing your basic faith with good character, spiritual understanding, alert discipline, passionate patience, reverent wonder, warm friendliness, and generous love, each dimension fitting into and developing the others. With these qualities active and growing in your lives, no grass will grow under your feet, no day will pass without its reward as you mature in your experience of our Master Jesus. Without these qualities you can't see what's right before you, oblivious that your old sinful life has been wiped off the books. 2 Peter 1:5-9 MSG

Each day we are faced with some type of issue or a difficult decision that is placed before us. Some are easy, but many are intense and can cause fretting, anxiety, confusion and questioning. Here is an important fact, without the orange being squeezed, you will never see what's inside. Trials and tribulations are never fun, but without them most people will never see what's inside themselves.
Consider it a sheer gift, friends, when tests and challenges come at you from all sides. You know that under pressure, your faith-life is forced into the open and shows its true colors. So don't try to get out of anything prematurely. Let it do its work so you become mature and well-developed, not deficient in any way. (James 1:2-4 MSG)
Remember! Father will never use what He paid for on the cross as a trial or tribulation. He can use them for good, but they are not from Him.
When your being squeezed allow the personality of the Spirit to come out.

~Dr Micheal Spencer

February 4

TODAY is an IMPORTANT DAY.

Be bold, stand up, share God's love, do good, go the extra mile. Your life, your children's lives and others lives depend on it!
TODAY, AND EVERY DAY, IS AN IMPORTANT DAY.

Teach us to realize the brevity of life.
(Psalms 90:12 NLT)

BREVITY:
Shortness of time or duration; briefness: the brevity of human life; the quality of expressing much in few words.

You are powerful, valuable and important!!!! Give a smile, share a hug, pray in faith with someone, call someone and encourage them, SERVE GOD with your day (not yourself).

~Pastor Rhonda Spencer

February 5

I'm In A RUT!

I am sure you have heard people say, "I'm in a RUT." WHAT IS A RUT?

It is a grave with both ends knocked out. It reminds me of one of the episodes of Duck Dynasty when they were teasing Will that he was no longer a redneck, but now was citified. He was driving and was going to show the men that this was not the case. He swerved into a field and started doing donuts with his truck, slinging mud everywhere! He then went into one of the ruts that he created and got STUCK. He tried forward, reverse, being pushed, and nothing worked. They got out of the truck and started to walk, and then Will fell flat in the mud! It was funny, but, not if this is happening in real life.

I have some GREAT NEWS for you TODAY! No matter how spiritual you are, no matter how many years you serve Jesus, there will always come some dry, stuck, seasons in your life. WHEW...isn't it good to know you are not alone?

The dry, rutty feeling is not the problem, because it will happen in your life multiple times. The problem is what you are going to do about that WHEN it comes.

Many people react in the, "I'M GIVING UP" mindset, but if that is what you do then you will never get past that dry, rutty spot in your spiritual life. You must make the determination that no matter how you FEEL, you are moving forward, never backward. It is a choice, a decision, that backwards, reverse has been dismantled in my life. There is not an option for that direction.

SO, WHAT DO WE DO TO GET OUT OF THE RUT? WHAT DO WE DO TO GET OUT OF THAT DRY PLACE?

One of the non-popular answers is CONSISTENCY. The fundamentals are always what keep us from getting into the mud. They are also that chain to hook onto when we seem to be stuck. DO NOT go out and just try new things to get out of the rut, because then we are training ourselves that experiences are the answer. There are Christians that jump from one experience to another to stay "fresh", but they never grow roots and mature. Stay steady. Get into the Word (make yourself if you have too), make your appointment with God daily to talk with Him, stay consistent.

DO NOT STOP GOING TO CHURCH!!

Be the tortoise, not the rabbit, and you will finish the race!

~Dr Micheal Spencer

February 6

Don't Run, Quit or Have a Pity Party

When you're in the fire and it gets hot, YOU'RE GOING TO A NEW LEVEL. The hot fire brings the dross (junk/impurities) to the surface....THIS IS A GOOD THING. Scrape off the dross and CONTINUE upward and onward, you've been being purified. Complain, run or quit and you've felt all that pain for nothing, then you'll have to go through it again someday. EMBRACE IT AND DEAL WITH THE JUNK . IT'S A GOOD THING. You'll come out better; pearls form under pressure, diamonds hold up under pressure and metals become more precious through the fire.

Proverbs 25:4 Remove the impurities from silver, and the sterling will be ready for the silversmith.

1 Peter 1:7
so that the proof of your faith, being more precious than gold which is perishable, even though tested by fire, may be found to result in praise and glory and honor at the revelation of Jesus Christ;

2 Corinthians 4:8-9, 16-18 We are hard-pressed on every side, yet not crushed; we are perplexed, but not in despair; persecuted, but not forsaken; struck down, but not destroyed. Therefore we do not lose heart. Even though our outward man is perishing, yet the inward man is being renewed day by day. For our light affliction, which is but for a moment, is working for us a far more exceeding and eternal weight of glory, while we do not look at the things which are seen, but at the things which are not seen. For the things which are seen are temporary, but the things which are not seen are eternal.

~Pastor Rhonda Spencer

February 7

Thoughts Change Our Landscape

Proverbs 23:7
For as he thinks in his heart, so is he. "Eat and drink!" he says to you, But his heart is not with you.

Today we are going to minister the Word of God on the THOUGHTS of man, and how they enable faith to be released, or they destroy faith before God can show up on the scene for a miracle or answered prayer.

Thoughts are amazing – Every one of us are one thought away from success – one thought away from a cure for cancer, one thought away from a new business, one thought away from healing, one thought away from that new idea that would transform our entire lives and those surrounding you.
Don't give me money, give me a thought from God!!
This church started with a God thought!

If you think little, you will get little!
If you think defeat, you will be defeated!
If you think poverty, you will live in poverty!
If you think in bitterness, you will live in bitterness!
If you think the Word, you will live the Word!

YOU ARE ONE THOUGHT FROM WHAT GOD DESIRES FOR YOU!

~Dr Micheal Spencer

February 8

Personal Prayer Time is a MUST

Your time alone with God should be your priority of the day for 3 reasons
You were CREATED to have fellowship with God

John 15:15, No longer do I call you servants, for a servant does not know what his master is doing; but I have called you friends, for all things that I heard from My Father I have made known to you.

Jesus DIED to make a relationship even possible

1 Corinthians. 1:9, God is faithful, by whom you were called into the fellowship of His Son, Jesus Christ our Lord.

You cannot be a HEALTHY, growing Christian unless you spend time with Jesus.

~Pastor Rhonda Spencer

February 9

TODAY! What are you going to do with it?

The Word of God covers 2 judgements.

The Christian will be going to the Bema Seat (Judgement Seat of Christ), and we will be judged for our works (what we have done, and have not done for Jesus), and our words. We will not be judged for sin because they have been forgiven.
Ravenhill said, "The most sobering thought for a Christian is the judgement."
Today you have a purpose, a mission! You are a key to someone's eternity.

1. Take 15, and build your relationship with Jesus.
2. Take 10, and do something that will have eternal value.
3. Encourage someone who is struggling with their walk with Jesus.
4. Share with a non-believer how Jesus has changed your life.
5. Enjoy your journey with the joy of the Lord and people will come to you today!

But instead warn (admonish, urge, and encourage) one another every day, as long as it is called Today, that none of you may be hardened [into settled rebellion] by the deceitfulness of sin [by the fraudulence, the stratagem, the trickery which the delusive glamor of his sin may play on him]. Hebrews 3:13 AMP
Don't let TODAY end with no eternal value!

~Dr Micheal Spencer

February 10

THE PRESENCE OF GOD

Your most important moments are spent in the presence of God...that is the place you will find what your life needs....

For she said to herself, If only I may touch His garment, I shall be made well. But Jesus turned around, and when He saw her He said, Be of good cheer, daughter; your faith has made you well. And the woman was made well from that hour.
Matthew 9:21, 22 NKJV

Don't forget Him today, it's the very thing you need...

MOMENTS IN HIS PRESENCE will cause divine, supernatural power and destiny to happen. Glory to Glory! Move out of your dry place, your desolation and get into His presence as often as you can. Let's live in power and overflow.

~Pastor Rhonda Spencer

February 11

Consistency is Everything

Hebrews 13:8
Jesus Christ is the same yesterday, today, and forever.
Isn't it an amazing quality that brings such peace, what is that quality, CONSISTENCY.

Jesus is constant and consistent. It gives us confidence that whenever we need Him, or want to talk with Him, He is right there. We also have confidence that what He says He will accomplish, will be accomplished. His consistency allows us to trust so much that we can collapse in His arms during intense times. He is our constant!!

What about us? We desire Him to be constant, but can He rely upon us, or is this just a one sided relationship? In today's Christianity, to get most Christians to come to God's house two weeks in a row is miraculous, the national average on consistent giving has dropped to only 2% of a tithe, ministry responsibilities are passed off in our sluggish attitudes. Jesus is calling His house, His family, His army back to CONSISTENCY.
Can Jesus rely on you, or do you just rely on Him?

~Dr Micheal Spencer

February 12

The Path That Few Find

So, chosen by God for this new life of love, dress in the wardrobe God picked out for you: compassion, kindness, humility, quiet strength, discipline. Be even-tempered, content with second place, quick to forgive an offense. Forgive as quickly and completely as the Master forgave you. And regardless of what else you put on, wear love. It's your basic, all-purpose garment. Never be without it. Let the peace of Christ keep you in tune with each other, in step with each other. None of this going off and doing your own thing. And cultivate thankfulness. Let the Word of Christ-the Message-have the run of the house. Give it plenty of room in your lives. Instruct and direct one another using good common sense. And sing, sing your hearts out to God! Let every detail in your lives-words, actions, whatever-be done in the name of the Master, Jesus, thanking God the Father every step of the way.
Colossians 3:12-17 MSG

We enter His gates with Thanksgiving EVEN when it's stormy....KEEP ON THE NARROW PATH OF THE WORD...few find it and fewer follow it.

Bible Reading: Psalm 119

~*Pastor Rhonda Spencer*

February 13

SEEKING EQUALS SUCCESS

Today is not just another day in the week, but it is this exact day that we will never be able to relive once it slips into time called PAST.
We have this moment to make an ETERNAL VALUE.
We cannot change yesterday, we can hope for tomorrow, BUT, we have this moment, this day to live for Jesus to make a difference.
Matt. 6:33-34, Seek the Kingdom of God above all else, and live righteously, and he will give you everything you need. "So don't worry about tomorrow, for tomorrow will bring its own worries. Today's trouble is enough for today.

Seek - ask for (something) from someone
Kingdom of God – who's kingdom? This is a key because TODAY we have a choice, to live our kingdom, or to live His Kingdom. If we live our kingdom, then we are the king, BUT, if we choose to live HIS KINGDOM, then He truly becomes the Lord of our day.
Josh. 1:7-8, Be strong and very courageous. Be careful to obey all the instructions Moses gave you. Do not deviate from them, turning either to the right or to the left. Then you will be successful in everything you do. Study this Book of Instruction continually. Meditate on it day and night so you will be sure to obey everything written in it. Only then will you prosper and succeed in all you do.
THINK – MEDITATE ON THE WORD OF GOD. SEEK HIS KINGDOM.
THINK on the Word, and then OBEY the Word and you will succeed in the day called TODAY!
LIVE YOUR LIFE ON PURPOSE, stop living out of reaction or mistake!
PROSPERITY, SUCCESS IS AVAILABLE TODAY FOR YOU – Seek Jesus, and it will come to you TODAY!

~Dr Micheal Spencer

February 14

Is your life living you, or are you living life?

Living by accident is when a Christian just allows the days to run past them rather than seizing the moments.
Ephesians 5:16, Redeeming the time, because the days are evil.
Today is the only day will be able to live today, and if you do not intentionally seize a moment to
invest eternal value, then it cannot be redeemed. Two things never cease on this earth, time and change. But we do not have to allow them to control our lives.
You are not an accident and today Jesus has placed you where you are, in the community, the job, the family and church so that you can make a difference. Your gifts are so important to the plan of God, without you someone will not go to heaven.
Purpose that today will be intentional. Ask the Holy Spirit to use your life to invest, impart, infuse the love of the Father into someone's life. If you ask, He will bring them. This will mean that you are looking to leave this day with eternal value credited to your account, that when you stand before the Bema Seat of Christ and are judged for your words and works that you will receive crowns you can throw at the Messiah's feet to give Him glory.

BE INTENTIONAL AND PURPOSED PEOPLE OF GOD*!*

~Dr Micheal Spencer

February 15

Only what is done for Christ will last!

Nehemiah 13:14
Remember me, O my God, concerning this, and do not wipe out my good deeds that I have done for the house of my God, and for its services!

The heart of Nehemiah was that our Father's house and city would be reestablished in the midst of all the evil nations of the earth. His passion and focus did not allow the haters to take him off the wall or to distract from the purpose. His rewards with the King of Kings will be great because he served the house of God. Only what we do for Jesus will remain at the Bema Seat judgement (1 Corinthians. 3:11-15). If you entered eternity today what services, ministry, eternal value have you accomplished for Jesus? Our time on this planet is short, speedy, head shaking and time marches on. What have you done in the house of God? How have you served heaven? Will He say, "well done", or will you just make it?

Don't let life live you, you live life and serve the King's house!!

~Dr Micheal Spencer

February 16

IMMOVABLE

People with their minds set on You, You keep completely whole, Steady on their feet, because they keep at it and don't quit. Depend on God and keep at it because in the Lord God you have a sure thing.
Isaiah 26:3, 4 MSG

He shall not be afraid of evil tidings; his heart is firmly fixed, trusting (leaning on and being confident) in the Lord. Psalm 112:7

I have set the Lord continually before me; because He is at my right hand, I shall not be moved. Psalm 16:8

Don't get off track, dig deep and be IMMOVABLE.

-Pastor Rhonda Spencer

February 17

Don't Settle for Seconds

Numbers 32:1,2,5
1 Now the children of Reuben and the children of Gad had a very great multitude of livestock; and when they saw the land of Jazer and the land of Gilead, that indeed the region was a place for livestock,
2 the children of Gad and the children of Reuben came and spoke to Moses, to Eleazar the priest, and to the leaders of the congregation, saying,
5 Therefore they said, "If we have found favor in your sight, let this land be given to your servants as a possession. Do not take us over the Jordan." NKJV

The key verse is verse 5 – they did not want to cross over into God's best, they were willing to settle with the other side of the Jordan. So many Christians are willing to just be satisfied with just getting to heaven. Jesus has the BEST for your life, not just getting to heaven, but a plan, purpose, anointing, a calling. Just settling for heaven is so sad, I want to fulfill my purpose for being here on this earth.

Don't settle for the ok, go for the BEST!

~Dr Micheal Spencer

February 18

GET A GRIP

I will not give my thoughts or my way credibility...I will not get a friend or mentor to come in agreement with them either...thoughts are what drive my life so I will meditate on what the Word says... Not my past, not my fears, not my woes...the Word.

I have been crucified with Christ; it is no longer I who live, but Christ lives in me; and the life which I now live in the flesh I live by faith in the Son of God, who loved me and gave Himself for me. Galatians 2:20 NKJV

Bible Reading: Psalm 94:19, Jeremiah 17:9

~Pastor Rhonda

February 19

One Shacking-Up Woman

Matthew 5:13-14 "You are the salt of the earth; but if the salt loses its flavor, how shall it be seasoned? It is then good for nothing but to be thrown out and trampled underfoot by men. You are the light of the world. A city that is set on a hill cannot be hidden."

So many times we forget how powerful one person is on this planet.
We get superstar-dazzled by names, individuals, places...
"What could li'l,'ole, me do?
Let me tell you...... YOU COULD CHANGE YOUR HOUSE! STREET! TOWN! CITY!
Me?
A sleeping around, shacking-up woman, came to get water and met Jesus! She experienced Jesus at the well, and her life was changed. She was so excited that she ran back to the city, and shared her experience, and urged people to come see Christ.

John 4:39 "And many of the Samaritans of that city believed in Him because of the word of the woman who testified, 'He told me all that I ever did.'"

YOU CAN MAKE THE DIFFERENCE!

~Dr Micheal Spencer

February 20

I DON'T FEEL LIKE IT!!!!
I don't feel like it today!

Today, I was laying in bed and it was warm and relaxing, but I knew that I needed to get up and write the morning devotions.
TRUTHFULLY, I wanted to stay in bed!
I know this does not sound real spiritual, supernatural in the least, but it is simply true.
I had a choice
1) Stay in bed
2) Get up and do what needs to be done no matter what my flesh says.
Ok, you can tell, I got up, but it was not what "I" wanted.

Therefore I do not run uncertainly (without definite aim). I do not box like one beating the air and striking without an adversary. But [like a boxer] I buffet my body [handle it roughly, discipline it by hardships] and subdue it, for fear that after proclaiming to others the Gospel and things pertaining to it, I myself should become unfit [not stand the test, be unapproved and rejected as a counterfeit].
1 Corinthians 9:26, 27 AMP

This is not about doing what we want, this is about being consistent in what will arrest the flesh.
I don't want to get up and read the Word and pray!
I don't want to go to church today!
I don't want to go to Bible Study!
I don't want to eat my vegetables!
I don't want to shower!
I don't, I don't, I don't, I don't.........

CONSISTENCY IS EVERYTHING!
Arrest the flesh, and do what builds your spirit, and you will become a GIANT IN THE KINGDOM!

~Dr Micheal Spencer

February 21

If you feel like your foundation is crumbling, it must be built on the wrong thing.

Friends, co-laborers, buildings, things, money...these things will always be changing and that is not a stable foundation...ONLY Jesus and His presence is solid ground...get into HIS PRESENCE and your foundation will not be questionable/unstable.
There is solid ground that awaits your life in HIS PRESENCE.
Psalm 20:7 NKJV
Some trust in chariots, and some in horses; But we will remember the name of the LORD our God.
Psalm 125:1 AMPC
Those who trust in, lean on, and confidently hope in the Lord are like Mount Zion, which cannot be moved but abides and stands fast forever.
Isaiah 26:3-4 AMPC
You will guard him and keep him in perfect and constant peace whose mind [both its inclination and its character] is stayed on You, because he commits himself to You, leans on You, and hopes confidently in You. So trust in the Lord (commit yourself to Him, lean on Him, hope confidently in Him) forever; for the Lord God is an everlasting Rock [the Rock of Ages].

Bible Reading: Psalm 38:15, Isaiah 40:31

~Pastor Rhonda Spencer

February 22

Heaven! We have a HOME!

John 14:1-3
"Let not your heart be troubled; you believe in God, believe also in Me. In My Father's house are many mansions;[a] if it were not so, I would have told you. I go to prepare a place for you. And if I go and prepare a place for you, I will come again and receive you to Myself; that where I am, there you may be also.

THIS IS NOT MY HOME.
Ephesians 2:19 Now, therefore, you are no longer strangers and foreigners, but fellow citizens with the saints and members of the household of God,

Heb 11:10, For he looked for a city which hath foundations, whose builder and maker is God.

Even though we live here, this is not our home and the reason we are here is because we have a job to do. We are the only plan that God has to reach the world with His Good News.

~Dr Micheal Spencer

February 23

HEAVEN! WHAT IT IS LIKE!

Father is making a new heaven and a new earth just for us. 2 Peter 3:13

There will be no more sun or moon needed because Father will be the LIGHT. (Revelation 21:23) There will be no more pain, no more suffering, no more death, no more sadness. (Revelation 21:4) We will have glorified bodies in heaven. (1 Corinthians 15:42-44)

Our bodies will be perfect – physical, yet not constrained. One man who saw heaven (Roy Reinhold) says that everyone in heaven is in their prime (25-35) and that we all know each other. All babies who have died and aborted children will be waiting for you when you get to heaven.

We will have the ability to do what Jesus did, going through walls (John 20:26).

There are family units in heaven.

When Colton Burpo arrived in heaven at the age of 4, his grandfather, Pops, came to see him and his two sisters, that had died before birth, came to see and hug, and be with him.

Jesse Duplantis said that when he saw heaven, there was a family eating a picnic in the middle of a waving field of wheat.

Don Piper said that he was surrounded with family members, friends that had preceded him and loved him. They looked really, really good!!

Matthew 17:1-3 – We will know people.

What does heaven look like? The music. The colors. The aromas. There are streets of gold.

Jesse said that he saw the mountains, trees, grass, rivers, gorgeous!

PEACE, JOY, HAPPINESS, LOVE, ACCEPTANCE, HEALTH

The New Jerusalem (1500 miles high, 1500 miles square) Revelation 21:10-21 describes the beauty of heaven.

Everything that heaven is, HELL is the opposite: There is no peace. There is no joy. There is only loneliness. There is no rest in hell.

~Dr Micheal Spencer

February 24

HEAVEN! THE GOAL – MEETING OUR FATHER!

1 Corinthians 13:12, We don't yet see things clearly. We're squinting in a fog, peering through a mist. But it won't be long before the weather clears and the sun shines bright! We'll see it all then, see it all as clearly as God sees us, knowing him directly just as he knows us!

Matthew 25:23 – Well done, good and faithful servant Our purpose is clear – if someone does not know Jesus as their Savior then they cannot go to heaven and be with the Father and see their family that knew Christ.

Matthew 25:23 – Well done, good and faithful servant Our purpose is clear – if someone does not know Jesus as their Savior then they cannot go to heaven and be with the Father and see their family that knew Christ.

~Dr Micheal Spencer

February 25

SEE YOUR VICTORY.

Our God is ALL POWERFUL, supernatural, He will blow our natural mind. He can do abundantly above all we can ask think or imagine!!!!
TODAY SEE WITH YOUR SPIRITUAL EYES AND HEAR WITH YOUR SPIRITUAL EAR!!!
VICTORY-BREAKTHROUGH-REPAIR-MIRACLES-SIGNS-WONDERS. Do not doubt or SEE with natural eyes or you will miss out.

CAN YOU HEAR IT? CAN YOU SEE IT?

Then Elijah said..." I hear a mighty rainstorm coming!" Then he said to his servant, "Go and look out toward the sea." The servant went and looked, then returned to Elijah and said, "I didn't see anything." Seven times Elijah told him to go and look. Finally the seventh time, his servant told him, "I saw a little cloud about the size of a man's hand rising from the sea."
1 Kings 18:41, 43-44 NLT

The officer assisting the king said to the man of God, "That couldn't happen even if The Lord opened the windows of heaven!" But Elisha replied, "You will see it happen with your own eyes, but you won't be able to eat any of it!" 2 Kings 7:2 NLT

~Dr Micheal Spencer

February 26

Success is not an accident, it's purposed!

Nehemiah 3:2-5
Next to Eliashib the men of Jericho built. And next to them Zaccur the son of Imri built. Also the sons of Hassenaah built the Fish Gate; they laid its beams and hung its doors with its bolts and bars. And next to them Meremoth the son of Urijah, the son of Koz, made repairs. Next to them Meshullam the son of Berechiah, the son of Meshezabel, made repairs. Next to them Zadok the son of Baana made repairs. Next to them the Tekoites made repairs; but their nobles did not put their shoulders to the work of their Lord.

Who is next to you? If you listen to these verses it says, "and next to them....".
Is the person who is next to you building in your life with Christ, or are they tearing down God's plan for your life?
Be careful who you allow next to you if you want to complete the building. Only allow those who are taking you to completion to be right next to you. Don't get distracted, finish the job.

Who is next to you?

~Dr Micheal Spencer

February 27

You BELONG!

Because of our Father's INTENSE love for us, He gave us the ability to part of His FAMILY!
Satan strives with all that is in him to destroy families, because they are the mirror of heaven. Daddy, Abba, loves you so much that He paid the ULTIMATE cost to have us be part of His family.
Here is what Father says to YOU today....
Are you ready?
Here you go......

Therefore you are no longer outsiders (exiles, migrants, and aliens, excluded from the rights of citizens), but you now share citizenship with the saints (God's own people, consecrated and set apart for Himself); and you belong to God's [own] household. Ephesians 2:19 AMP

- You are no longer an outsider
- You are a citizen, with the rights of a new born child in the Father's Kingdom
- You BELONG!

I love that! We BELONG! This is where we are supposed to be, in His home.
YOU ARE NOT LESS THAN!
YOU ARE NOT A SURVIVOR!
YOU ARE NOT PEERING INTO THE WINDOW WATCHING SOMEONE ELSE'S FAMILY!
YOU ARE SITTING ON THE COUCH, EATING FROM THE FRIDGE. IT IS WHERE YOU BELONG!
Get it in your spirit today, you belong in Daddy's house.

~Dr Micheal Spencer

February 28

The scene: The boat is filled with 4 Christians that have their life jackets on (salvation) & they are in the boat (the local church).
The first person – they have jumped from the boat & are not calling out for help, but you try to throw them a life vest. They start saying how they tried the God stuff but it did not work for them. They don't need Jesus, they don't need church, they want to be left alone. They simply say, "I am living my own life & want nothing to do with you or the Jesus stuff"
They drown – when taken away – THEY BEGIN SCREAMING, "I was wrong, I want a second chance, I will do it right this time......"
The second person – they take off their life vest, jump out of the boat because they chose a girl or a guy over Christ. When they realize that a person can never replace God, they start to call for help. They start calling for help, and the Christian responds by throwing them a life vest and they grab it and get back in the boat. They are thankful and begin to worship God for restoring them.
The third person – jumped out of the boat with the second person. They are an obnoxious personality, offensive in nature.
They realize they wanted Christ again and started calling out for help. WE IGNORE THEM BECAUSE THEY OFFENDED US IN THE PAST & ARE AN IRRITANT. We turn to each other in the boat and simply let them drown......
They are taken away by the demons, weeping.....
WE ARE CALLED TO RESTORE, NOT IGNORE
Galatians 6:1, Brethren, if a man is overtaken in any trespass, **you who are spiritual restore** such a one in a spirit of gentleness, considering yourself lest you also be tempted.
Trespass – to fall beside or near something, a lapse or deviation from truth & uprightness, a sin, misdeed
Restore – to render, i.e. to fit, sound, complete, to mend (what has been broken or rent), to repair, to complete, to fit out, equip, put in order, arrange, adjust, to fit or frame for one's self, prepare, ethically: to strengthen, perfect, complete, make one what he ought to be
Gentleness – gentleness, mildness, meekness
HAVE YOU ATTEMPTED TO RESTORE THEM?
GET THEM BACK IN THE BOAT or WILL YOU IGNORE THEM, AND LET THEM DROWN? *~Dr Micheal Spencer*

February 29

Are YOU a Life Preserver?
2 Corinthians. 4:18 while we do not look at the things which are seen, but at the things which are not seen. For the things which are seen are temporary, but the things which are not seen are eternal.
Matthew 5:14-16 "You are the light of the world.
WE ARE THE LIGHTHOUSE Living in New England, one of the cool things to go to is a lighthouse. When my sister lived in Maine we would go to this lighthouse when we visited. It was gorgeous, but it had GREAT PURPOSE!
The purpose of a lighthouse is to warn the ships when they were getting too close to land, so that they would not run aground or shipwreck against the rocks.
When the fog is thick, when the storm is the harshest, the lighthouse beam would burn through and bring hope, safety, relief, salvation to the ship, but also to the crew. We are the LIGHT of the World!
WE ARE CALLED TO BRING HOPE, SAFETY, RELIEF, SALVATION to the world around us, but the majority of Christians never share their faith. When surveyed 55% say they have shared their faith in the last 12 months (according to Barna) but most churches are not growing, or seeing salvations.
With 83.6% of America not attending a conventional church on a given weekend "Fuller Theological Seminary did a research study that found that if a church is 10 or more years old, it takes 85 people to lead 1 person to Christ. If a church is less than 3 years old, it takes only 3 people to lead 1 person to Christ." (http://simplechurchathome.com/Why.html)
Do NOT be part of the statistics!!
THE WAY IT USUALLY HAPPENS
EXAMPLE OF THE GUY IN THE BOAT, WITH THE LIGHT BEHIND HIM. THE BOAT IS FILLED WITH LIFE PRESERVERS. THE LIGHTS ARE LOW IN THE BUILDING, AND FROM THE DARKNESS CALLS OF HELP COME. THEY SWIM TOWARD THE BOAT WHERE THE LIGHT IS SHINING. THE PERSON IN THE BOAT HAS LIFE PRESERVERS, BUT THROWS NONE TO THE PEOPLE SWIMMING. THEY ALL DROWN. DEMONS COME AND DRAG THEM AWAY.
Excuses: I'm shy, I do not feel comfortable talking with people about my faith, I don't like that person, I don't know that person, I was hurt by that person, I am going through things now and don't have time, I have to take care of me
"I, I, I, I, I, I, I, ..." THEY NEED YOU,
YOU ARE THEIR ONLY HOPE! *~Dr Micheal Spencer*

March 1

Victorious Confessions of the Word-1

The mind lies, our thoughts try to be higher than God's Word, we must take them captive!!

GOD DOESN'T WANT YOU! --- LIE!!!!

I AM – a son or daughter of God HIMSELF
John 1:12 – He gave me the right to be called His child.

I AM The Apple of My Father's Eye
Deuteronomy 32:10; Psalm 17:8

I AM chosen by God and adopted as His child.
Ephesians 1:3-8

YOU SINNED TOO MUCH AND GOD WON'T ACCEPT YOU! --- LIE!!!

I AM – TOTALLY FORGIVEN and brand new in Jesus.
I AM free from condemnation. Romans 8:1-2
I AM brand new in Jesus. 2 Corinthians 5:17
I HAVE newness of life. Romans 6:4

GOD HAS GIVEN UP ON YOU. YOU MESSED UP TOO MUCH! --- LIE!!!

~Dr Micheal Spencer

March 2

Victorious Confessions of the Word-2

The mind lies, thoughts try to be higher than God' Word, we must take them captive!!

YOU WILL NEVER BE FREE FROM YOUR PROBLEMS, NO HOPE FOR YOU! --- LIE!!!

I AM FREE

I stand fast in the liberty wherewith Christ has made me free ~ Galatians 5:1

I am FREE in Jesus from anything that would try to destroy me ~ John 8:36

YOU WILL ALWAYS BE A LOSER! --- LIE!!!

I AM and HAVE complete Victory in Jesus

I am more (not just) than a conqueror~ (Romans 8:37)

I am a success. I am an over-comer. I am a new creation.

I give thanks unto God who always causes me to triumph in Christ Jesus. ~ 2 Corinthians 2:14

I can do all things through Christ, who strengthens me ~ Philippians 4:13

I COMMAND MY MIND TO COME INTO SUBJECTION TO THE WORD OF GOD!

YOU ARE TOO WEAK! --- LIE!!!

I AM STRONG in Jesus

I AM strong in the Lord and in his mighty power. I am more than a conqueror through Christ who loved me. Eph6:10/Rom8:17

I AM young, and I am strong, and the word of God abides in me and I have overcome the evil one.1Jn2:14

I have not been given the spirit of fear but of power, love and a sound mind ~ 2 Timothy 1:7

~Dr Micheal Spencer

March 3

Victorious Confessions of the Word-3

The mind lies, thoughts try to be higher than God's Word, we must take them captive!!

YOU ARE TOO TIRED, JUST GIVE UP! --- LIE!!!

I AM NEVER GIVING UP, Daddy will give me strength! *My God quickens my mortal body* by his Holy Spirit who dwells in me and I build up myself upon my most holy faith by praying in the Holy Ghost. Romans 8:11/Jude 20

When I am weak, HE is strong ~ 2 Corinthians 12:10

My faith stands in the power of God and not in the wisdom of man. All things are possible unto me because I can believe. 1 Corinthians 2:5/Mark9:23

YOU WILL NEVER WIN! --- LIE!!!

I CANNOT LOSE with Jesus on my side!

I overcome the enemy by the blood of the Lamb and by the word of my testimony. Revelation 12:11

My God supplies all my need according to his glorious riches by Christ Jesus. I lack for nothing for the Lord is my shepherd. Philippians 4:19/Psalm 23:1

I am the righteousness of God in Christ Jesus and I can do all things through Christ who strengthens me. 2 Corinthians 5:21/Philippians 4:13

SPEAK THE WORD – So if the Son liberates you [makes you free men], then you are really and unquestionably free. John 8:36 AMP

~Dr Micheal Spencer

March 4

You are not alone

Jesus, Himself is praying for you!!!!

And the Lord said, Simon, Simon! Indeed, Satan has asked for you, that he may sift you as wheat. But I have prayed for you, that your faith should not fail.
Luke 22:31, 32 NKJV

Likewise the Spirit also helps in our weaknesses. For we do not know what we should pray for as we ought, but the Spirit Himself makes intercession for us with groanings which cannot be uttered. Now He who searches the hearts knows what the mind of the Spirit is, because He makes intercession for the saints according to the will of God. Romans 8:26-27

Bible Reading: Isaiah 53:12, Romans 8:34, Hebrews 7:25

~Pastor Rhonda Spencer

March 5

Snatchers List

Luke 19:10
for the Son of Man has come to seek and to save that which was lost.

Jesus didn't come to sit and save, but to seek, and save. That means He put action to His passion.

TAKE OUT A PEN, AND PAPER PLEASE.
Write the names of 5 people you want to reach with the Gospel this year.
We are targeting those 5 people for salvation this year. This means by the last day of this year, you are expecting them to be sitting next to you during worship.

Now pray this 3 times a day over those people:
In the name of Jesus, I bind the devil that blinds their minds, and I loose the Word of God, the angels of God, and the saints of God, by the Holy Spirit to plant seeds, water, and we will watch God bring the increase.
I decree in Jesus name that Satan must let them go, and that they will come to Jesus this year.
In the name of Jesus!

NOW WATCH WHAT JESUS WILL DO!

~Dr Micheal Spencer

March 6

DEPRESSION is a tool of Satan - I

Fear is not just a tormentor, but it also is the door to open up a myriad of other emotions and or sicknesses that can hold you in prison.
DEPRESSION – definition
1. a mental state characterized by a pessimistic sense of inadequacy and a despondent lack of activity. Sad feelings of gloom and inadequacy. A sunken geological indenture.

Depression medication – The proportion of Americans using antidepressants in a given year nearly doubled from 5.8% in 1996 to 10.1% in 2005, according to a paper just published: National Patterns in Antidepressant Medication Treatment, by Mark Olfson and Steven Marcus.
I think everyone of us at some point and time have dealt with some level of depression.
There are also three major causes for depression that Jesus desires to set you free from.
1. Physical 2. Mental 3. Demonic
Psalm 42:5 Why are you cast down, O my soul? And why are you disquieted within me? Hope in God, for I shall yet praise Him, for the help of His countenance.
MEDICAL DEPRESSION
In the old days majority of churches believed that depression was a demon and that it was not real in people's lives. Depression is real, It can be caused by a physical illness of the mind. Causes of physical depression: Lower levels of serotonin (neurotransmitter) or genetic, biochemical.

If a person is sick, physically then Jesus desires to heal you, even in your MIND.
-2 Tim. 1:7, For God has not given us a spirit of fear, but of power and of love and of a sound mind.
God desires to make you mind SOUND, physically.
-If you are on medication then as God heals your mind you will be able to go back to the doctor and they will be able to see the healing and take you off the medication.
-You need a physical healing in your brain and Jesus is the healer!

~Dr Micheal Spencer

March 7

DEPRESSION is a tool of Satan - 2

THE STRONGEST CAUSE OF DEPRESSION = THINKING

This is the NUMBER ONE reason for depression.
How you think and speak can begin the spiral toward depression and captivity.
The horrific part of depression is that it takes you out of the game.
It can be totally debilitating and keeps you from producing fruit for Jesus.
In war, one of the wisest things you can do is wound someone. When you would someone you take at least 2 or 3 people off the battlefield because people have to help the wounded.
The devil knows that if he can get us depressed then we will lose focus and he will steal many souls.

> I Kings 19:4, But he himself went a day's journey into the wilderness, and came and sat down under a broom tree. And he prayed that he might die, and said, "It is enough! Now, Lord, take my life, for I am no better than my fathers!"
> How you think and the voices you allow to run around your head can steal your faith and hope in life and you will enter the spiral decent of depression!

Satan is striving to get you to stop believing and confessing the Word of God. If he can get you to believe the facts above the TRUTH, then you will always struggle with depression.

2 Corinthians 5:7 For we walk by faith, not by sight.
Are you thinking the Word today, or are you allowing your unclean, non-renewed mind to mandate your joy?

Nehemiah 8:10 Then he said to them, "Go your way, eat the fat, drink the sweet, and send portions to those for whom nothing is prepared; for this day is holy to our Lord. Do not sorrow, for the joy of the Lord is your strength."

~Dr Micheal Spencer

March 8

HOW TO THINK

If stinking thinking is what gets majority of people into depression, then let's change the way we think to cut off that option.
Most people talk negative.
The talk is just what is already in their heart.
Matt. 12:34-37, Brood of vipers! How can you, being evil, speak good things? For out of the abundance of the heart the mouth speaks. A good man out of the good treasure of his heart brings forth good things, and an evil man out of the evil treasure brings forth evil things. But I say to you that for every idle word men may speak, they will give account of it in the day of judgment. For by your words you will be justified, and by your words you will be condemned.

The negative is already in our hearts before we speak it out of our mouths. By our words, we are either justified, or condemned. Our words, that are determined by our thoughts, condemn or save us.
The Word teaches us how to think so that we can understand how to have VICTORY in our minds.

2 Corinthians. 10:4-6, For the weapons of our warfare are not carnal but mighty in God for pulling down strongholds, casting down arguments and every high thing that exalts itself against the knowledge of God, bringing every thought into captivity to the obedience of Christ, and being ready to punish all disobedience when your obedience is fulfilled.

~Dr Micheal Spencer

March 9

People think themselves into depression!
It's the number #1 cause!

When my thoughts start to spiral out of control, what do I do?

First things first
Verbally, even loudly if you need, tell you mind to be quiet!
Take CAPTIVE your thoughts!
"In Jesus name, I command you to be quiet, NOW!"
Second
Begin to think the Word.
Speak the Word and let the Word work!
Speak LIFE and not death!

If you are struggling with getting control; call a FAITH FRIEND. This is a person who will speak life to you and build you up, not sympathize with you. This is a person who will speak life to you and build you up, not sympathize with you. (Sympathy is feeling sorry for the person. Empathy is helping the person.)
• Get hands laid on you to break the cycle.
• Get into the Word, know who you are and speak it.
• Break the power of ungodly thoughts that imprison your mind and steal your hope & faith!

~Dr Micheal Spencer

March 10

THINK THIS WAY

Philippians 4:4-9 MSG Rejoice in the Lord always. Again I will say, rejoice! Let your gentleness be known to all men. The Lord is at hand. Be anxious for nothing, but in everything by prayer and supplication, with thanksgiving, let your requests be made known to God; 7and the peace of God, which surpasses all understanding, will guard your hearts and minds through Christ Jesus. Finally, brethren, whatever things are true, whatever things are noble, whatever things are just, whatever things are pure, whatever things are lovely, whatever things are of good report, if there is any virtue and if there is anything praiseworthy—meditate on these things. Summing it all up, friends, I'd say you'll do best by filling your minds and meditating on things true, noble, reputable, authentic, compelling, gracious—the best, not the worst; the beautiful, not the ugly; things to praise, not things to curse. Put into practice what you learned from me, what you heard and saw and realized. Do that, and God, who makes everything work together, will work you into his most excellent harmonies.

ALWAYS think this way & ALWAYS rejoice.
Dance in the rain, Praise in the prisons...even in your sorrows, rejoice and know it is producing good in you.

Bible Reading: 2 Corinthians 10:4-6, Proverbs 16:3, Jeremiah 17:8-10

~Pastor Rhonda Spencer

March 11

STRENGTH IS FOR SERVICE, NOT STATUS

Those of us who are strong and able in the faith need to step in and lend a hand to those who falter, and not just do what is most convenient for us. STRENGTH IS FOR SERVICE, NOT STATUS. Each one of us needs to look after the good of the people around us, asking ourselves, "How can I help?"

That's exactly what Jesus did. He didn't make it easy for himself by avoiding people's troubles, but waded right in and helped out. "I took on the troubles of the troubled" is the way the Scripture puts it. Even if it was written in Scripture long ago, you can be sure it's written for us. Romans 15:1-4 MSG

STRENGTH IS FOR SERVICE, NOT STATUS!!! Ask today, "How can I help?" Wade right in and help out. You'll surely walk away the one that was truly blessed.

~Pastor Rhonda Spencer

March 12

That Is So Petty!

Yesterday I was driving and came to a set of lights that takes a long time to get through. I decided in the moment to change my music from some jazz to a worship. It literally took seconds, but during those seconds the light must have changed and when I looked up the car in front of me was moving. I quickly got going, and was only a car length behind the lead car. The guy behind me was irate! He could not wait to get along side and swing his arm in disgust at me. I kind of chuckled to realize that he lost his joy and peace over a car length at a light.

Nehemiah 8:10b, for this day is holy to our Lord. Do not sorrow, for the joy of the Lord is your strength."

But what happens when we live God's way? He brings gifts into our lives, much the same way that fruit appears in an orchard—things like affection for others, exuberance about life, serenity. We develop a willingness to stick with things, a sense of compassion in the heart, and a conviction that a basic holiness permeates things and people. We find ourselves involved in loyal commitments, not needing to force our way in life, able to marshal and direct our energies wisely. Galatians 5:22, 23 MSG
Never allow someone to steal your joy, especially over stupid things that will make no difference. Things might irritate us, but why allow those things, or those people to take away what Jesus has given you.
MAKE A DECISION!
I will not surrender my joy and my peace, over stupid little, petty things that make no eternal impact. I choose to live in the joy of my God, smile, and have a step in my walk. Today people will notice that I am different, and that in those small things I refuse to allow to steal my joy!!
SMILE, AND SHARE THE JOY BY DEBUNKING PETTY WHINING, OR IRRITATION OVER FOOLISHNESS.

~Dr Micheal Spencer

March 13

Why Are People Petty?

Investigate my life, O God, find out everything about me; Cross-examine and test me, get a clear picture of what I'm about; See for yourself whether I've done anything wrong— then guide me on the road to eternal life. Psalm 139:23, 24 MSG

The main reason people get petty is because they have things in their lives that they do not want to face and deal with, so it is easier to focus on everyone else, instead of dealing with themselves.

When others or (let's get more personal) ourselves, start picking out foolish flaws in people we are just avoiding dealing with the BIG issues in our own hearts. We can hide our unforgiveness, our anger, our home life, and our spiritual lives, as long as we distract ourselves and others, we are safe from dealing with us.

Petty people are pulling that shell game, and just hope that nobody finds the pea under the shell, especially themselves.

FOCUS ON THE MAJORS That would be our own hearts to make sure that we are in a good place with Christ, and showing His fruit wherever we are, and in whatever we are doing.

But what happens when we live God's way? He brings gifts into our lives, much the same way that fruit appears in an orchard—things like affection for others, exuberance about life, and serenity. We develop a willingness to stick with things, a sense of compassion in the heart, and a conviction that a basic holiness permeates things and people. We find ourselves involved in loyal commitments, not needing to force our way in life, able to marshal and direct our energies wisely. Galatians 5:22, 23 MSG

When you find yourself getting petty, picky or nasty, check inside first, because it is not them with the problem, IT'S US!

When we find others being petty, instead of pulling attitude with them, pray for them. They need your prayer, they are running from issues.

~Dr Micheal Spencer

March 14

Get out of the old things that hold you back...

Neither is new wine put in old wineskins; for if it is, the skins burst and are torn in pieces, and the wine is spilled and the skins are ruined. But new wine is put into fresh wineskins, and so both are preserved. Matthew 9:17 AMP

It's never too late to start, today is a new day.
His mercies are new every morning. You choose. You can either stay where you are because this is where life brought you; or you can GET OUT OF THE OLD AND STEP INTO THE NEW.

Yes, it is that easy. You are in control of where you are going, start fresh and new today.

old things have passed away; behold, all things have become new. 2 Corinthians 5:17b

This could be something big or something even small that has you stuck like: small mindedness, fear of failure, gossip, eating habits....GET OUT OF THE THINGS THAT ARE HOLDING YOU BACK. DO IT!!!!

Bible Reading: Philippians 3:12-13, Romans 12:1-2, Lamentations 3:22-24, 2 Corinthians 5:17

~Pastor Rhonda Spencer

March 15

DECISIONS DETERMINE YOUR LIFE

It is the decisions we make that set us up for failure or success.
There are so many Christians that believe in FATE.
As a Christian FATE is a foolish perception.

Psalm 37:23 The steps of a good man are ordered by the Lord, And He delights in his way.

Your choices to obey, or disobey, God and His Word, determines your success or failure.

Moses obeyed God when he was told to take the staff and extend it over the Red Sea; it rolled it back, and Israel walked across on dry ground. Not fate, but obedience brought success.

2 Kings 5:9-14, when Naaman obey the Prophet and dipped 7 times in the Jordan, he became clean of leprosy. Nothing to do with fate; it was obedience.

Proverbs 3:5-6 Trust in the Lord with all your heart, and lean not on your own understanding; in all your ways acknowledge Him, and He shall direct your paths.

~Dr Micheal Spencer

March 16

NEGATIVE NANCY!

The Spring season was said to have sprung!
When I looked outside, there was a fresh dusting of snow, and it was about 30 degrees out. When we look at that, and feel the cold against our faces, it is sometimes difficult to believe that it is Spring.
BUT when I went outside this morning, I STOPPED, I LISTENED, and I HEARD SPRING!
The birds were singing songs! I heard a morning dove, and I saw a flaming red cardinal. I looked out my window a little later and saw a robin.
We cannot live by how it looks! If we live by how it looks only, then we will live in depression, discouragement, and struggle most of the time. We need to be like God's creation – they are already singing with expectation! They have returned knowing that there might be some cold days, but when Spring breaks, they want to be where it is!
Stop always looking at what is in front of you – listen to the birds sing and know......SPRING WILL BREAK THROUGH – NEW BEGINNINGS ARE HERE!

Psalm 42:11, Why are you cast down, O my soul? And why are you disquieted within me? Hope in God; for I shall yet praise Him, the help of my countenance and my God.

2 Corinthians 4:18, While we do not look at the things which are seen, but at the things which are not seen. For the things which are seen are temporary, but the things which are not seen are eternal.

~Dr Micheal Spencer

March 17

Conviction over our Words

There is therefore now no condemnation to those who are in Christ Jesus, who do not walk according to the flesh, but according to the Spirit. Romans 8:1 NKJV

I want to remind you of the difference between conviction, and condemnation.

Conviction is your friend, it tells you when you're doing something wrong presently, or have in your past. It is the way the Holy Spirit keeps our relationship with God clear, because sin separates. Conviction is your friend!

Condemnation is not your friend. It throws your forgiven past in your face, and holds you down from moving forward. Condemnation is never from God, because once you have been forgiven its forgotten.

Why did I say all of that?

We have been teaching on the power of thoughts and words, and how we will be judged for the words that come out of our mouths. As you begin to learn the Holy Spirit starts working the Word in your life. It becomes more than a sermon preached, and it becomes a lifestyle of living the Word of God. The Holy Spirit is the one who tells us when we are wrong, and stepping out of the Word.

The other day I saw a person who has missed much church. They love God, but His house is not priority.

I jokingly said some words that were not meant to be a curse, but when released and activated could cause serious damage. I don't even know if that individual had a clue, BUT, the Spirit of God woke me up and convicted me of sin. He said that I was wrong and what I spoke was not right and that I needed to recant, repent, and then ask the person for forgiveness.

The power of words; they release life or death. Pay attention, and be willing to ask forgiveness from God and others for words you allow to escape from your lips.

SPEAK LIFE TODAY!

~Dr Micheal Spencer

March 18

NEW

We can't do just whatever we feel like doing, we must be followers of Christ; obedient to His Holy Word.

So roll up your sleeves, put your mind in gear, be totally ready to receive the gift that's coming when Jesus arrives. Don't lazily slip back into those old grooves of evil, doing just what you feel like doing. You didn't know any better then; you do now. As obedient children, let yourselves be pulled into a way of life shaped by God's life, a life energetic and blazing with holiness. God said, "I am holy; you be holy." You call out to God for help and he helps—he's a good Father that way. But don't forget, he's also a responsible Father, and won't let you get by with sloppy living. Your life is a journey you must travel with a deep consciousness of God. It cost God plenty to get you out of that dead-end, empty-headed life you grew up in. He paid with Christ's sacred blood, you know.
1 Peter 1:13, 17, 18 MSG

We are a NEW creation,. We are NOT to be conformed to this world. If you've slipped back into the old way of living; make the choice to obey God's Word and FOLLOW HIM.

Bible Reading: James 4:16-17 Isaiah 59:1-2, Matthew 25:1-13

~Pastor Rhonda Spencer

March 19

LOVE is the greatest commandment of the Kingdom of the King!

Everything that is manifested is generated by LOVE, even judgement.
Salvation came because of LOVE! Faith even works through LOVE!
We MUST INCREASE IN LOVE!
Insist on walking in the commandment of LOVE.

John 13:34-35 A new commandment I give to you, that you love one another; as I have loved you, that you also love one another. By this all will know that you are My disciples, if you have love for one another."
We have a debt – THE DEBT OF LOVE
We are responsible to love Him.
It's the love of God that shows the world that God is alive, and that comes through us.

Matthew 5:46-48 For if you love those who love you, what reward have you? Do not even the tax collectors do the same? And if you greet your brethren only, what do you do more than others? Do not even the tax collectors do so? Therefore you shall be perfect, just as your Father in heaven is perfect.
You have to walk in love even with the haters.
HOW DID GOD LOVE? John 3:16 – God gave!

Even if I dole out all that I have [to the poor in providing] food, and if I surrender my body to be burned or in order that I may glory , but have not love (God's love in me), I gain nothing. 1 Corinthians 13:3 AMP
There is profit to love. How do you get perfected in love? PRACTICE.

~Dr Micheal Spencer

March 20

It Wont Kill You.

Look, the people of the children of Israel are more and mightier than we; Therefore they set taskmasters over them to afflict them with their burdens. But the more they afflicted them, the more they multiplied and grew. Exodus 1:9, 11, 12 NKJV

It won't kill you, but it WILL make you stronger. You may be crushed but you WILL NOT be destroyed.

We are hard-pressed on every side, yet not crushed; we are perplexed, but not in despair; persecuted, but not forsaken; struck down, but not destroyed—
2 Corinthians 4:8-9

All these things are making you stronger!

Bible Reading: 2 Corinthians 4:16-18, James 1:1-3, Romans 5:3

~Pastor Rhonda Spencer

March 21

True or False

Matthew 7:24-27 " Therefore whoever hears these sayings of Mine, and does them, I will liken him to a wise man who built his house on the rock: and the rain descended, the floods came, and the winds blew and beat on that house; and it did not fall, for it was founded on the rock. But everyone who hears these sayings of Mine, and does not do them, will be like a foolish man who built his house on the sand: and the rain descended, the floods came, and the winds blew and beat on that house; and it fell. And great was its fall."

How many times have we heard or even sung this verse?
BUT, Do we believe it?
Jesus is the Word that became flesh, Jesus only said what the Father told Him to say, the Words that He spoke were Spirit and life.
Jesus was the presentation of the Word of heaven to earth.
Many Christians like the Word as long as it complies with their beliefs and desires.
The Word MUST become our filter.
Our entire thought life, reactions, actions, interactions, must be filtered through the Word. Is what I'm doing and saying lining up with the Word of God? There comes a time in our maturing process that we must make a commitment beyond getting out of the lake of fire.
We must decide to LIVE for Him!
How do we know if we are living correctly for Him?
Measure it with the Word!
I challenge you today to decide to LIVE by the Word. Live the Word! It is correct, it is TRUTH, all other thoughts, imaginations, words, actions, reactions and interactions MUST be filtered through the WORD.

~Dr Micheal Spencer

March 22

His Word = My Greatest Treasure

My heart stands in awe of Your word. I rejoice at Your word As one who finds great treasure.
Psalm 119:161-162 NKJV

The Word, The Word, The Word....live by it. Eat it. Drink it. Do it. Every moment should be governed by the Word of God...people, philosophies, psychology, feeling and emotions will let you down, lead you astray and fail you.....
BUT GODS PERFECT WORD NEVER FAILS.

Maybe today you need to rethink your path if it is not a direct result of your time in the Word, if your direction came from ANY other source....
OPEN THE WORD AND WALK DAILY, MOMENT BY MOMENT, ACCORDING TO IT.
Joy unspeakable IS YOURS, peace that passes all understanding IS YOURS, Love unconditional IS YOURS!

His Word = my treasure.

~Pastor Rhonda Spencer

March 23

I'm NOT FEELING It!

The roller coaster ride with Jesus is not exhilarating, it's exhausting!!
What do I mean?
He loves me, He loves me not!
Remember when we were kids in the school yard, and we watched the girls play that game with a flower? Sadly, many Christians live in this zone!
They are not stable, they are not established, they are still vacillating because they have never grown up.
Most Christians live more in the FEELING world, than in the faith and growing up world.

" Therefore whoever hears these sayings of Mine, and does them, I will liken him to a wise man who built his house on the rock: and the rain descended, the floods came, and the winds blew and beat on that house; and it did not fall, for it was founded on the rock. But everyone who hears these sayings of Mine, and does not do them, will be like a foolish man who built his house on the sand: and the rain descended, the floods came, and the winds blew and beat on that house; and it fell. And great was its fall." Matthew 7:24-27

To get off the roller coaster ride with Jesus you must decide to be CONSISTENT in building your faith walk on the ROCK, who is Jesus.
We must decide to consistently build our faith by getting into the Bible daily, and talking with Jesus every day.
We must also be faithful to Daddy's house, and being taught and trained.

And they continued steadfastly in the apostles' doctrine and fellowship, in the breaking of bread, and in prayers. Acts 2:42

~Dr Micheal Spencer

March 24

It Brings Out The Best in You

Take your everyday, ordinary life—your sleeping, eating, going-to-work, and walking-around life—and place it before God as an offering. Embracing what God does for you is the best thing you can do for him. Don't become so well-adjusted to your culture that you fit into it without even thinking. Instead,
fix your attention on God. You'll be changed from the inside out. Readily recognize what he wants from you, and quickly respond to it. Unlike the culture around you, always dragging you down to its level of immaturity, God brings the best out of you, develops well-formed maturity in you. I'm speaking to you out of deep gratitude for all that God has given me...
Romans 12:1-3 MSG

Bible Reading: 2 Corinthians 6:16-18,
1 Corinthians 14:20, Philippians 3:14-16

~Pastor Rhonda Spencer

March 25

Faith, the Conflict of the Mind

while we do not look at the things which are seen, but at the things which are not seen. For the things which are seen are temporary, but the things which are not seen are eternal. 2 Corinthians 4:18

I have heard people say, "I am a realist and I can't get into this faith stuff." People allow their flesh to dictate to them who they are, and what they do, over the Word of God!

"This is just the way I am", really? Who lied to you? Why are you believing a lie? Why would you accept what others, and or, who your flesh says you are, over who God says you are? Who has the loudest voice in your life? The King, or..........

Who we ALLOW to have the loudest voice in our lives is who has the greatest influence over our lives.
This is why the Word says in Romans 10:17 "So then faith comes by hearing, and hearing by the word of God." The more Word, the more faith, the more faith, the more trust.

For we walk by faith, not by sight. 2 Corinthians 5:7

Pick up the Word today and arrest your mind. Allow the Word to be your truth over your facts.

~Dr Micheal Spencer

March 26

Buckle in Baby!

2 Thessalonians 2:3 Let no one deceive you by any means; for that Day will not come unless the falling away comes first, and the man of sin is revealed, the son of perdition,

Jesus is coming!! Can I hear a shout of praise! BUT

Before He comes there will be a great falling away.
Falling away? You cannot fall from somewhere you are not, or have not been. Where is that place?
In relationship, in your walk, your calling of life.

Let no one deceive you, the Word says. The greatest deceiver is ourselves. Living a life that is not pleasing to the Father, choosing to ignore Him in our daily life, choosing to subtract ourselves from His church. Yet, we sit back and say, “I prayed that prayer”, or, “I used to, but He knows my heart.”.
If we are not beyond where we were last year in our walk with Him, then we are backsliding, and deceiving ourselves that all is well. If you barely come to God’s home, barely pray, never pick up the Word and believe all is well, then your deceived.

AWAKE, RISE FROM THE SPIRITUAL SLUMBER!
Don’t let the flesh, the temporary world, or Satan himself get you to FALL away. Repent, call out, and Jesus will restore, realign and rejuvenate your passion for Him!
Do it TODAY!

~Dr Micheal Spencer

March 27

GOD IS FOR YOU!!!!!

And we know that God causes everything to work together for the good of those who love God and are called according to his purpose for them.
What shall we say about such wonderful things as these? If God is for us, who can ever be against us? Romans 8:28, 31 NLT

no weapon that is fashioned against you shall succeed, and you shall refute every tongue that rises against you in judgment. This is the heritage of the servants of the LORD and their vindication from me, declares the LORD." Isaiah 54:17

God is our refuge and strength, a very present help in trouble. Psalm 46:1

This I declare about the LORD :
He alone is my refuge, my place of safety; he is my God, and I trust him. For he will rescue you from every trap and protect you from deadly disease. He will cover you with his feathers. He will shelter you with his wings. His faithful promises are your armor and protection. Psalms 91:2-4 NLT

The LORD himself watches over you!
The LORD keeps you from all harm and watches over your life. The LORD keeps watch over you as you come and go, both now and forever. Psalms 121:5, 7-8 NLT

GOD IS FOR YOU---CONTINUE. PRESS ON.

~Pastor Rhonda Spencer

March 28

Be a HEALER today

There is one who speaks like the piercings of a sword,
But the tongue of the wise promotes health.
Proverbs 12:18

Normally, when things are going well our mouths are speaking life, and not death. It is not till pressure is applied that we truly get to see what is resident in our hearts. Out of the abundance of the heart, the mouth speaks.

When pressure is applied, immediately, what we think about ourselves and what we think about others comes streaming out. What many do not realize is that our words applied to ourselves, our situation, and to others will either produce life or death.

Today, when pressure is applied, govern your tongue. Arrest your words! Make sure that what comes out promotes health and faith. Faith does not deny facts, faith declares truth. Speak the TRUTH over your situation and watch God produce health in the circumstance.
If you choose not to do this, then you are digging your own mental, emotional, marital, and business grave. There will be nobody to blame but yourself. The words we speak can bring healing, or can spread disease.
BE A HEALER TODAY!!!!

~Dr Micheal Spencer

March 29

Disciple

Who are you discipling? We are called to be disciples and make disciples. Take time this week to reach out to and build 3 people that God places on your heart and continue to stick with them.

You'll not only be obeying God's Word and be a blessing to them, it will complete and fulfill you.

Matthew 28:19 Therefore, go and make disciples of all the nations, baptizing them in the name of the Father and the Son and the Holy Spirit.

John 15:8 By this my Father is glorified, that you bear much fruit and so prove to be my disciples.

2 Timothy 2:2 And what you have heard from me in the presence of many witnesses entrust to faithful men who will be able to teach others also.

Romans 10:14-15 How then will they call on him in whom they have not believed? And how are they to believe in him of whom they have never heard? And how are they to hear without someone preaching? And how are they to preach unless they are sent? As it is written, "How beautiful are the feet of those who preach the good news!"

John 17:18 As you sent me into the world, so I have sent them into the world.

Mark 1:17 And Jesus said to them, "Follow me, and I will make you become fishers of men."

~Pastor Rhonda Spencer

March 30

Let's Do It!

For if anyone is a hearer of the word and not a doer, he is like a man observing his natural face in a mirror; James 1:23

Therefore, to him who knows to do good and does not do it, to him it is sin. James 4:17

We can hear about it, talk about it, read about it, pray about it.....

BUT

There comes a time when you just have to DO IT!

For the next 3 days find a person that others would consider different, unlovely, or unwanted and start speaking LIFE into them.

You can quote the Word, speak encouragement, speak acceptance and love. Watch Jesus change their life by speaking life and not death.

You have nothing to lose, but they have everything to gain!!

BE PURPOSED.

~Dr Micheal Spencer

March 31

I AM, still here.

It's time to REDEDICATE yourself back to the one that you know is your God.

JEHOVAH IS MY GOD - He is my source, my ONLY source.

In THE MIDDLE OF the storm, it's so important to ask yourself:
WHO DO I SAY THAT HE IS?
Do I trust Him?
Is He still my healer, my protector, my refuge?

WHO DO YOU SAY THAT I AM?
I am the same yesterday, TODAY and forever, am I STILL the same to you today?

Hebrews 13:8 Jesus Christ is the same yesterday, today and forever.

~Pastor Rhonda Spencer

April 1

Guard Your Heart in the Last Days

You can be certain that in the last days there will be some very hard times. People will love only themselves and money. They will be proud, stuck-up, rude, and disobedient to their parents. They will also be ungrateful, godless, heartless, and hateful. Their words will be cruel, and they will have no self-control or pity. These people will hate everything that is good. They will be sneaky, reckless, and puffed up with pride. Instead of loving God, they will love pleasure. Even though they will make a show of being religious, their religion won't be real. Don't have anything to do with such people.
2 Timothy 3:1-5 CEV

What is most interesting about the description is that he is talking about the church. They will have the LOOK of religion, smell of CHURCH, but they deny the power of God.

They live like a heathen, yet declare they are born again. Living for Jesus takes the power of God, and if there is no power there is usually a loose life.

The Word of God, our personal time with Jesus, the corporate anointing, the Spirit of God within will keep us from becoming like the world.

Take 15 today in the Word & prayer, and when u do that you will be ready to LIVE for Jesus!
Take 10 and share Jesus with someone who needs Him!

~Dr Micheal Spencer

April 2

The Bunny CHIRPS?

Easter eggs, ham, mashed potatoes, corn, asparagus, Cadbury eggs, chocolate bunnies.....ahhhhhh!
I feel a fattening day coming on!
The greatest food we can ever eat is the Word of God, and the best, most refreshing drink, is the Holy Spirit. FOOD

Jesus said to them, "My food is to do the will of Him who sent Me, and to finish His work. John 4:34 NKJV

DRINK but whoever drinks of the water that I shall give him will never thirst. But the water that I shall give him will become in him a fountain of water springing up into everlasting life." John 4:14

Easter is not the celebration of food, and a short little bunny that clucks like a chicken. We are celebrating the day that Jesus finalized the forecast for the failing devil, called Satan.

[God] disarmed the principalities and powers that were ranged against us and made a bold display and public example of them, in triumphing over them in Him and in it [the cross]. Colossians 2:15 AMP

And when I saw Him, I fell at His feet as dead. But He laid His right hand on me, saying to me, "Do not be afraid; I am the First and the Last. I am He who lives, and was dead, and behold, I am alive forevermore. Amen. And I have the keys of Hades and of Death. Revelation 1:17, 18 NKJV

A Good Friday for us, but it was not a Good Friday for Satan, and his cohorts!!!!
We are VICTORIOUS THROUGH JESUS CHRIST!
The DEATH, and RESURRECTION of our JESUS, nailed the coffin for Satan, and WE ARE THE CHAMPIONS!

~Dr Micheal Spencer

April 3

Jesus is DEAD!

He claimed to be the Son of God! He claimed He was the Resurrection and the Life! BUT I saw Him dead on that tree. I saw the blood and water come out His side when He was pierced. I saw Joseph take Him down and do the ceremonial washing, and mummification. I saw them put Him in that tomb, and roll the 2 ton stone against the door. JESUS IS DEAD! Where is Jesus? How could He die? I know He was the Son of God, and now, He is gone!

WHERE ARE YOU JESUS? I have great news for you. It is not always how it seems. You cannot go by what you see! 2 Corinthians 4:18, while we do not look at the things which are seen, but at the things which are not seen. For the things which are seen are temporary, but the things which are not seen are eternal.
Things are happening in the eternal. Activity, action, power and, for Satan, his defeat is seconds, milliseconds away in eternities time clock. JESUS might be dead in this realm at this moment, BUT, He was active in the eternals.

JESUS WAS WHOOPING ON THE DEVIL DURING HIS MOMENTS OF DEPARTURE FROM THIS WORLD. HE WAS SETTING US UP FOR COMPLETE VICTORY OVER THE DEVIL AND HIS ANGELS.

"I don't see Jesus doing anything." Just because you cannot see Him working, does not mean He is not changing your entire life.

John 11:25-27 Jesus said to her, "I am the resurrection and the life. He who believes in Me, though he may die, he shall live. And whoever lives and believes in Me shall never die. Do you believe this?"She said to Him, "Yes, Lord, I believe that You are the Christ, the Son of God, who is to come into the world."
THE END.... is NOT a part of this TRUTH.

~Dr Micheal Spencer

April 4

Bash the Devils head UNDER THE FOOT!

The very first prophetic word is found in Genesis 3:15,
And I will put enmity between you and the woman, and between your seed and her Seed; he shall bruise your head, and you shall bruise His heel."
A few days ago Satan was shouting in victory that his diabolical plot to kill Jesus would not only be a victory over God, but would also destroy the opportunity for God to save us. He thought he was that sly ol' fox, bursting with pride as the Son of God was sealed in a tomb.
Satan's shouting was coming to an end as he could hear the PRAISE erupting from Abraham's Bosom. The blood of the animals only covered the sins of the Old Testament saints, but something was happening! The blood of the Lamb slain before the foundations of the earth was being applied, and now every sin that a saint of the old covenant committed was washed away, and they now are transported to the presence of glory!
Ephesians 4:9-10, (Now this, "He ascended"—what does it mean but that He also first descended into the lower parts of the earth? He who descended is also the One who ascended far above all the heavens, that He might fill all things.)
Now it was Satan's turn to be whooped, and to be shown that he is not competition to the One True God!
Revelation 1:18, I am He who lives, and was dead, and behold, I am alive forevermore. Amen. And I have the keys of Hades and of Death.
Satan has LOST! He is ABSOLUTELY DEFEATED
Colossians 2:15 Having disarmed principalities and powers, He made a public spectacle of them, triumphing over them in it.
Jesus even made sure that DEATH LOST ITS POWER OF FEAR to the believer!
1 Corinthians 15:54-56 So when this corruptible has put on incorruption, and this mortal has put on immortality, then shall be brought to pass the saying that is written: "Death is swallowed up in victory." "O Death, where is your sting? O Hades, where is your victory?" The sting of death is sin, and the strength of sin is the law.
TODAY, WE ARE VICTORIOUS IN EVERY SITUATION BECAUSE OF THE POWER OF THE RESURRECTION. YOU ARE NOT WEAK, YOU ARE STRONG, AND CAN DO ANYTHING THROUGH JESUS, THE RISEN KING.

~Dr Micheal Spencer

April 5

Kill the Flesh!

I say then: Walk in the Spirit, and you shall not fulfill the lust of the flesh. Galatians 5:16

The appetite of the flesh is constantly striving for more. What is the flesh?
It is our soulish man: our intellect, emotions, and will.
It is what we want, our passions, our desires. When a person is driven by their flesh, then sin is a constant, and spiritual victory is the struggle.

For those who are according to the flesh and are controlled by its unholy desires set their minds on and pursue those things which gratify the flesh, but those who are according to the Spirit and are controlled by the desires of the Spirit set their minds on and seek those things which gratify the [Holy] Spirit. Now the mind of the flesh [which is sense and reason without the Holy Spirit] is death [death that comprises all the miseries arising from sin, both here and hereafter]. But the mind of the [Holy] Spirit is life and [soul] peace [both now and forever]. [That is] because the mind of the flesh [with its carnal thoughts and purposes] is hostile to God, for it does not submit itself to God's Law; indeed it cannot. So then those who are living the life of the flesh [catering to the appetites and impulses of their carnal nature] cannot please or satisfy God, or be acceptable to Him. Romans 8:5-8 AMP

We must do what Paul did to succeed against having our flesh rule our lives.
But [like a boxer] I buffet my body [handle it roughly, discipline it by hardships] and subdue it, for fear that after proclaiming to others the Gospel and things pertaining to it, I myself should become unfit [not stand the test, be unapproved and rejected as a counterfeit].
1 Corinthians 9:27 AMP

KILL THE FLESH TODAY! Whatever is controlling you besides Jesus, break its power today.
~Dr Micheal Spencer

April 6

WORK OUT THE HURT

Pain is a highly concentrated thought (focusing intently on one thing). When you are focused intently on the pain (what hurt you), it will effect your physical self... it can cause sickness and disease.
It's important to get over hurt quickly by training yourself in the Word... every time you go on vacation from your training, you have got to start all over again. (My husband and I did P90X exercise program for 2 months and lost inches, then we went on vacation and didn't resume the exercise program and lost all of our progress.) We need to practice (exercise) the Word daily...moment by moment and not take a "break" from it.

We put more faith (practice/exercise) in emotions, than the Word of God.

Greater is he that is in you than he that is in the world.
1 John 4:4 ASV

The same way hurt works in big situations, is the way it works in everyday "little" things of life. If I execute it in the little things (practice/exercise) I'll be better prepared in the big things.

EMPOWER YOUR LIFE WITH THE WORD AND FIGHT YOUR EMOTIONS (HURTS) OFF.

Bible Reading: 1 Corinthians 2:5, Proverbs 17:22, Ephesians 6:16

~Pastor Rhonda Spencer

April 7

TRUTH – What is it?

There is a way that seems right to a man, But its end is the way of death. Proverbs 14:12

TRUTH – it is what we base our decisions on.

The interesting thing about TRUTH is that so many times truth, to us, is what we believe is truth.
Our truth is based on our thoughts, feelings, experiences. We literally allow our finite minds to make decisions in an infinite world. If we feel something is right or truth, we move into, or on it. When a circumstance looks right, or truthful, then we allow that experience to BE TRUTH, and we make decisions that change lives forever because of that experience. "It just feels right to me," "this makes sense to me," "I believe I am making the right decision," or worse yet, we allow someone else to determine truth for us.
Have you ever talked yourself into something because you wanted it so bad, and then it exploded right in front of you? We blame God, we blame man, we will even blame the
devil, but we really chose that decision because we believed, we're convinced by our own minds.
As a Pastor I have watched MANY make choices of death, and no matter what was said, the individuals could never be talked out of it because they believed it to be TRUTH.
LET'S SET THE BOUNDARIES OF TRUTH – the Word of God is the absolute TRUTH, consistent TRUTH, the voice of the Father in our lives. Any decision that does not lined up with the Word is NOT truth, it is a lie.
The day we allow our thoughts, feelings, experiences, or anyone else to dictate truth to us we begin to walk in error.
KNOW THE WORD! AND YOU WILL KNOW THE TRUTH!!

~Dr Micheal Spencer

April 8

YOU HAVE AUTHORITY

We are not taught about our authority enough. It is easy to blame God or the devil, but **we, who are authorized,** don't want to take responsibility for anything. Jesus said behold I give you authority and nothing by any means hurt you.

Luke 10:19 NKJV Behold, I give you the authority to trample on serpents and scorpions, and over all the power of the enemy, and nothing shall by any means hurt you.

Grab hold of YOUR authority and get some work done in your life today....NOTHING can stay unless YOU allow it!

Bible Reading: Matthew 8:8-10, Mark 13:33-35, Luke 9:1-3

~Pastor Rhonda Spencer

April 9

GOD WON'T COMPETE

Every time you turn your life over to your emotions or feelings, you have made them god of your life. You have put them in charge and this is where that puts God.
HE IS NOT GOING TO COMPETE FOR CONTROL.

Now, whereas God WOULD HAVE shown up in your life IF you said Lord, I take authority over these feelings/ thoughts/emotions, I'm going to overcome evil with good, I'm going to do like I'm supposed to do...THEN God shows up and does something mighty in your life.

Romans 12:21 Do not be overcome by evil, but overcome evil with good.

If you put those emotions/thoughts/feelings in check and do it right and walk in the Word of God and the Love of God, THEN you are EMPLOYING GOD and heaven to work on your behalf. BUT when we selfishly respond in the wrong way or we let our emotions take charge of our life then God CANNOT get involved because our will has made something else to be the god; so, HE won't get involved in the situation.
I wonder if some of the things that happen in our lives, maybe God couldn't get involved in because we chose another god.....
Every time you step in the place of responsibility, HE WON'T.

Bible Reading: Deuteronomy 5:9; 6:5; 10:12, Joshua 22:4-6, Isaiah 59:1-2, Proverbs 19:23, Matthew 22:37

~Pastor Rhonda Spencer

April 10

CHASING FOXES

It is not usually the large issues that take our eyes off Jesus, or disengage us from our calling, but the little beasts that seem to grab our focus.

One of the contrary things for our flesh is to not become distracted. Many people love the foxes, those little fires that keep life shot up with adrenaline. The problem is when you have to have that rush of emotion, drama, excitement, you have to stop moving forward.

A body set in motion tends to stay in motion. The Dog Whisperer said that dogs live in the now, and as long as we are moving forward, they will move forward.

Stop looking for, or even participating with the little foxes.

Hebrews 12:2 looking unto Jesus, the author and finisher of our faith, who for the joy that was set before Him endured the cross, despising the shame, and has sat down at the right hand of the throne of God.

Colossians 3:2 Set your mind on things above, not on things on the earth.

STOP STOPPING!!!

~Dr Micheal Spencer

April 11

HE GAVE YOU THE SHIELD

Put on the whole armor of God, that you may be able to stand against the wiles of the devil. For we do not wrestle against flesh and blood, but against principalities, against powers, against the rulers of the darkness of this age, against spiritual hosts of wickedness in the heavenly places. Therefore take up the whole armor of God, that you may be able to withstand in the evil day, and having done all, to stand. Stand therefore, having girded your waist with truth, having put on the breastplate of righteousness, and having shod your feet with the preparation of the gospel of peace; above all, taking the shield of faith...
Ephesians 6:11-16 NKJV

The only way you can get hurt is when you put the Word of God down and lift up what someone else has said.

You have to hold up the shield.
Put it down and you are exposed and people will hurt you. You are giving them more power than the Word of God and what God says about you.

Always, always hold up what God says about you above what others say.

Bible Reading: Ecclesiastes 7:21-22,

~Pastor Rhonda

April 12

NATURE

In which at one time you walked [habitually]. You were following the course and fashion of this world [were under the sway of the tendency of this present age], following the prince of the power of the air. [You were obedient to and under the control of] the [demon] spirit that still constantly works in the sons of disobedience [the careless, the rebellious, and the unbelieving, who go against the purposes of God]. Ephesians 2:2 AMP

Before we knew Christ we had the normal nature of our father, who is Satan. When a person does not know Jesus as their Savior, they live according to the normal nature of disobedience. Why are you shocked when a sinner lies, cheats and steals? Why are we shocked when the "F" bomb drops out of their mouth every other word? It is their nature, it is who they are as they mimic their father, the devil. BUT!
As a Christian, we no longer have that nature of disobedience. We have the nature of our Father, God!

2 Peter 1:4, by which have been given to us exceedingly great and precious promises, that through these you may be partakers of the divine nature, having escaped the corruption that is in the world through lust.

Habitual sin is not part of who we are any longer!

Romans 6:18, And having been set free from sin, you became slaves of righteousness.
I challenge you today to live by our Dad's nature, which is Divine. Don't say yes to sin, you are free from its clutches.

1 Corinthians 10:13, No temptation has overtaken you except such as is common to man; but God is faithful, who will not allow you to be tempted beyond what you are able, but with the temptation will also make the way of escape, that you may be able to bear it. You can OVERCOME!!

~Dr Micheal Spencer

April 13

What To Do In The Valleys

Yea, though I walk through the valley of the shadow of death, I will fear no evil; For You are with me; Your rod & Your staff, they comfort me. Psalm 23:4

VALLEY OF DEATH

Historically the Valley of the Shadow of Death
Death is the mountain range. The valley was so deep and the mountain was so high that it created a place where the sun does not shine. It is between Jerusalem and Jericho in the same span where the Samaritan man was beaten and left for dead.
It was a place where robbers hid, where animals waited for their prey, damp, dark, and a place that creates and fosters fear.
In our history we can all relate to situations, places and difficult times that have strove to debilitate, arrest, cripple, and have FEAR overtake us.

WE MUST WALK THROUGH

Sheep – we are called His sheep, and Jesus is our Shepherd. Sheep, when it gets dark, tend to lay down. Sheep do not like tight spaces or wet places – they like the wide open. Sheep, when they become afraid, sometimes freeze and fall over. They get very nervous and have a flight zone; they run. For the sheep to live, when they go through the Valley of the Shadow of Death they have to keep moving, move as a flock, and do not lay down!

GOING THROUGH!

Don't give up-Don't lay down-Don't let fear get you to run.

~Dr Micheal Spencer

April 14

Am I Mature?

Brethren, if a man is overtaken in any trespass, you who are spiritual restore such a one in a spirit of gentleness, considering yourself lest you also be tempted.
Galatians 6:1 NKJV

BRETHREN, IF any person is overtaken in misconduct or sin of any sort, you who are spiritual [who are responsive to and controlled by the Spirit] should set him right and restore and reinstate him, without any sense of superiority and with all gentleness, keeping an attentive eye on yourself, lest you should be tempted also.
Galatians 6:1 AMP

Live creatively, friends. If someone falls into sin, forgivingly restore him, saving your critical comments for yourself. You might be needing forgiveness before the day's out. Galatians 6:1 MSG

It is interesting when I hear people say they are mature in the Kingdom, but they have no fruit.
DON'T JUDGE ME, is often heard, but we judge ourselves by the fruit on the tree.
Look around and ask yourself this question, "who have I seen fall away, and did I go after them to forgive and restore?"
The main reason people are not restored is because we are not mature. We are self focused, self driven, and so self absorbed, that a soul flounders and instead of pursuit, we condemn.
BE MATURE, AND RESTORE!!!!

~Dr Micheal Spencer

April 15

Are You a Life Giver?

Death and life are in the power of the tongue, And those who love it will eat its fruit. Proverbs 18:21 NKJV
This is one of my favorite verses as it shows the power that we wield both positive and negative!
We are His Ambassadors.
2 Corinthians 5:20, Now then, we are ambassadors for Christ, as though God were pleading through us: we implore you on Christ's behalf, be reconciled to God.

In this real world we have the ability today to bring life to our environment.

You have been given so much power that your company is blessed because you are there! When you speak life, when you prophesy over the environment, when you prophesy over the business, when you prophesy over the owners, you will release the eternal to touch the temporal.

In the same sense, if you curse the environment, business and owners you release the demise of that company.

This is also the same principle with your family, church and life! The Word says you will eat of the fruit of your mouth. What you prophesy is what you will eat, either cursing or blessing. Speak life and you will eat good; speak death and you will be licking the dry bones.

Be that healthy, life-giving apple in the midst of spoiled, rotten apples. You have been granted this power, how will you wield your tongue today?

~Dr Micheal Spencer

April 16

Spiritually Over-Weight!
When I was a kid I was thin as a rail! BUT
Now, the rail is still there, but, a little harder to find....lol!
What is the main difference?
The teaching on weight loss, and health comes down to eating, and the satanic word called exercise.
I know the amount of calories to eat in a day to keep my weight down, but even if the weight isn't there without that evil word called exercise I am still not in shape.
Spiritually it is the same thing.
Exercise daily in God—no spiritual flabbiness, please! Workouts in the gymnasium are useful, but a disciplined life in God is far more so, making you fit both today and forever. 1 Timothy 4:8 MSG

EXERCISE IS THE WAY DADDY CREATED US TO STAY ALIVE, AND HEALTHY.
But solid food is for full-grown men, for those whose senses and mental faculties are trained by practice to discriminate and distinguish between what is morally good and noble and what is evil and contrary either to divine or human law. Hebrews 5:14 AMP

Jesus wants to grow us up! That means we must exercise our faith. Most Christians go to church, eat the Word, and do nothing with it. They remain spiritually fat, and never exercise their faith beyond the building.
LET US EXERCISE TODAY....ASK THE HOLY SPIRIT WHO YOU NEED TO SHARE HIM WITH TODAY.
HOW CAN YOU EXERCISE YOUR FAITH IN SOMEONE ELSE'S LIFE TODAY?
BE A GIVER, NOT A TAKER!

~Dr Micheal Spencer

April 17

Think BIG!

Now to Him Who, by (in consequence of) the [action of His] power that is at work within us, is able to [carry out His purpose and] do super-abundantly, far over and above all that we [dare] ask or think [infinitely beyond our highest prayers, desires, thoughts, hopes, or dreams]– To Him be glory in the church and in Christ Jesus throughout all generations forever and ever. Amen (so be it). Ephesians 3:20, 21 AMP

Father wants us to stretch our faith to believe that He is HUGE!

God has never planned us to be failures, or just to barely make it. Father's plan is that your life will draw attention to Him so people will ask about His goodness.

Listen to these words:
super-abundantly, far over and above all that we [dare] ask or think

That doesn't sound like survival to me! Let's start dreaming, start thinking, start asking BIG! Father wants us to step into a new level of success & blessing. Start today! What would you ask for if there was no restrictions? Be brave, pray, believe for it today.

~Dr Micheal Spencer

April 18

BEING HURT WILL ONLY ROB FROM YOU

BEING HURT WILL ONLY ROB FROM YOU.
It doesn't hurt the other person, it hurts you. I have heard it said that its like drinking poison and expecting the other person to die.

Pause and think- Let your thinking be in line with the Word.... Let your thinking be in line with the love of God and the character of God.

Proverbs 12:18 Wrong words are like the piercing of a sword but a man of wisdom brings healing.

Bible Reading: Matthew 15:11, Proverbs 6:2,
1 Peter 5:8, Galatians 6:7

~Pastor Rhonda Spencer

April 19

We All Want To Be Liked

Yes, and all who desire to live godly in Christ Jesus will suffer persecution. 2 Timothy 3:12

We all want to be liked and accepted by people who surround us. When you choose to truly live for Jesus, there are going to be people who will dislike you, even though you didn't do anything against them. They will gossip about you, lie about you, treat you like dirt, and for no other reason but that you love Jesus.
Please know that it is not against you but because you house the Spirit of God. Remember, we fight not against flesh & blood.

2 Corinthians 10:3-5, For though we walk in the flesh, we do not war according to the flesh. For the weapons of our warfare are not carnal but mighty in God for pulling down strongholds, casting down arguments and every high thing that exalts itself against the knowledge of God, bringing every thought into captivity to the obedience of Christ,

Don't take it personal, the spirit they carry is reacting to the Spirit who lives inside you. What do you do?

1. Pray for them
2. Do good to them
3. Do not let anyone steal your joy

Matthew 5:44, But I say to you, love your enemies, bless those who curse you, do good to those who hate you, and pray for those who spitefully use you and persecute you.

~Dr Micheal Spencer

April 20

DON'T LET YOUR THINKING TALK YOU OUT OF YOUR DESTINY

Because when they knew and recognized Him as God, they did not honor and glorify Him as God or give Him thanks. **But instead they became futile and godless in their thinking [with vain imaginings, foolish reasoning, and stupid speculations] and their senseless minds were darkened** Romans 1:21 AMP

We aren't getting to the blessings or destiny of what God has- not because God can't,
"But I've been praying--- why didn't God do it".

Why? -- You show your why....emotions have moved you into negativity and complaining.
This is pointing you in THAT direction.

Complaining= **another way of talking yourself out of where you are supposed to be!!!**

Bible Reading: Numbers 11:1, Philippians 2:14, Ecclesiastes 5:3

~Pastor Rhonda Spencer

April 21

Pee In Your Coffee?

With it [the tongue] we bless our God and Father, and with it we curse men, who have been made in the similitude of God. Out of the same mouth proceed blessing and cursing. My brethren, these things ought not to be so. Does a spring send forth fresh water and bitter from the same opening? Can a fig tree, my brethren, bear olives, or a grapevine bear figs? Thus no spring yields both salt water and fresh. James 3:9-12 NKJV

Of course you would not pee in your coffee.....I hope!! BUT! We do!

Our mouth determines our success or failure, it is the microphone of our hearts. When we speak doubt, unbelief, discouragement, or just sheer defeat over our lives, then we have just contaminated our life.

Today govern yourself, evaluate yourself. How many times to you speak death to your situation rather than life?

Faith is not ignoring the fact, it's declaring the TRUTH!

~Dr Micheal Spencer

April 22

DON'T CUT GOD OFF

Some hurt comes from not understanding why God didn't do something you asked, BUT you can't get offended with God. He's the only one that can get you out of your mess--- if you get offended at God you're leaving yourself stranded.

We've given authority over to our emotions rather than to God.

Job 15:11-13 (CEV) And you have been offered comforting words from God. Isn't this enough? Your emotions are out of control, making you look fierce; that's why you attack God with everything you say.

Turn to God even if you don't understand. The last thing you need is to cut of the SUPERNATURAL from your life, yet many times that's exactly what we do.

Remember God is good all the time and never bad.

Bible Reading: Proverbs 3:5, Isaiah 31:1, Psalm 9:10; 18:2; 20:7

~Pastor Rhonda Spencer

April 23

STONE ROLLER

And they went out and preached everywhere, the Lord working with them and confirming the word through the accompanying signs. Amen. Mark 16:20

Jesus said, "Take away the stone." John 11:39a

God has chosen to use man in working His works. Abraham, Moses, Deborah, the entire nation of Israel was saved by Esther, Chuza, Suzanna, children of Israel.....
God has always used people to lead, work, and give in the accomplishing of His will. God in His Sovereignty has chosen to use people to get His will done.
The story of Lazarus is so powerful, and it is found in John 11. We always focus on Lazarus in this historical experience, but today I want to see some different champions.
John 11:38-44, Then Jesus, again groaning in Himself, came to the tomb. It was a cave, and a stone lay against it. Jesus said, "Take away the stone."Martha, the sister of him who was dead, said to Him, "Lord, by this time there is a stench, for he has been dead four days." Jesus said to her, "Did I not say to you that if you would believe you would see the glory of God?" Then they took away the stone from the place where the dead man was lying.

1) Roll away the stone!
2) If you desire to see the miracle, if you desire to see my glory, if you want what you are believing for, ROLL BACK THE STONE!
3) Lazarus would have remained in the grave IF some people did not roll back the stone! God's glory would not have been seen if PEOPLE did not ROLL BACK THE STONE! Thank God for Lazarus raising from the dead, but the miracle would not have happened without the UNKNOWN, UNIDENTIFIED PEOPLE who rolled the stone back!
4) Today God has raised you and I up as STONE ROLLERS so His glory will be seen! We are the ones He has chosen to lead, work and give so He can show His love to people.

~Dr Micheal Spencer

April 24

You Are Never Alone

You have never had an alone moment in your life! Stop speaking that you are so alone.

Why would you ever complain, O Jacob, or, whine, Israel, saying, "God has lost track of me. He doesn't care what happens to me"? Don't you know anything? Haven't you been listening? God doesn't come and go. God lasts. He's Creator of all you can see or imagine. He doesn't get tired out, doesn't pause to catch his breath. And he knows everything, inside and out. He energizes those who get tired, gives fresh strength to dropouts. For even young people tire and drop out, young folk in their prime stumble and fall. But those who wait upon God get fresh strength. They spread their wings and soar like eagles, They run and don't get tired, they walk and don't lag behind. Isaiah 40:27-31 MSG

YOU ARE NOT ALONE.
Challenge: Cover your mouth. The saying "if you don't have anything good to say; don't say anything at all" is true. Stop complaining and put your trust in God, the Creator of the universe is with you.

Bible Reading: Hebrews 13:5, Joshua 1:5

~Pastor Rhonda Spencer

April 25

NO REGRET

Work at getting along with each other and with God. Otherwise you'll never get so much as a glimpse of God. Make sure no one gets left out of God's generosity. Keep a sharp eye out for weeds of bitter discontent. A THISTLE OR TWO GONE TO SEED CAN RUIN A WHOLE GARDEN in no time. Watch out for the Esau syndrome: trading away God's lifelong gift in order to satisfy a short-term appetite. You well know how Esau later regretted that impulsive act and wanted God's blessing - but by then it was too late, tears or no tears. (Hebrews 12:15-17 MSG)

~Pastor Rhonda Spencer

April 26

Your Success is not an Accident!

1 Corinthians 9:24-27 NLT Don't you realize that in a race everyone runs but only one person gets the prize? So run to win! All athletes are disciplined in their training. They do it to win a prize that will fade away, but we do it for an eternal prize. So I run with purpose in every step. I am not just shadowboxing. I discipline my body like an athlete, training it to do what it should. Otherwise, I fear that after preaching to others, I myself might be disqualified.

WE ARE RUNNING THE RACE TO WIN, NOT LOSE! God has told us that we are to CHAMPION this race, and Jesus has given us everything we need to accomplish the VICTORY. We CANNOT LOSE unless we are not PURPOSED and DISCIPLINED.

There is a horrible plot that has unraveled in American churches. The average person goes to church only once a month. Most American Christians are on a 3-week rotation because they have other things that are more important than the invitation of the King to come to His house every week and eat from His table. We have so many other priorities in our lives. I know families who take the summer off to "camp" while others cannot come because their children have "sports". I actually have had adults say they could not come because they were afraid of thunder and lightening.

UNDISCIPLINED PEOPLE PRODUCE NO RESULTS. They start running the race but are swelled up with fatigue because they never took the race seriously.

BE PURPOSED! BE DISCIPLINED! BE SUCCESSFUL! No results in your walk with Christ? ASK YOURSELF IF YOU ARE PURPOSED AND DISCIPLINED. Even Paul said, "Otherwise, I fear that after preaching to others I might myself be disqualified."

~Dr Micheal Spencer

April 27

CHOOSE YOUR BATTLES

We immediately want to jump to defend ourselves and destroy people who have wronged us. These actions are prideful, selfish, unwise and carnal. We need to realize we are a sample of Christians to our society and when we choose to battle we need to do it according to the Word of God AND the Love of God.

Proverbs 15:18 A wrathful man sirs up strife, but he who is slow to anger allays contention.
Proverbs 17:4 The beginning of strife is like releasing water; therefore stop contention before a quarrel starts.
2 Timothy 2:23 But avoid foolish and ignorant disputes, knowing that they generate strife.
1 Corinthians 3:3 for you are still carnal. For where there are envy, strife, and divisions among you, are you not carnal and behaving like mere men?
Galatians 5:15 But if you bite and devour one another, be careful that you (and your whole fellowship) are not consumed by one another.
James 3:16 For where envy and self-seeking exist, confusion and every evil thing are there.

No one wins when you fight according to your flesh... walk in the Love of God, chose your battles wisely and WIN EVERY TIME.

~Pastor Rhonda Spencer

April 28

WHY PEOPLE ARE NOT BLESSED

God never blesses disobedience
Deuteronomy 28:15 "But it shall come to pass, if you do not obey the voice of the Lord your God, to observe carefully all His commandments and His statutes which I command you today, that all these curses will come upon you and overtake you:"

When we curse ourselves with our tongue (speech).
Proverbs 18:21 Death and life are in the power of the tongue, And those who love it will eat its fruit.

When we allow our mind, thoughts to supersede the Word (unbelief).
Romans 11:20 Well said. Because of unbelief they were broken off, and you stand by faith. Do not be haughty, but fear.
Hebrews 3:19 So we see that they could not enter in because of unbelief.

When we have false humility (believe ourself to be holier because they have nothing).
Mark 7:13 making the word of God of no effect through your tradition which you have handed down. And many such things you do.

When we beat ourselves up; Satan condemns; people condemn (not worthy of God's blessing).
Romans 8:1 There is therefore now no condemnation to those who are in Christ Jesus, who do not walk according to the flesh, but according to the Spirit.

~Dr Micheal Spencer

April 29

Hyper Faith!!

But without faith it is impossible to please and be satisfactory to Him. For whoever would come near to God must [necessarily] believe that God exists and that He is the rewarder of those who earnestly and diligently seek Him [out]. Hebrews 11:6 AMP

I have had people say to me, "You are one of those hyper faith preachers!"
My answer is always, "Yes, of course, and thank you for the compliment."

The Word says that it is impossible to PLEASE our Father without trusting, putting faith in Him. I don't know about you, but I want to please my Daddy more than anything. According to His Word, I have to have faith, and the more faith I have in Him, the more He is pleased with me.

Those individuals meant their statement as an attack on my beliefs, but it was a tremendous compliment that others see that I have faith that is growing, and able to believe that a BIG God is able to do BIG things in our lives.

We all have a measure of faith, how full is your cup?

Romans 10:17 So then faith comes by hearing, and hearing by the word of God.

GET INTO THE WORD TODAY!!!!!

~Dr Micheal Spencer

April 30

The Race is NOT over

I have fought the good fight, I have finished the race, I have kept the faith. Finally, there is laid up for me the crown of righteousness, which the Lord, the righteous Judge, will give to me on that Day, and not to me only but also to all who have loved His appearing.
2 Timothy 4:7-8

The race is daily, sometimes hourly, and in times of great pressure, the race can be defined by the seconds. When the race gets intense, the defining moments are not those seconds, but the time that was spent preparing for the race. TAKE 15 (taking 15 minutes daily and spending time with Jesus), reading the Word, and being in Church and classes, is God's strengthening plan. No Word, prayer or fellowship, makes you weak. Experiences are gauged by the preparation before the experience. Most of the time, we wait for hell to lick our toes before we prepare, but this is why the experience can cripple our hearts. When you're in the Word, in prayer and in fellowship, the experience isn't any less real, but it ends up not controlling you, you control it. I am not saying it goes away, but it will not own the thoughts, actions, and passions that belong to Jesus. Don't give up, don't be discouraged. Get into the Word, get into prayer, get into fellowship, and you will FINISH the race, and strong!

If then you were raised with Christ, seek those things which are above, where Christ is, sitting at the right hand of God. Set your mind on things above, not on things on the earth. Colossians 3:1-2

~Dr Micheal Spencer

May 1

You're Gonna Poke Your Eye Out!

Hebrews 12:2 looking unto Jesus, the author and finisher of our faith, who for the joy that was set before Him endured the cross, despising the shame, and has sat down at the right hand of the throne of God.

Matthew 6:22-23 The lamp of the body is the eye. If therefore your eye is good, your whole body will be full of light. But if your eye is bad, your whole body will be full of darkness. If therefore the light that is in you is darkness, how great is that darkness!

I get it now more than ever before. Your entire personage, your spirit, your soul and your body have been created to go where we aim our eyes (attention).
If you are ever going to ride a bicycle, motorcycle or even drive a car, one of the first things they teach you is that where you look, you go! On a motorcycle when you go into a curve, you do not look at the road right in front of you, but you fix your eyes on the curve many yards ahead, and your body will automatically lean the amount needed to navigate through that curve.
Where are our eyes focused?
Where, and what are our minds thinking?
Whose that's are controlling our navigation system?
Our eyes, attention, acknowledgment, literally screams the light or darkness that is in our soul.

If your right eye causes you to sin, pluck it out and cast it from you; for it is more profitable for you that one of your members perish, than for your whole body to be cast into hell. Matthew 5:29

~Dr Micheal Spencer

May 2

Don't Lay on the Sword! Part 1

For the word of God is quick, and powerful, and sharper than any two-edged sword, piercing even to the dividing asunder of soul and spirit, and of the joints and marrow, and is a discerner of the thoughts and intents of the heart. Hebrews 4:12

The devil is a wise adversary. He is not going to get you to deny the Word, or stop believing the Word, but he will get you to lay down the sword so you are DEFENSELESS.
THE WORD IS POWER AGAINST THE DEVIL

Jesus used the Word against the devil
Mat 4:3-11 And when the tempter came to him, he said, If thou be the Son of God, command that these stones be made bread. But he answered and said, It is written, Man shall not live by bread alone, but by every word that proceedeth out of the mouth of God. Then the devil taketh him up into the holy city, and setteth him on a pinnacle of the temple, and saith unto him, If thou be the Son of God, cast thyself down: for it is written, He shall give his angels charge concerning thee: and in their hands they shall bear thee up, lest at any time thou dash thy foot against a stone. Jesus said unto him, It is written again, Thou shalt not tempt the Lord thy God. Again, the devil taketh him up into an exceeding high mountain, and showeth him all the kingdoms of the world, and the glory of them; and saith unto him, All these things will I give thee, if thou wilt fall down and worship me. Then saith Jesus unto him, Get thee hence, Satan: for it is written, Thou shalt worship the Lord thy God, and him only shalt thou serve. Then the devil leaveth him, and, behold, angels came and ministered unto him.

The Word is the greatest weapon coupled with prayer to tear down the devils strongholds.
The antichrist and beast will be destroyed by the sword that comes from the mouth of Jesus (Revelation 19:20-21)

~Dr Micheal Spencer

May 3

Don't Lay on the Sword! Part 2

The devil will try to get you to lay down the sword
1. He will do it by lulling people to sleep. Matthew 26:40-41 And he cometh unto the disciples, and findeth them asleep, and saith unto Peter, What, could ye not watch with me one hour? Watch and pray, that ye enter not into temptation: the spirit indeed is willing, but the flesh is weak.
2. Steal it -Matthew 13:19 When any one heareth the word of the kingdom, and understandeth it not, then cometh the wicked one, and catcheth away that which was sown in his heart. This is he which received seed by the way side.
3. Choke it -Matthew 13:22 He also that received seed among the thorns is he that heareth the word; and the care of this world, and the deceitfulness of riches, choke the word, and he becometh unfruitful.
4. Making it religious – Mark 7:13 Making the word of God of none effect through your tradition, which ye have delivered: and many such like things do ye.

WE need a fresh passion for HIS WORD.

Psalm 51:10 – Create in me a clean heart O God & renew a right spirit within me.
Acts 6:7 And the word of God increased; and the number of the disciples multiplied in Jerusalem greatly; and a great company of the priests were obedient to the faith.
Acts 12:24 But the word of God grew and multiplied.
Acts 19:20 So mightily grew the word of God and prevailed.
Colossians 3:16 Let the word of Christ dwell in you richly in all wisdom; teaching and admonishing one another in psalms and hymns and spiritual songs, singing with grace in your hearts to the Lord.

~Dr Micheal Spencer

May 4

THOUGHTS + HEART = MOUTH

There are two types of thoughts.
God thoughts or Flesh thoughts.

For as he thinks in his heart, so is he. Proverbs 23:7

Our thoughts are first, which shows the condition of the heart, the mouth is just the evidence of what is already resident.

A good man out of the good treasure of his heart brings forth good; and an evil man out of the evil treasure of his heart brings forth evil. For out of the abundance of the heart his mouth speaks. Luke 6:45

The first need is to THINK THE THOUGHTS OF GOD = THE WORD.
Our hearts will respond to the Word with FAITH. Our mouth will then evidence what is abundant in our heart.

Bible Reading: Philippians 4:7-9; 1 Chronicles 28:9; Heb 4:11-13

~Pastor Rhonda Spencer

May 5

Seed + God's Plan = Harvest! (Part 1)

As for what was sown on good soil, this is he who hears the Word and grasps and comprehends it; he indeed bears fruit and yields in one case a hundred times as much as was sown, in another sixty times as much, and in another thirty. Matthew 13:23 AMP

The good ground.

1. What is good ground?
a. The only is ONE reason for planting
   – PRODUCTION!
b. How do you know that the ground you are planting your seed in is GOOD GROUND?
   i. It is balanced soil. The Word of God is the priority. It is the grounding, and foundational principles of the Kingdom. (Hebrews 5:12-6:3)
   ii. It is productive soil.
      -People are saved.
      -People are healed.
      -People are filled with the Spirit.
      -People are delivered.
      -People grow.
      -People reproduce.

~Dr Micheal Spencer

May 6

Seed + God's Plan = Harvest! (Part 2)

2. We determine our own harvest.
   a. Joshua 1: 8 This book of the Law shall not depart out of your mouth, but you shall meditate on it by day and by night, so that you may be careful to do according to all that is written in it. For then you shall make your way prosperous, and then you shall act wisely.
   b. Obedience to the Word – 1 Samuel 15:22 And Samuel said, Does Jehovah delight in burnt offerings and sacrifices as in obeying the voice of Jehovah? Behold, to obey is better than sacrifice! To listen is better than the fat of rams!
   c. Feeding on the Word – Ephesians 5:25-27 Husbands, love your wives, even as Christ also loved the church and gave Himself for it, that He might sanctify and cleanse it with the washing of water by the Word, that He might present it to Himself as the glorious church, without spot or wrinkle or any such things, but that it should be holy and without blemish.
   d. 1 Corinthians 3:8-9 So he planting, and he watering, are one, and each one shall receive his own reward according to his own labor. For of God we are fellow-workers, a field of God, and you are a building of God.

We determine our own harvest.
How we water, fertilize, protect – the more intense the attention, the more crop production.

~Dr Micheal Spencer

May 7

Seed + God's Plan = Harvest! (Part 3)

"Study this story of the farmer planting seed. When anyone hears news of the kingdom and doesn't take it in, it just remains on the surface, and so the Evil One comes along and plucks it right out of that person's heart. This is the seed the farmer scatters on the road. "The seed cast in the gravel-this is the person who hears and instantly responds with enthusiasm. But there is no soil of character, and so when the emotions wear off and some difficulty arrives, there is nothing to show for it. (Matthew 13:18-21 MSG)
The destructive ground

3. The Cares of the world
   a. So many Christians live by sight and not by faith.
   2 Corinthians 4:18 While we look not at the things which are seen, but at the things which are not seen: for the things which are seen are temporal; but the things which are not seen are eternal.
   b. Distracted by life
   c. Demas, who worked with Paul, he saw all the miracles, heard all the teaching, but sold out. / 2Timothy 4:10 For Demas hath forsaken me, having loved this present world, and is departed unto Thessalonica; Crescens to Galatia, Titus unto Dalmatia.
   d. One of the greatest ways the devil Steals the gospel from your heart (Stealing the seed) is by getting you so involved with even good things, so we do Not take care of the BEST things.
   e. Work, love, family, sleep, sports, friends: It is not that any of these things are BAD, but If the enemy can get us to pay more attention to the cares of the world, then the distractions will destroy the seed.

Do not let the Devil Distract with temporary things.
Keep the seed safe.

~Dr Micheal Spencer

May 8

Consider Others

Fill up and complete my joy by living in harmony and being of the same mind and one in purpose, having the same love, being in full accord and of one harmonious mind and intention. Do nothing from factional motives [through contentiousness, strife, selfishness, or for unworthy ends] or prompted by conceit and empty arrogance. Instead, in the true spirit of humility (lowliness of mind) let each regard the others as better than and superior to himself [thinking more highly of one another than you do of yourselves]. Let each of you esteem and look upon and be concerned for not [merely] his own interests, but also each for the interests of others. Philippians 2:2-4 AMP

Live in unity and consider others more important than yourself...I just love His Word that teaches us how we should live. So lets LIVE IT.

Bible Reading: 2 Corinthians 12:19-21; Romans 13:12-14; 1 Corinthians 3:3; 1 Corinthians 12:11-13; Ephesians 4:2-4

~Pastor Rhonda Spencer

May 9

Stop Being Negative!

Psalm 95:2 Let us come before His presence with thanksgiving; Let us shout joyfully to Him with psalms.

THE COMPLAINING & NEGATIVE
Newspapers and just human nature, we usually steer towards the negative of the situation rather than being a person of thanksgiving and praise.
The children of Israel did this well
Complaining when they came to the Red Sea: They were being led by a pillar of fire at night, and a cloud by day, hummmm, think God was with them?
Red Sea – Ex. 14:11, Then they said to Moses, "Because there were no graves in Egypt, have you taken us away to die in the wilderness? Why have you so dealt with us, to bring us up out of Egypt?
God delivers them on dry ground and the Sea comes back and drowns the entire Egyptian Army.
Bitter water made sweet at Marah & Bread from heaven: Ex. 16:3, And the children of Israel said to them, "Oh, that we had died by the hand of the Lord in the land of Egypt, when we sat by the pots of meat and when we ate bread to the full! For you have brought us out into this wilderness to kill this whole assembly with hunger." Thirst – water comes from the Rock
If we took just our morning today, would our conversation be more complaining or thankfulness?
WE ARE A VERY BLESSED PEOPLE
Some would say, "You have no idea how bad it is"
"Be thankful for what you have and you can be trusted to appreciate more"
-You have JESUS AND ETERNITY-You have the WORD OF GOD-You have BREATH-You have FREEDOM-You have LOVE-You have FAMILY-You have A PLACE TO LAY YOUR HEAD-You have CLOTHES ON YOUR BACK-
The list is massive. Take a moment and write down 10 things you are thankful for in your life.

~Dr Micheal Spencer

May 10

GUARD YOUR MOUTH

A man shall eat well by the fruit of his mouth,
But the soul of the unfaithful feeds on violence. He who guards his mouth preserves his life, But he who opens wide his lips shall have destruction.
Proverbs 13:2-3

Set a guard, O Lord, over my mouth;
Keep watch over the door of my lips. Psalm 141:3

Satan's plan – Satan actually believes what Jesus teaches. Satan takes Jesus at His Word. Satan actually watched God create with words and he understands the power of words.
He actually heard Jesus establish and fortify the principle of the spoken word of faith in Mark 11:23-24.
Satan knows that if he get you to speak death, doubt and unbelief, you shall have what you say......
Satan's goal is to get you to have faith in him, your circumstances, instead of having faith, trust in the Word of God.
Who you agree with, you speak about, which establishes your destiny.

BE CAREFUL OF YOUR THOUGHTS, ESTABLISH THEM ON THE WORD, THEN YOUR FAITH WILL RISE AND YOU WILL BE ABLE TO LOOK AT THE MOUNTAINS IN YOUR LIFE AND SPEAK TO THEM, AND THEY WILL CHANGE!

~Pastor Rhonda Spencer

May 11

I Really HATE You!

We all cannot deny the emotions of hurt, but we do have control of them.

When we are saved we now have control over our soul (intellect, emotions & will), instead of it controlling us.

We might not be able to able to arrest the initial flood of emotions, but we MUST take control of them as soon as possible or they will give the devil a foothold.
Ephesians 4:27 nor give place to the devil.
Here is the start of healing your wound.

1. Ask Jesus to heal you
2. Matthew 5:23-25
Therefore if you bring your gift to the altar, and there remember that your brother has something against you, leave your gift there before the altar, and go your way. First be reconciled to your brother, and then come and offer your gift. Agree with your adversary quickly, while you are on the way with him, lest your adversary deliver you to the judge, the judge hand you over to the officer, and you be thrown into prison.
3. Luke 6:27-28
" But I say to you who hear: Love your enemies, do good to those who hate you, bless those who curse you, and pray for those who spitefully use you.

Never let hatred own your life! Be FREE in Jesus!!!

~Dr Micheal Spencer

May 12

Have Nothing To Do With It

But refuse (shut your mind against, have nothing to do with) trifling (ill-informed, unedifying, stupid) controversies over ignorant questionings, for you know that they foster strife and breed quarrels. And the servant of the Lord must not be quarrelsome (fighting and contending). Instead, he must be kindly to everyone and mild-tempered [preserving the bond of peace]; he must be a skilled and suitable teacher, patient and forbearing and willing to suffer wrong. He must correct his opponents with courtesy and gentleness, in the hope that God may grant that they will repent and come to know the Truth [that they will perceive and recognize and become accurately acquainted with and acknowledge it], And that they may come to their senses [and] escape out of the snare of the devil, having been held captive by him, [henceforth] to do His [God's] will.
2 Timothy 2:23-26 AMP

Don't fall for the trap of division in your life today.

Bible Reading: Proverbs 26:20-22; Joel 2:13; Galatians 5:22

~Pastor Rhonda Spencer

May 13

THE DEMON OF DOUBT

James 1:6-8 But let him ask in faith, with no doubting, for he who doubts is like a wave of the sea driven and tossed by the wind. For let not that man suppose that he will receive anything from the Lord; he is a double-minded man, unstable in all his ways.

If FAITH is our Victory, then DOUBT is our defeat!
Doubt should be hated as much as the devil is hated because it will steal the blessing.
We know that is John 10:10, Satan has come to steal, kill and destroy
We also know that if Faith is our Victory, the DOUBT is our Failure, which makes doubt our enemy.
In the very Garden of Eden – Satan seeded doubt of God's Word to Eve, and when the seed of doubt took root, their minds were divided and the direction was the wrong fork in the road.
Doubt is when we question what we know is true.
You cannot doubt what you do not believe.
So you believe the Word is true, you have faith, BUT, when doubt comes it creates that fork in the road.
We must hate doubt!
It is the road of failure and discouragement. It is the road of unanswered prayers!
The saddest part about doubt is what it does to us.
Our lives become governed by the tides of life, and when the storm surge comes, it floods every part of our lives
It means that we are now governed by every word and statement, every environment, every newscast, every circumstance. We are now owned, and ruled, by the world.

HATE DOUBT!!

~Dr Micheal Spencer

May 14

He Is With You

"Fear not, for I have redeemed you; I have called you by your name; You are Mine. When you pass through the waters, I will be with you; And through the rivers, they shall not overflow you. When you walk through the fire, you shall not be burned, Nor shall the flame scorch you. For I am the Lord your God. Fear not, for I am with you. Isaiah 43:2-3, 5 NKJV

It's awesome to know that the King of Kings, Creator of the whole world is with you. Me? YES, YOU!

HE IS WITH YOU.

Bible Reading: Psalm 23; Hebrews 13:5; 2 Corinthians 6:16

~Pastor Rhonda Spencer

May 15

What's In YOUR BOX?

There it is.....the purse, the wallet...a zipper, a padlock, an alarm device when the Pastor begins talking about tithing, alms and seed.
Giving is one of the hottest topics in church on a Sunday morning.
When we talk about giving in the church, this is the portion of the service, and our lives, when we literally show the very nature of God through our natural practical lives.
When we obey God with the tithe we are declaring – YOU ARE MY SOURCE!
When we give an alms (giving to the poor), we are showing the nature of caring of our God.
When we give seed, we are showing the creative nature of our God.
Our lives should be the CHARACTER OF GIVING.
"For God loved the world so much that he gave his one and only Son, so that everyone who believes in him will not perish but have eternal life. John 3:16 NLT
"No one can serve two masters. For you will hate one and love the other; you will be devoted to one and despise the other. You cannot serve both God and money. Matthew 6:24 NLT
While he was eating, a woman came in with a beautiful alabaster jar of expensive perfume and poured it over his head. The disciples were indignant when they saw this. "What a waste!" they said. "It could have been sold for a high price and the money given to the poor." But Jesus, aware of this, replied, "Why criticize this woman for doing such a good thing to me? You will always have the poor among you, but you will not always have me. She has poured this perfume on me to prepare my body for burial. I tell you the truth, wherever the Good News is preached throughout the world, this woman's deed will be remembered and discussed." Matthew 26:7-13 NLT
She would be remembered and discussed because she gave ALL to the Master. What is in your box?

~Dr Micheal Spencer

May 16

INSIDE OUT PEOPLE

For as many as are led by the Spirit of God, these are sons of God. Romans 8:14
I have been crucified with Christ; it is no longer I who live, but Christ lives in me; and the life which I now live in the flesh I live by faith in the Son of God, who loved me and gave Himself for me. Galatians 2:20
WE are different from the world.
The world lives from the outside in – that means that what touches their life from their environment directly affects, and directs their lives. They seek from the outside all their needs, physical, emotional, spiritual, and monitory, everything comes from the outside.
So if life is difficult, the outside in people seek help from the natural world system to meet the need. This is how we have been trained to live. The reason it does not work is because our lives will never stabilize. The world, natural life is never the same, it is unpredictable, and unstable. As a person works from the outside in, they will never achieve stability because there is none.
WE ARE INSIDE OUT PEOPLE!
We are governed, directed, established, not by what we see, not by what the environment dictates, but we are established from the ONE who lives inside us, out.
2 Corinthians 5:7, For we walk by faith, not by sight.
Our lives should be effecting the outside, because of who lives on our inside.
Colossians 1:27, To them God willed to make known what are the riches of the glory of this mystery among the Gentiles: which is Christ in you, the hope of glory.
You and I, who are governed, directed, given peace, given wisdom, given favor, are people who live from the INSIDE OUT.
ALLOW JESUS TO LIVE INSIDE OUT OF YOU TODAY!

~Dr Micheal Spencer

May 17

STOP LOOKING AT YOUR SHOES

There was a branch of the religious group called the Pharisee's called the "no see-ums" They did not want to look at evil so they never looked up. They were funny to watch as they were explained in the books because they constantly bumped into things. They would just never look up...DUH!
Christians do this all the time too.
They start looking down at their shoes, instead of looking up where our help comes from.

My help comes from the Lord,
Who made heaven and earth. Psalm 121:2

If you are always looking at your shoes when trouble comes, then you will never see your help coming, and you will lose HOPE.

Hope deferred makes the heart sick,
But when the desire comes, it is a tree of life.
Proverbs 13:12
STOP! LOOK UP!
OK, steady yourself!
READY?
FOCUS on Jesus......
Colossians 3:1-2, If then you were raised with Christ, seek those things which are above, where Christ is, sitting at the right hand of God. 2 Set your mind on things above, not on things on the earth.
WALK AND PRAISE AND YOU WILL SEE YOUR LIFE DIFFERENTLY!

~Dr Micheal Spencer

May 18

The Greatest Possession

Yes, furthermore, I count everything as loss compared to the possession of the priceless privilege (the overwhelming preciousness, the surpassing worth, and supreme advantage) of knowing Christ Jesus my Lord and of progressively becoming more deeply and intimately acquainted with Him [of perceiving and recognizing and understanding Him more fully and clearly]. For His sake I have lost everything and consider it all to be mere rubbish (refuse, dregs), in order that I may win (gain) Christ (the Anointed One), And that I may [actually] be found and known as in Him, not having any [self-achieved] righteousness that can be called my own, based on my obedience to the Law's demands, but possessing that [genuine righteousness] which comes through faith in Christ (the Anointed One), the [truly] right standing with God, which comes from God by [saving] faith. [For my determined purpose is] that I may know Him [that I may progressively become more deeply and intimately acquainted with Him, perceiving and recognizing and understanding the wonders of His Person more strongly and more clearly], and that I may in that same way come to know the power outflowing from His resurrection. Philippians 3:8-10 AMP

Jesus is OUR GREATEST TREASURE!

Bible Reading: Psalm 119:162; 2 Corinthians 2:2-5

~Pastor Rhonda Spencer

May 19

NO COMPROMISE Part 1

If compromise is an option in your walk with Christ – YOU WILL COMPROMISE!

The enemy will make compromising opportunities to come into your life consistently.

CHRISTIANS MIGHT NOT BE CONSISTENT, BUT SATAN IS....

But if not, let it be known to you, O king, that we do not serve your gods, nor will we worship the gold image which you have set up." Daniel 3:18

The Hebrew boys had determined that compromise, bowing down to another god, was not an option.

What is an idol?
It is anything, or anyone, that you put in front of God.
Money, work, man, woman, sex, TV, sleep, booze......
ANYTHING THAT TAKES PRIORITY OVER JESUS.
The Hebrew boys determined that no matter what the cost, they would never trade their living God for a temporary satisfaction and acceptance.

~Dr Micheal Spencer

May 20

NO COMPROMISE Part 2

Nebuchadnezzar was so irate that they would not bow that he brought them in front of him again, and gave them one last chance to bow! HERE IS ONE LAST CHANCE:
Then Nebuchadnezzar, in rage and fury, gave the command to bring Shadrach, Meshach, and Abed-Nego. So they brought these men before the king. Nebuchadnezzar spoke, saying to them, "Is it true, Shadrach, Meshach, and Abed-Nego, that you do not serve my gods or worship the gold image which I have set up? Now if you are ready at the time you hear the sound of the horn, flute, harp, lyre, and psaltery, in symphony with all kinds of music, and you fall down and worship the image which I have made, good! But if you do not worship, you shall be cast immediately into the midst of a burning fiery furnace. And who is the god who will deliver you from my hands?" Daniel 3:13-15

Daniel 3:17-18, The God who we serve will deliver us, and if he doesn't, WHATEVER, we will still never BOW any other God, but Him!!!!
Here it is king....listen clear...God will deliver us, BUT, if he doesn't, we will still NEVER BOW!
The king threw them into the furnace, stirred 7 times hotter than normal, and when he looked in he saw one more than what was thrown in. He saw the faithful, the salvation, the protector, The Lord, the KING OF KINGS standing with them.

HE IS STANDING WITH YOU TODAY......
NO COMPROMISE

~Dr Micheal Spencer

May 21

NO COMPROMISE Part 3
UNTIL YOU MAKE THE DECISION IN YOUR HEART THAT COMPROMISE IS NOT AN OPTION.....You will compromise!
The devil & life will always make sure you have opportunities to walk away from your faith.
Daniel 3:18 But if not, let it be known to you, O king, that we do not serve your gods, nor will we worship the gold image which you have set up
Daniel and these three young men were stolen.
Lost their home, Lost their mom & dad, Lost their freedom of religion, Lost their names.
Hananiah (God has favored) – Shadrach (a great scribe)
Mishael (Who is what God is) – Meshach (guest of a king)
Azariah (Jehovah has helped) – Aded-Nego (servant of Nebo)
These boys had everything going for them, until the trial of faith came upon them!
THEY HAD THE EXCUSES – THE REASONS TO STOP SERVING GOD
COMPROMISE, turning back, was not an option!
Nebuchadnezzar was so full of himself that he had a 9ft x 90ft image created of gold.
He commanded everyone at the sound of the instruments would fall down and worship the image.
Daniel 3:6, and whoever does not fall down and worship shall be cast immediately into the midst of a burning fiery furnace."
What do you do? You know the cost! Your life!
You know you cannot hide, and if you remain standing the consequences!!
JUST BOW, GOD UNDERSTANDS.
JUST BOW, YOU DON'T REALLY MEAN IT IN YOUR HEART.
JUST BOW, YOU CAN ASK FORGIVENESS LATER...
They refused to bow their heart, their trust, their faith to anyone, but THEIR GOD!
WHEN YOU ALLOW COMPROMISE TO BE AN OPTION, it will start small, then that slippery slope grabs you and before you realize it, you are in the cesspool of the world.

~Dr Micheal Spencer

May 22

Are you stumbling away without even realizing it?
The enemies tactic REVEALED.

Mark 4:16-17
And in the same way the ones sown upon stony ground are those who, when they hear the Word, at once receive and accept and welcome it with joy; And they have no real root in themselves, and so they endure for a little while; then when trouble or persecution arises on account of the Word, they immediately are offended (become displeased, indignant, resentful) and they stumble and fall away.

Matthew 24:10
And then **many will be** offended and repelled and will **begin to distrust and desert [Him Whom they ought to trust and obey] and will stumble and fall away and betray one another and pursue one another with hatred.**

Fight the good fight- warfare.
The enemy of our soul is on task 24/7. He doesn't rest in his job to steal kill and destroy. We must daily fight the good fight.
WE HAVE TO GET RID OF THE OFFENSES WE ALREADY HAVE AND MAKE SURE AT THE SAME TIME WE AVOID THE EVERY-MOMENT OPPORTUNITY FOR A NEW OFFENSE TO COME IN.

~Pastor Rhonda Spencer

May 23

Here Are Some Encouraging TRUTHS!

Can you be any more reassured of your SUCCESS, than to know that Jesus is PRAYING for YOU!
Luke 22:32
But I have prayed for you, that your faith should not fail; and when you have returned to Me, strengthen your brethren."
It is cool to know that we all people that believe in us, and we can go to them and know that they will speak life and encouragement in our lives, BUT.......
CAN IT GET ANY BETTER THAN THIS –
Jesus believes in you, and is before the Father right this very moment praying for you personally, your needs, your concerns, your struggles! Jesus, the One who died for our sins, rose from the dead, has not forgotten you, you are not a number to Him, you are His focus!!
Life might be being life right now to you, discouragement might be trying to steal your faith and trust, BUT, hold firm, fix your eyes, don't waver, JESUS IS PRAYING FOR YOU! He is releasing His angels to strengthen and work on our behalf!
Hebrew 1:14
Are they not all ministering spirits sent forth to minister for those who will inherit salvation?
If you are struggling with sin – KNOW THAT JESUS IS PRAYING FOR YOUR FREEDOM!
You are not alone – Matt. 28:20b,....and lo, I am with you always, even to the end of the age." Amen.
BE ENCOURAGED TODAY - Romans 8:31, What then shall we say to these things? If God is for us, who can be against us?

~Dr Micheal Spencer

May 24

Constant

The Spirit of **God IS A CONSTANT** on the earth, what is not constant is us...our emotions, our walking in the flesh or the Spirit, our decisions. **BUT GOD AND HIS POWER NEVER CHANGES!!!!** We find our solid place in Christ, security is in Him.

Be firm in faith [against his onset--rooted, established, strong, immovable, and determined], knowing that the same (identical) sufferings are appointed to your brotherhood (the whole body of Christians) throughout the world. Be steadfast and persevere in it.
1 Peter 5:9, 12 AMP

Bible Reading: Mark 11:22; Mark 13:33-34; Mark 14:38; Acts 2:42-47; Romans 12:12; 1 Corinthians 1:7

~Pastor Rhonda Spencer

May 25

I HATE Myself

The hardest person in the to stop hating is OURSELVES. It is actually easier to forgive someone else, than to forgive ourselves, BUT, today, right now, this is the time to set yourself free from the past. Mutilation, depression, separation, medication, all the -ion's show the torment that we place upon ourselves when we do not forgive.

IF JESUS CAN FORGIVE YOU, YOU CAN FORGIVE YOURSELF!

Unforgiveness is a prison that we put others in, and even ourselves. The major individual to lose with this jail, is us.

Therefore if the Son makes you free, you shall be free indeed. John 8:36

If Jesus set you free from your sin, it is time for you to set yourself free from that sin.

Today
1. Pray for yourself
2. Speak out loud, "the past has no hold on me past this second, I am FREE"
3. Every time the thought comes up, take authority over it immediately. Speak this, "In Jesus name, get out of my head. Thought, you have to come under the authority, now get out"
4. Start thanking Jesus for your FREEDOM!!

~Dr Micheal Spencer

May 26

Live in the NEW NATURE, the NEW MAN

For you are still [unspiritual, having the nature] of the flesh [under the control of ordinary impulses]. For as long as [there are] envying and jealousy and wrangling and factions among you, are you not unspiritual and of the flesh, behaving yourselves after a human standard and like mere (unchanged) men?
1 Corinthians 3:3 AMP

UNITY IN THE BODY OF CHRIST IS NOT AN OPTION...Check your heart today for any wrangling or factions. It's a sign of walking in the flesh, not the Spirit. You have power over that sin nature, because of the cross, it has no hold on you.

Bible Reading: Psalm 133:1; Romans 16:17,
1 Corinthians 12:25; Galatians 5:19-21; Jude 1:18-20

~Pastor Rhonda Spencer

May 27

Padlock those Lips

For assuredly, I say to you, whoever says to this mountain, 'Be removed and be cast into the sea,' and does not doubt in his heart, but believes that those things he says will be done, he will have whatever he says. Mark 11:23

DO IT GOD'S WAY
The first act we see the Father do in the Word is creation: Calling those things which were not as though they already are

> Romans 4:17, (as it is written, "I have made you a father of many nations"[d]) in the presence of Him whom he believed—God, who gives life to the dead and calls those things which do not exist as though they did;

God SAID: Genesis 1:3, 6, 9, 11, 14, 20, 24, 29
We are the only creation that God spoke into existence that He gave the ability to do what He does, SPEAK THE WORD
Genesis 1:26, Then God said, "Let Us make man in Our image, according to Our likeness;
He has given us the authority, the ability, and direction, the example of how He works this universe and yet the Christians do not pay attention to the direction and example of the Father. Then we complain when we do not see the results we desire.
Jesus said in John 6:63, "It is the Spirit who gives life; the flesh profits nothing. The words that I speak to you are spirit, and they are life."
Jesus also taught us clearly not only the principle, but He then turned and used the principle to validate our rights and responsibility to say and speak.
Mark 11:23-24, So Jesus answered and said to them, "Have faith in God. For assuredly, I say to you, whoever says to this mountain, 'Be removed and be cast into the sea,' and does not doubt in his heart, but believes that those things he says will be done, he will have whatever he says. Therefore I say to you, whatever things you ask when you pray, believe that you receive them, and you will have them.

~Dr Micheal Spencer

May 28

Final Destination? REALLY?

ETERNITY! If only it was more of a reality!
I am only speaking for myself right now. We know it is TRUTH. We know that we are LITERALLY seconds away from stepping into ETERNITY, but we live like it is 10 billion years away.
Can you imagine if we had that REALITY, that AWAKENING, that AWARENESS that it is FOREVER, and that once you are there, there is no way out?
We would live different. We would act different.
Our goals would be different. Our passions would be different.
We would not look at people the same.
We would not curse them so easily.
Oh that we would see them in their eternal state, not in their Calvin Klein's.
HEAVEN or THE LAKE OF FIRE – those are the only options. They are for keeps.
God has only designed ONE plan to save them – His name is Jesus.
God has only designed ONE plan to tell them – US.
If WE do not reach out and share the plan, then they have NO HOPE or OPPORTUNITY.
Pray this with me:
Jesus, give me a reality of eternity. Let me really get a hold of this please. Give me a heavy burden for people that are not going to heaven, and do not let me get consumed with my life. Use my life you gave me to tell others of your plan to save them. Give me BOLDNESS please, so I am not intimidated by what the haters say about me. Thank you for saving me, now use me to reach others. Thank you Jesus!
Mark 16:15 And He said to them, " Go into all the world and preach the gospel to every creature.

~Dr Micheal Spencer

May 29

Sit & Spin

You grab your computer because you have an important item to research. Hit the on button, it sslloowwllyy comes up, you hit the Internet icon, and up it comes.... that spinning circle.... and it spins, and spins, and spins, and spins..........you wait, and wait, and wait, and wait!!
You are ready to take that computer and throw it out the door because this is important and all you get it the sit and spin mode!
Have you ever felt that way in life?
It is that hurry up and wait mode...ahhhhh!!
With life and Christ that is a mode to pay attention to. With the computer, it is time to take it for some disease control.
There are times in life when that sit and spin icon seems to be present in our lives. We have a plan, we have an idea, we know what we want, but God seems to throw the icon up, and nothing moves forward.
This is a time to STOP, and LISTEN, because He is trying to SHOW you something that you cannot see.
For all who are led by the Spirit of God are children of God. Romans 8:14 NLT
Look here, you who say, "Today or tomorrow we are going to a certain town and will stay there a year. We will do business there and make a profit." How do you know what your life will be like tomorrow? Your life is like the morning fog—it's here a little while, then it's gone. James 4:13, 14 NLT
If Jesus is throwing the sit and spin icon up in your life it is not to hold you back, but to protect you from something you cannot see because you and I do not know what tomorrow holds. We must learn to trust Him, He has our best interest, He has the perfect plan for our lives, He knows what will bring success.
TRUST HIM AND YOU WILL SEE FULFILLMENT AND PEACE!
Trust in the Lord with all your heart; do not depend on your own understanding. Seek his will in all you do, and he will show you which path to take. Proverbs 3:5, 6 NLT
What the sit and spin icon comes up, STOP, LISTEN & WAIT till He says GO!

~Dr Micheal Spencer

May 30

Be still and know that I am God

GOD IS our Refuge and Strength [mighty and impenetrable to temptation], a very present and well-proved help in trouble. Therefore we will not fear, though the earth should change and though the mountains be shaken into the midst of the seas, Though its waters roar and foam, though the mountains tremble at its swelling and tumult. Selah [pause, and calmly think of that]! There is a river whose streams shall make glad the city of God, the holy place of the tabernacles of the Most High. God is in the midst of her, she shall not be moved; God will help her right early [at the dawn of the morning]. **Let be and be still, and know (recognize and understand)** that I am God. I will be exalted among the nations! I will be exalted in the earth! The Lord of hosts is with us; the God of Jacob is our Refuge (our High Tower and Stronghold). Selah [pause, and calmly think of that]! Psalm 46:1-5, 10, 11 AMP

Bible Reading: Psalm 33:8; Job 37:14-18

~Pastor Rhonda Spencer

May 31

I FEEL LIKE GIVING UP!

Why are you cast down, O my soul? And why are you disquieted within me? Hope in God, for I shall yet praise Him for the help of His countenance. Psalms 42:5

Why are you down in the dumps, dear soul? Why are you crying the blues? Fix my eyes on God— soon I'll be praising again. He puts a smile on my face. He's my God.
Psalm 42:5 MSG

Sometimes no matter how much you are praying and believing, there are times we begin to get discouraged. It doesn't start with discouragement, it usually begins with just simply getting tired, and that is the foothold (Ephesians 4:27 nor give place to the devil.) for the enemy to come in with discouragement.

Galatians 6:9 And let us not grow weary while doing good, for in due season we shall reap if we do not lose heart.

How come we just seem to get so tired, and how can I fix that in my life? Here are some steps to break that cycle in your life:

1. Live out of your excess – We should never be so dry in the Spirit that we have to live and give out of our need. You must do devotions every day; get into the Word to feed and water your spirit.
2. 1 Peter 5:7, casting all your care upon Him, for He cares for you. This literally means to throw them like a stone. Throw your burdens, situations, concerns and cares to Him. I mean, go ahead and do it right now. Literally, throw your cares to Him!!
3. Pray in the Holy Spirit often and always – Jude 1:20, But you, beloved, building yourselves up on your most holy faith, praying in the Holy Spirit,
4. Find a Faith Friend - find someone that will speak life and encouragement to you and to your situation, and not doubt. We never need sympathy, we need empathy. Sympathy says how sad it is while empathy says, "let's get this thing fixed".

He is waiting to strengthen you today. You do not have to be discouraged or tired; get your strength from above!

~Dr Micheal Spencer

June 1

I Really HATE You. You Hurt Me!

If we are all going to be honest, **we have ALL been really hurt and wounded by people, AND, we have also really hurt and wounded people.**

The emotions that rise when we have been hurt by a person we trust are like a tornado that takes a barn and shreds it over the next county. Our minds race, our hearts ache, and each moment we strive to make sense of the situation we get even more angry because it makes no sense!

Many go into defensive mode, by lashing out.

Yesterday, my dogs (the rat dog, 25lbs vs. the horse, 100lbs), went at it in the yard because they both wanted the same thing. The big dog threw the little dog around, BUT, that little dog got right back up and went for the big dogs ears. Any weak spot he saw he was going to bite!

Most Christians do the same thing when we are hurt!

We are like the rat dog! I will hurt you!

Many allow the hurt to mature into HATRED, and BITTERNESS!

Hebrews 12:15 Looking carefully lest anyone fall short of the grace of God; lest any root of bitterness springing up cause trouble, and by this many become defiled;

HATRED is a horrible SIN!

It is against the God, yourself and the person you now despise!

Matthew 6:14-15 " For if you forgive men their trespasses, your heavenly Father will also forgive you. But if you do not forgive men their trespasses, neither will your Father forgive your trespasses."

This is serious!

You MUST NOT HATE even those who have wounded you!

"You don't understand Pastor! You don't know what they did to me!" I do understand this –

WHAT DID WE DO TO GOD, AND SHOULD HE FORGIVE OR HATE US?

~Dr Micheal Spencer

June 2

NOTHING IN THIS WORLD CAN REMOVE YOU FROM YOUR DESTINY OR ETERNITY

....Nothing but your own thoughts, your own will and your own choices.
The things in this life we give so much attention to and so much value to HAVE NO EFFECT ON OUR ETERNAL BEING. This joy, love, peace and hope that I have...the world didn't give it to me and the world can't take it away.

For I am persuaded that neither death nor life, nor angels nor principalities nor powers, nor things present nor things to come, nor height nor depth, nor any other created thing, shall be able to separate us from the love of God which is in Christ Jesus our Lord.
Romans 8:38, 39 NKJV

For we do not wrestle against flesh and blood, but against principalities, against powers, against the rulers of the darkness of this age, against spiritual hosts of wickedness in the heavenly places.
Ephesians 6:12 NKJV

AND YOU HAVE AUTHORITY OVER THE ENEMY-
YOU WIN!

Behold, I give you the authority to trample on serpents and scorpions, and over all the power of the enemy, and nothing shall by any means hurt you. (Luke 10:19 NKJV)

SO AGAIN NOTHING YOU ARE FEELING OR FACING CAN EFFECT YOUR ETERNAL DESTINY OR YOUR PLACE IN CHRIST
...so go THROUGH bold and unwavering!

~Pastor Rhonda Spencer

June 3

WE HAVE APPROVAL

APPROVAL – Noun

The action of officially agreeing to something or accepting something as satisfactory.
The belief that someone or something is good or acceptable.

Being approved is important.
When we take medications, we want them approved!
When we use a product, we want it approved!
When we get saved, WE HAVE BEEN APPROVED, and marked with the stamp of approval!

2 Corinthians 1:22
who also has sealed us and given us the Spirit in our hearts as a guarantee.

Today do not let the devil, people or even yourself tell you that you are not important and approved by God through the blood of Jesus.
If you are feeling conviction (the feeling of not doing right), then ask Jesus to forgive you and to wash your sin away!

1 John 1:9
If we confess our sins, He is faithful and just to forgive us our sins and to cleanse us from all unrighteousness.

~Dr Micheal Spencer

June 4

Preparedness Produces Victory Part 1

Daniel refused to SURRENDER his love for God because of fear or intimidation.
Daniel 6
Vs 3 – God elevated Daniel, and he was a man of distinction above all the natives
Vs 4 - Whenever you are in the blessing of God people are going to try to destroy you (Joseph). They are jealous of the hand of God on your life and will work to bring false accusation, or strive to get you to trip up.
Daniel was faithful. He was walking before his God, and there were no valid accusations that would stick.
Vs 7-9 – The governors, administrators, managers all decided to get Daniel. They devised a plan. Go to Darius and get him to sign a bill that whoever wants something for the next 30 days, must come pray to him or be thrown into the lions den.
Vs 10 – Daniel knew of the decree and its validity, but refused to bow to anyone or anything beside the ONE TRUE GOD.
He was not ashamed. He went home, where his window was open, and knelt and prayed to God; not once a day, three times a day, Daniel gave thanks to God.
This was constant through his early days – CONSISTENCY IS EVERYTHING
EVERYONE WANTS VICTORY WHEN TROUBLE COMES, BUT VICTORY IS NOT AN ACCIDENT – IT MUST BE PREPARED FOR.

FAITH COMES THROUGH RELATIONSHIP WITH GOD – Daniel has a living, consistent relationship with God, daily, 3 times a day he spent time with God.
HAVE A DANIEL SPIRIT TODAY.

~Dr Micheal Spencer

June 5

Preparedness Produces Victory Part 2
Daniel 6
Vs 11 – The HATERS are always waiting to get you in trouble, to strive to break down your testimony. You will never be perfect, but the closer you walk with Christ the less you will choose sin.
Vs. 12-15 – They got the king to fulfill the decree

Vs 16 – The king told Daniel his testimony
So the king gave the command, and they brought Daniel and cast him into the den of lions. But the king spoke, saying to Daniel, **"Your God, whom you serve continually, He will deliver you."**

Vs 22-23
My God sent His angel and shut the lions' mouths, so that they have not hurt me, because I was found innocent before Him; and also, O king, I have done no wrong before you."23 Now the king was exceedingly glad for him, and commanded that they should take Daniel up out of the den. **So Daniel was taken up out of the den, and no injury whatever was found on him, because he believed in his God.**
Don't wait for the den to get your faith, trust, confidence in Christ and His Word up
Daniel BELIEVED GOD – you don't trust someone, till you know someone!
HAVE A DANIEL SPIRIT TODAY

~Dr Micheal Spencer

June 6

Watch Your Mouth, You're Planting Seeds

And they have overcome (conquered) by means of the blood of the Lamb and by THE UTTERANCE OF THEIR TESTIMONY. Revelation 12:11 AMP

Speak the answers over your situations!!! TESTIFY and you will overcome by the blood of the lamb. Refuse to speak about the problem.
Your words are seeds and you are only fertilizing the problem when you speak about it.
INSTEAD DECLARE the answer, the supernatural, and then you are sowing victory. Everything you need for life, victory and Godliness has already been accomplished....so speak the Word of God only and lay hold on the supernatural (it's yours).

Victory today.

~Pastor Rhonda Spencer

June 7

I Can't FEEL ANYTHING, Am I OK? Part I

These are the times when we lay in our beds and the lights are off and we just talk with The Lord and wonder WHY, HOW, WHAT DO I DO NEXT.

We get up in the morning and want to be filled with hope and the fire, but it feels like our fire is starting to flicker, and the air is seeping out of the balloon.

We go to church and it seems like we are there, but not really.

WHAT DO I DO?

This can be some of the most difficult times when we do not FEEL what we used to, BUT, today I want you to know that this is actually a GOOD THING, not bad.

HOW CAN YOU SAY THAT?

We live so much by how we feel. We base LOVE on feelings, HAPPINESS on feelings, SUCCESS on feelings. Our lives are wrapped up in feelings, and they are good, in their place.

There comes a time when our faith must be stretched beyond our emotions.

There comes a time when we learn that it is not how we FEEL, it is what the WORD says.

When this time comes, we MUST push through, not stop, not flounder, not step back,

these are the times we must PRESS THROUGH.

If the devil can get you to stop in this trial of your faith, then he will always know how far you will go before you give up.

Learning to stand even when feelings are not there is a strong GROWTH PLATE for your life.

2 Corinthians 5:7, For we walk by faith, not by sight.

I know this is a hard trial, but you must press through!!!

CONSISTENCY IS EVERYTHING!

~Dr Micheal Spencer

June 8

I Can't FEEL ANYTHING, Am I OK? Part 2

When I was in Bible College my first year was such an amazing experience with Jesus. It was powerful every time I prayed or went to church. It was like Jesus was there every second. My second year started off different. I prayed...nothing. I went to church...nothing. I had people pray for me...nothing. I did everything I was supposed to...nothing, not feeling God or His presence. I finally, in my top bunk of the dorm room truthfully asked Jesus if I was back-slidden, lost. He said to me, "son, this is not about feelings, and I cannot take you to the next level until you are led by my Word, and not your emotions." I made a decision! No matter how I felt, I know what the Word says about me and my walk....period. It all changed, and faith rose, and my walk went to the next level.

2 Corinthians 5:7, For we walk by faith, not by sight.

YOU CAN MAKE IT....GO TO THE NEXT LEVEL!

~Dr Micheal Spencer

June 9

WHERE SHALL WE CAMP TODAY?

I saw the Lord constantly before me, for He is at my right hand that I may not be shaken or overthrown or cast down [from my secure and happy state]. Therefore my heart rejoiced and my tongue exulted exceedingly; moreover, my flesh also will DWELL IN HOPE [will encamp, pitch its tent, and dwell in hope in anticipation of the resurrection]. For You will not abandon my soul, leaving it helpless in Hades (the state of departed spirits), nor let Your Holy One know decay or see destruction [of the body after death]. You have made known to me the ways of life; You will enrapture me [diffusing my soul with joy] with and in Your presence. Acts 2:25-28 AMP

WHAT A GREAT PASSAGE TO START MY DAY ......I am going to pitch a tent of hope in Him.

~*Pastor Rhonda* Spencer

June 10

IMPRESSIONS

Do you remember as a child taking Silly Putty or Play-Doh and making a mold of something, or taking the impression from the local newspaper?
It was so cool being able to look and actually see what you took off the page, or be able to see what the Play-Doh had molded.
We do the same thing!
We leave impressions on people when we are in their presence. People watch us as pressure is put on, or how we conduct ourselves each day. They are watching to see if following Jesus is really worth it.
Do we have something they want or need?
Do they see the Jesus in us, or are we the same as them, but go to church?
Today, watch your steps!
Today, watch your words!
Today, watch your testimony!
They are watching......SO.......what are they seeing?

Philippians 1:27 Only let your conduct be worthy of the gospel of Christ, so that whether I come and see you or am absent, I may hear of your affairs, that you stand fast in one spirit, with one mind striving together for the faith of the gospel,
Colossians 1:10 that you may walk worthy of the Lord, fully pleasing Him, being fruitful in every good work and increasing in the knowledge of God;
WHAT IMPRESSION ARE YOU LEAVING, AND WHAT REFLECTION CAN THEY SEE?

~Dr Micheal Spencer

June 11

eXcuses, means you have an "X"

Daniel- King Nebuchadnezzar of Babylon came to Jerusalem and took it over. The king wanted some of the Israelites royal blood to be taken back into captivity. They were taught the language, trained in Babylonian ways to serve the king. Daniel refused to defile himself and took a stand and a test about eating unclean foods. He gained favor with the chief officers. God elevated Daniel through the supernatural ability like Joseph, to interpret dreams. Daniel rose in position and posture in the kingdom of the Babylonians, even though he was a Jewish captive.
God can elevate you even in the worst conditions
Be consistent and faithful to Him, and He will raise you up!
Daniel 6:3-4 Then this Daniel distinguished himself above the governors and satraps, because an excellent spirit was in him; and the king gave thought to setting him over the whole realm. 4 So the governors and satraps sought to find some charge against Daniel concerning the kingdom; but they could find no charge or fault, because he was faithful; nor was there any error or fault found in him.
Daniel was stolen from his home.
Daniel was taken from his mom and dad.
Daniel was brought to a foreign country.
Daniel was being reprogrammed by the Babylonian kingdom.
Daniel could not practice his spirituality like he used to in Jerusalem.
THE LIST OF EXCUSES OF WHY DANIEL COULD NOT HAVE ASPIRED TO GREATEST IS LIMITLESS.
He could have blamed Neb! He could have blamed God!
He could have blamed his circumstances! He could whine & complain
BUT he chose not to use "X"cuses, but to be faithful to His God.
He was known as a man with an EXCELLENT SPIRIT.
He was known as a man that was FAITHFUL.
He was known as a man without fault, or charge.
He was not perfect, but Daniel walked before His God.
HOW ARE YOU KNOWN IF YOUR NAME WAS IN THE BOOK?
WHAT ADJECTIVES WOULD BE NEXT TO YOUR NAME

~Dr Micheal Spencer

June 12

I HATE Life!!

For whatever is born of God is victorious over the world; and this is the victory that conquers the world, even our faith. 1 John 5:4 AMP

Have you had those days, no, those years when you hated your life? It seems like everything that could go wrong has and will again!!!

When this occurs there are choices to make

1. Lay down and give up
2. Whine and go into depression
3. Get up and GRAB YOUR VICTORY!

Ok, this is what I do...

I am going to be transparent.....

I usually whine and complain for about an hour. I allow myself that time for a pity party. It never fixes anything, but, it feels good to the flesh.

You can HATE your life, your situation, your family, your job, your church, but that is not the problem. It will not change anything to HATE your life.

Jesus did not come for you to HATE your life, He came to give you life and life more abundant (John 10:10).

VICTORY comes over your situation when you decide that laying in the mud does not fix anything. We are still so very blessed in our lives in America.

Do me a favor today

1) Write down the bad things in your life on a piece of paper

2) Write down all the blessings, and begin to thank Him right out loud.

a. Psalms 30:12, To the end that my glory may sing praise to You and not be silent.

O Lord my God, I will give thanks to You forever.

b. Psalms 150:6, Let everything that has breath praise the Lord.

Praise the Lord!

~Dr Micheal Spencer

June 13

FREAK OUT

Worry, stress, anxiety and FREAKING OUT cause nothing but harm to our minds and bodies. This is not the will of God!!
Philippians. 4:6-7, Don't worry about anything; instead, pray about everything. Tell God what you need, and thank him for all he has done. Then you will experience God's peace, which exceeds anything we can understand. His peace will guard your hearts and minds as you live in Christ Jesus.
Come on now preacher, you need to be real, you expect me not to worry?
The Word of God says that a Christian does not have to worry! In fact it says that worry, anxiety, & FREAKING OUT is not God's will for your life, and that He has a plan to take away the worry, stress and anxiety.
One of the basic principles of worry, stress, and anxiety is that it does NOTHING! It accomplishes NOTHING! It changes NOTHING! It only eats away at the inside of our minds and creates FEAR.
This is how it works. We think first, then we have an emotion second, then we manifest that in our physical body third (vocal, body language, motion). Our thoughts create for us the emotional reaction called worry, stress, overwhelmed or anxiety.
One of the first things to recognize is that we have to start controlling what we think and what we allow to enter into our minds. We cannot just allow any thought to run free in our heads. A thought is a seed and when we allow that seed to take root, then it will begin to grow. Once it takes root, then we have entered into worry, fret, stress, or anxiety.
2 Corinthians 10:4-6, We use God's mighty weapons, not worldly weapons, to knock down the strongholds of human reasoning and to destroy false arguments. We destroy every proud obstacle that keeps people from knowing God. We capture their rebellious thoughts and teach them to obey Christ. And after you have become fully obedient, we will punish everyone who remains disobedient.
THIS IS NOT THE WILL OF GOD FOR YOU!
HIS PLAN IS THAT YOU AND I LIVE A STRESS FREE LIFE!

~Dr Micheal Spencer

June 14

STILL Freaking Out

Philippians 4:6-7, Don't worry about anything; instead, pray about everything. Tell God what you need, and thank him for all he has done. Then you will experience God's peace, which exceeds anything we can understand. His peace will guard your hearts and minds as you live in Christ Jesus.

So worry, fret, anxiety, stress and overwhelming sensations, are not your portion as a believer. The world, "those who do not know Jesus" have those emotions as a norm because they live out of their soul. As a believer in Jesus, this is not what, or how, we should be living. We serve a HUGE God, who has UNLIMITED power, and UNLIMITED LOVE for His children.

Someone has lied to you! Too many Christians have bought the lie that stress, anxiety and worry are a normal part of life. Why are you allowing someone to deposit seed in your life that is contrary to the Word of God? This lie, when it is allowed to seat, is the open door for the polar opposite of faith, and that is fear. FEAR IS NOT OF GOD! FEAR IS THE OPPOSITE OF FAITH! FEAR IS THE FEEDING GROUND OF SATAN! There is NO FEAR in the Father!

1 John 4:18, Such love has no fear, because perfect love expels all fear. If we are afraid, it is for fear of punishment, and this shows that we have not fully experienced his perfect love.

THIS IS HOW YOU CONTROL FEAR, STRESS, ANXIETY, WORRY IN YOUR LIFE!

There is nothing wrong with concern. There are times we should be concerned, but concern is not worry or fear, it gives us a direction to pray and believe. If there are never any concerns, then we are in perfect control of our lives and nothing negative is ever happening. Wouldn't we all love that! When a concern comes into your life, not if a concern comes, but when, stop and make a decision. I refuse to allow a seed of worry, doubt, fear to get into my head or heart. That decision is imperative for your immediate direction of a stress-free life.

WHAT IS YOUR FIRST STEP OF A WORRY-FREE LIFE? SAY IT OUT LOUD PLEASE!

~Dr Micheal Spencer

June 15

FREAKED OUT to PEACE

Philippians 4:6-7, Don't worry about anything; instead, pray about everything. Tell God what you need, and thank him for all he has done. Then you will experience God's peace, which exceeds anything we can understand. His peace will guard your hearts and minds as you live in Christ Jesus.

We all want the PEACE! BUT, To get the peace you have to do it God's way!

Over the last few days we have already covered that stress, worry, fret, and anxiety are not of God, and we have showed that our thoughts must be controlled. Our thoughts must be brought into submission, or they will rule, which will produce stress, worry, anxiety and fear.

CONCERN- We have a concern. It is a very real situation, and normally worry and fear would start overtaking you. You made the decision that you will not go that route again. So now what do you do?

PRAY- There is a difference between saying words and praying to the Father.

Hebrews 4:16, So let us come boldly to the throne of our gracious God. There we will receive his mercy, and we will find grace to help us when we need it most.

1 John 5:14-15, And we are confident that he hears us whenever we ask for anything that pleases him. And since we know he hears us when we make our requests, we also know that he will give us what we ask for.

James 5:16b, The earnest prayer of a righteous person has great power and produces wonderful results.

When we pray, we talk to Daddy, knowing that He cares and is able and willing to be there for our concerns. Once you have shared your concern with Father, the real question comes down to, "DO WE REALLY BELIEVE HE WILL HANDLE IT?"

If we really believe He will handle our concerns, and that He is moving on them, then we will start to praise and thank Him for our answer. If we continue to get overwhelmed with it, then we do not really believe that He is strong enough to take care of us. We are perfected in our praise. Praise releases the power of God. It is that declaration that we trust Him and He will take care of it.

THEN...THE PEACE OF GOD WHICH PASSES ALL UNDERSTANDING WILL KEEP OUR HEARTS & MINDS IN CHRIST!

It is not until we follow that truth that the peace will come. Why will the peace come? Because we trust, know, and rely completely on Jesus, knowing He is working on the scene for His kids. GRAB YOUR PIECE OF THE PEACE TODAY!

Determine – I WILL NOT WORRY OR FEAR – I WILL TRUST IN MY GOD!

~Dr Micheal Spencer

June 16

KEEP YOUR GUARD UP

You're not the only ones plunged into these hard times. It's the same with Christians all over the world. So keep a firm grip on the faith. The suffering won't last forever. It won't be long before this generous God who has great plans for us in Christ-eternal (and glorious plans they are!) will have you put together and on your feet for good. He gets the last word; yes, he does.
1 Peter 5:9-11 MSG

YOU ARE NOT ALONE...Sometimes it feels like we are the only ones going through stuff because we don't see into the lives of others. Everyone's got something. Keep your guard up and fight the good fight with your brothers and sisters in the faith.

Bible Reading: 1 Corinthians 10:13, Galatians 6:1-2, Psalm 23:4

~Pastor Rhonda Spencer

June 17

The Clock is TICKING...tic, tic, tic, tic.....

Have you ever watched one of those movies where a bomb was going to go off? You are actually so engulfed in the plot unfolding and the ticking of the seconds away that you find yourself leaning forward with nervous anticipation.
Tic, tic, tic, tic..... 5, 4, 3, 2.........
The last second feels like it takes forever, and at the same moment if feels like it is an out of control train getting ready to crash. Your nerves bunch up, your eye balls are glued, your blood pressure rises, your heart beats quicker........
BOOOOOOOOOM!!!
Oh that the church will again be engulfed with the reality of TIME, and how close we are to the coming of the end of this age.
Matthew 16:1-3 Then the Pharisees and Sadducees came, and testing Him asked that He would show them a sign from heaven. He answered and said to them, " When it is evening you say, 'It will be fair weather, for the sky is red'; and in the morning, 'It will be foul weather today, for the sky is red and threatening........
Not a fear monger tactic, a reality that time is ticking and so short must get the church on the edge of her seat again, or the lost will be lost.
If you knew that in 1 hour Jesus would come, who would you tell?
If you knew that you only had 15 minutes remaining on the clock of time, and all who did not respond would be cast into the Lake of Fire forever, who would you call, who would you confront, who would you be passionate to share Jesus with?
There are no prophecies left to be fulfilled before Jesus returns. The clock of Biblical time is literally, not figuratively, on the last seconds counting. Jesus is coming, it is a serious time, tic, tic, tic, tic.....
WHO WILL YOU GRAB TODAY AND SHARE THE LOVE OF JESUS WITH?
2 Peter 3:9, The Lord is not slack concerning His promise, as some count slackness, but is long-suffering toward us, not willing that any should perish but that all should come to repentance.

~Dr Micheal Spencer

June 18

You Were A WHAT?

Sometimes people have been saved too long......
What do you mean by that Pastor?
There are some Christians who have forgotten where they have come from. I have watched pompous, religion-filled "Christians" who are holier-than-thou look down their faces at others. You want to run up and slap the stupid out of them!!
Sometimes we have been saved so long that we forget what it feels like to be lost without Jesus, and therefore we have no drive to help someone else get born again. We are not BETTER than others, we are washed in the blood and forgiven!!
1 Timothy 1:15, This is a faithful saying and worthy of all acceptance, that Christ Jesus came into the world to save sinners, of whom I am chief.
Paul did not forget where he came from and was driven to reach others who were lost too.
Be a Paul today. Don't forget that we were all forgiven much, and that there is someone in your journey today that needs the love, acceptance, and forgiveness that you received. I didn't say deserves, I said needs. We all DESERVE to be punished for our own sin, BUT, Jesus!
Thank you Jesus, and we will never forget!
SEND US SOMEONE TODAY TO SHARE WHAT WE RECEIVED – LOVE & FORGIVENESS!

Heal the sick, cleanse the lepers, raise the dead, cast out demons. Freely you have received, freely give.
Matthew 10:8

~Dr Micheal Spencer

June 19

Get along even with your brothers and sisters in Christ

...I urge Euodia and Syntyche to iron out their differences and make up. God doesn't want his children holding grudges. And, oh, yes, Syzygus, since you're right there to help them work things out, do your best with them. These women worked for the Message hand in hand with Clement and me, and with the other veterans—worked as hard as any of us. Remember, their names are also in the Book of Life.
Philippians 4:2, 3 MSG

Pursue peace with all people, and holiness, without which no one will see the Lord: looking carefully lest anyone fall short of the grace of God; lest any root of bitterness springing up cause trouble, and by this many become defiled; Hebrews 12:14, 15 NKJV

It's a command to walk in unity and pursue peace so lets go after it. GET ALONG!

Bible Reading: Psalm 34:14; 2 Timothy 2:22; 1 Peter 3:11

~Pastor Rhonda Spencer

June 20

WHERE ARE YOU GOD? I THOUGHT YOU CARED!

We have all been at this point! Life seems to be falling around us, and we have prayed, and prayed and it feels like the heavens are brass.

At first we hold on to our faith. We are like Jairus, we get hit with one serious, harsh truth of a hardship.

Mark 5:22-23 And behold, one of the rulers of the synagogue came, Jairus by name. And when he saw Him, he fell at His feet and begged Him earnestly, saying, "My little daughter lies at the point of death. Come and lay Your hands on her, that she may be healed, and she will live."

He stepped out in faith. He was a man who should never have come to Jesus in the first place, but here he is speaking in faith that if Jesus touches her, she will be healed.

Jesus went with him!! That means everything is going to be perfect from this second! That means no more bad news, no more trial, no more hardship! Then, the news does not get better, it gets worse.......

Mark 5:35 While He was still speaking, some came from the ruler of the synagogue's house who said, "Your daughter is dead. Why trouble the Teacher any further?"

Not just worse, THE WORST IT COULD GET!

Where are you Jesus?

I thought everything was going to be perfect! I thought you CARED!

Jesus knew the rush of emotions, and the seepage of faith that would immediately come. So he spoke to Jairus.

Mark 5:36 As soon as Jesus heard the word that was spoken, He said to the ruler of the synagogue, " Do not be afraid; only believe."

OH, BY THE WAY... SHE DID DIE, BUT JESUS IS THE RESURRECTION AND THE LIFE! She came back from the dead... He can resurrect your situation, if you keep the faith like Jairus!

HEAR JESUS TODAY. Do not allow your faith to slip. So many have lost their miracle, their answer as it is getting ready to cross the threshold of heaven to be delivered to earth. The reason it is lost is because we started to get mad at God, rather than keep faith in God.

THE ANSWER MIGHT BE TAKING A BIT OF TIME, BAD NEWS MIGHT HAVE GOTTEN EVEN WORSE, BUT KEEP THE FAITH!

I would rather die a believer, than die a doubter!!

~Dr Micheal Spencer

June 21

MIXED UP CHURCH

What is that? That is when the church has lost its sight of purpose and design. The concept of church has changed so much from what the Father intended. She has veered from her intention, and design.
Church has become about being happy, agreeing with everything, liking everyone, or I will just go find another "CHURCH".
The self-satisfying, placating church has become plump in its spirituality, yet emaciated in its results.
We have become a religious society of consumers who never take ownership of destiny, only adjust our geography to appease our spiritual addiction to the next experience.
This is not about an EXPERIENCE, or ENJOYMENT, this is about purpose and fulfilling God's will!!
CHURCH, We have a PURPOSE!!
We are called to FINISH what Jesus began, not sit in our corner with Jack Horner eating our Christmas pie.
Until we get our heads out of the clouds, it will still be about US, our happiness, our satisfaction, our spiritual high, our new experience, our refreshing, our needs, our wants, "our, our, our, our, our, our..."
instead of Luke 22:42, saying, " Father, if it is Your will, take this cup away from Me; nevertheless not My will, but Yours, be done."
OUR PURPOSE IS CLEAR – Finish the work. WHAT IS THE WORK?
Luke 19:10, for the Son of Man has come to seek and to save that which was lost."
John 4:35, Do you not say, "There are still four months and then comes the harvest'? Behold, I say to you, lift up your eyes and look at the fields, for they are already white for harvest!
YOU CAN HAVE ALL THE SPIRITUAL EXPERIENCES YOU WANT, BUT UNTIL THEY PRODUCE SOULS, THEY ARE ONLY A SELF INDUCED SPIRITUAL ECSTASY DRUG THAT BRINGS THE ILLUSION OF SPIRITUALITY.

What has your Christianity PRODUCED?

~Dr Micheal Spencer

June 22

DISCOURAGED?
Have you ever been just going along in life and all is good, then, BAM, out of nowhere you get hit with a situation and it literally takes your breath away?
A great word picture is seeing a kid riding his Schwinn BMX bike down a street and the evil neighborhood kid throwing a stick in the front spokes...over the handlebars we fly...thud, thud, thud is the sound as he hits the pavement.
WHY? WHAT JUST HAPPENED?
WHAT AM I GOING TO DO? GOD, WHAT DO I DO NEXT?
All the questions start to fly as emotionally, and maybe even physically you shriek in pain.
It is almost like someone ran up behind you and popped your balloon.
Today, right now, Jesus desires you to know that He has not left you, He has not abandoned you (Matt. 28:20b,....and lo, I am with you always, even to the end of the age." Amen.).
YOU ARE NOT ALONE, and do not allow discouragement to start to take root.
Discouragement means that you believe that there is no hope, or no way through the hurt and heartache. It is the opposite of encouragement, and it attacks, and can eliminate our COURAGE.
Don't allow that emotion a place in your life. It is NEVER from Father.
Psalms 42:5 Why are you cast down, O my soul? And why are you disquieted within me? Hope in God, for I shall yet praise Him for the help of His countenance.
Joshua 1:9 Have I not commanded you? Be strong and of good courage; do not be afraid, nor be dismayed, for the Lord your God is with you wherever you go."

LIFT UP YOUR HEAD AND HEART – YOU ARE GOING TO MAKE IT!!! JESUS IS PRAYING FOR YOU, AND GOD IS WORKING THIS THROUGH! DO NOT LOSE HOPE, DO NOT ALLOW YOUR COURAGE TO BE STOLEN! KEEP THE FAITH – HE IS FAITHFUL!!

~Dr Micheal Spencer

June 23

Do You Really CARE? Part 1

We really do care, but what do we care MOST about? Let's all be very honest here, we mainly care about OURSELVES. Making sure that we are taking care of, and that we are happy.
THAT FIGHT OF SACRIFICE IS LONG TERM, but, WE CAN WIN THIS WAR!
Have you ever gone somewhere and someone says, "How are you doing?" I usually say back, "Do you really care?" It is hilarious seeing the results. People are shocked, their head tips, and they immediately sputter looking for a response.
The TRUTH is, most of us could care less about anyone else, just mostly about ourselves.
Today is an easy devotion. Today, I want you to pray this prayer with me right out loud. Are you ready?

"Jesus, thank you for giving me life. Thank you for loving me even though many times I am unlovable. Thank you for never giving up on me. Thank you for my purpose and destiny. I am asking today for one thing. Please give me your heart. Please give me your love for people. Burden me with a desire to love others above myself. Let me start seeing people the way you see them. In Jesus name.....AMEN."

Don't be selfish; don't try to impress others. Be humble, thinking of others as better than yourselves. Don't look out only for your own interests, but take an interest in others, too.
You must have the same attitude that Christ Jesus had.
Philippians 2:3-5 NLT

~Dr Micheal Spencer

June 24

Do You Really CARE? Part 2

Don't be selfish; don't try to impress others. Be humble, thinking of others as better than yourselves. Don't look out only for your own interests, but take an interest in others, too.
You must have the same attitude that Christ Jesus had.
Philippians 2:3-5 NLT

Have you ever seen a car accident?
One day I was driving with a friend and we came over a bridge, and in front of us was a 4 way stop. We watched a car blow the sign and hit a small SUV. The SUV literally went up in the air and landed on its roof. The back hatch swung open and out ran a dog. We drove up to the accident. The girl was in her 20s and in the back seat. She was crying and freaking out. We started talking and calming her down until help arrived.
I felt helpless, weak, and unable to do anything but talk with her. Have you ever felt that way? Even if it was a person I did not like I would have felt sorry for them. I didn't have the tools or skills to help, except to be calming.
People who do not know Jesus are in a more dangerous situation. They are on the threshold of eternal torment and separation from Daddy. Many times we do not see them in that situation because we are not startled by a physical death, but the eternal death is far worse, and long lasting.
I might not have known the skills to help the girl in the SUV, but we have the skills to share the answer, and His name is Jesus!

CARE TODAY HELP SOMEONE FROM THEIR SOON IMPENDING ACCIDENT AND DEATH.

SHARE JESUS TODAY!

~Dr Micheal Spencer

June 25

CHEAP GRACE

"If you love me, keep my commandments" John 14:15

Well then, should we keep on sinning so that God can show us more and more of his wonderful grace? 2 Of course not! Since we have died to sin, how can we continue to live in it? Romans 6:1-2

WE FORGET THE COST THAT WAS PAID FOR OUR SALVATION.
There are many Christians that forget that just because God's love is unconditional, it does not mean there is no justice.
Micah 6:8, No, O people, the Lord has told you what is good, and this is what he requires of you, to do what is right, to love mercy, and to walk humbly with your God.
1 Peter 4:17, For the time has come for judgment, and it must begin with God's household. And if judgment begins with us, what terrible fate awaits those who have never obeyed God's Good News?
God loves us unconditionally, but because this is a RELATIONSHIP, it takes two to create it and keep it healthy.
There is a sweeping deception going across the world that because God loves unconditionally that we can live any manner that we desire, because He has to forgive.
That is called CHEAP GRACE, and it is not the truth.
THIS IS A MATTER OF THE HEART!
"Cheap grace is the grace we bestow on ourselves. Cheap grace is the preaching of forgiveness without requiring repentance, baptism without church discipline, Communion without confession.... Cheap grace is grace without discipleship, grace without the cross, grace without Jesus Christ, living and incarnate." *Dietrich Bonhoeffer*
"Grace is never cheap. It is absolutely free to us, but infinitely expensive to God... Anyone who is prone to use grace as a license for irresponsible, sinful behavior, surely does not appreciate the infinite price God paid to give us His grace."
Jerry Bridges

~Dr Micheal Spencer

June 26

CHEAP GRACE Day 2

"If you love me, keep my commandments" John 14:15
Well then, should we keep on sinning so that God can show us more and more of his wonderful grace? 2 Of course not! Since we have died to sin, how can we continue to live in it? Romans 6:1-2

SINNING FREELY

Today's Christian sins freely without the understanding of the true meaning of love. Love is NOT JUST – it is multifaceted. When you look at a diamond shimmering in the sunlight, you are seeing the one diamond, but the facets are what are reflecting the wholeness. It is the multiplicity of facets that make the totality. God's love is the whole, but within the love is justice and discipline. Without them the diamond would have one whole side missing.

A facet of love is justice – discipline / Heb. 12:10-11, For our earthly fathers disciplined us for a few years, doing the best they knew how. But God's discipline is always good for us, so that we might share in his holiness. 11 No discipline is enjoyable while it is happening—it's painful! But afterward there will be a peaceful harvest of right living for those who are trained in this way.

Because God's love is unconditional, does it mean we can live our sinful life, and He has to forgive us?

Do not be confused with His unconditional love that never ceases. With the justice of God, they are on the same diamond of whole love.

Gal. 6:7-8, Don't be misled—you cannot mock the justice of God. You will always harvest what you plant. 8 Those who live only to satisfy their own sinful nature will harvest decay and death from that sinful nature. But those who live to please the Spirit will harvest everlasting life from the Spirit.

Have you ever been around someone who takes advantage of people? They get as much out of them as possible.

They use the people around them for what they can get out of the them. They abuse them because the other person is generous.

Is that a true relationship?

We do not sin because we cannot – we do not sin because we do not want to hurt the One we love the most!

IF, IF, IF you love ME, keep my commandments.

~Dr Micheal Spencer

June 27

CHEAP GRACE Day 3

"If you love me, keep my commandments" John 14:15
Well then, should we keep on sinning so that God can show us more and more of his wonderful grace? 2 Of course not! Since we have died to sin, how can we continue to live in it?
Romans 6:1-2
SINNING FREELY
NO IMMEDIATE CONSEQUENCES. Many people ask Jesus into their lives to save them from hell, but do not live in Christ. Their lifestyle does not change
They drink the same way. They cuss the same way. They sleep around the same way. They shack up the same way.
In the OT when a person did a sin it was immediate retribution. If a person was caught sleeping around they would stone them to death.
Death was often the consequence of sin. Korah – the earth opened up and swallowed them....ummm, I wouldn't hang around that dude.
In the NT Jesus shows us grace and we do not see IMMEDIATE consequences for our sin – that is God's grace & mercy, or consequence–this does not mean there is not a price.
Obedience is an expression of a right relationship with God in Christ. It's a relationship of love. Jesus said, "If ye love me, keep my commandments" (John 14:15). If one really knows and loves Christ, it's bound to show in their actions. Where there is essentially no obedience there is every reason to question whether Christ actually resides in the heart. The apostle Paul taught: "For by grace are ye saved through faith; and that not of yourselves; it is the gift of God: Not of works, lest any man should boast. For we are his workmanship, created in Christ Jesus unto good works, which God hath before ordained that we should walk in them" (Ephesians 2:9-10). Without question, we are saved by grace through faith alone in Christ and His finished work of redemption on our behalf, but a genuine conversion experience results in good works — a characteristic obedience to the Lord's commands — a dynamic and increasingly growing biblical worldview approach to life. WE SERVE HIM BECAUSE WE LOVE HIM! WE CHOOSE NOT TO SIN BECAUSE WE LOVE HIM! DO NOT FORGET HIS LOVE IS UNCONDITIONAL–BUT WE MUST RESPOND TO HIS LOVE
We should hate sin like we hate Satan. Sin separates us from our Father, and Satan is striving to steal, kill and destroy you! If you play with sin, you will lose, and the consequences are eternal. IF you really love Jesus, you will keep His commandments.

~Dr Micheal Spencer

June 28

Pass Me a BEER!!

"You are the light of the world—like a city on a hilltop that cannot be hidden. No one lights a lamp and then puts it under a basket. Instead, a lamp is placed on a stand, where it gives light to everyone in the house. In the same way, let your good deeds shine out for all to see, so that everyone will praise your heavenly Father. Matthew 5:14-16 NLT

The drama is over, so now I can wait till next year to tell the rest of my friends about Jesus! NO..........

That presentation of the Gospel might be over, but now the GREATEST salvation testimony unfolds to your friends, family and enemies.

IT'S YOUR EVERY DAY LIFE WITH JESUS.

You do not have to run around with a 10lb Bible, shouting GLORY all over the place to be a good witness.

People are watching our every move when we live for Christ. It is not that you have to be perfect, but we do need to pay attention to make sure we have a good testimony.

People are looking for the GENUINE, not the FAKE. If you are perfect, then you are fake. People are looking at our lives as Christians to see that God is real to us and not some freaky religious kick. That is shown in every day, real life, crap hit the fan at work, life.

You cannot expect to keep your testimony when you go to the bar with them and take someone home that you don't even know, or that you are so drunk, they give you a ride home to keep you from driving. You cannot expect they will believe your genuine about Jesus when you are dropping the "F" bomb every other word, or are the one gossiping, and backbiting at work.

We have to be aware that the greatest Bible most will ever see is......US!

Don't hide your light, SHINE BABY, SHINE!

"I would rather go to church with a few hypocrites, than go to the Lake of Fire with all of them."

~Dr Micheal Spencer

June 29

What Is Your Mess?

There is one thing for sure.....
WE ARE NOT PERFECT YET....Can I hear an amen!
No matter how many years you have been serving The Lord there is always something that He is working on to make us more like Him.
We pray to be more like Him, we sing songs that say the same thing. During the sermon on Sunday you even want to more than normal, BUT, when push comes to shove, will you choose change, or stay the same?
There will always be a mess in the backyard, but our willingness to change makes the pile smaller.
Ok, here is some transparency from your Pastor:

> This week God has been dealing with me about sharing my opinion. I always seem to have an opinion, something to add, something to say. Like my opinion really matters! It is the Word that matters not my opinion!

Let no corrupt word proceed out of your mouth, but what is good for necessary edification, that it may impart grace to the hearers. Ephesians 4:29
The Lord keeps reminding me what my mom used to say, "If you have nothing good to say, be quiet."
It isn't even that my opinion is bad, but why do I feel I have to give it?
Good learning..... no fun..... but good learning!
WHAT IS THE HOLY SPIRIT TEACHING YOU THIS WEEK?
WHAT MESS IN THE PILE IS HE TELLING YOU TO CLEAN UP?
Get out that spiritual shovel and let's become more like Jesus.

~Dr Micheal Spencer

June 30

HOPE is OXYGEN

Most people that come to me for help have lost HOPE in their situation of life!
Proverbs 13:12, Hope deferred makes the heart sick, but when the desire is fulfilled, it is a tree of life.
When a person has no hope, then they cannot activate faith. When their is no faith, then we cannot activate the eternal opportunities. **When a person loses hope it literally effects their entire personage. They become sad, depressed, unhappy in their soulish man, their physical body manifests it through their posture (slumping, shuffling when they walk, head down), and in their spirit they lose faith in God.**
NEVER GIVING UP HOPE is a key to making the impossible come to fruition.
Psalm 42:5, Why are you cast down, O my inner self? And why should you moan over me and be disquieted within me? Hope in God and wait expectantly for Him, for I shall yet praise Him, my Help and my God.

TODAY I HAVE GREAT NEWS FOR YOU!
JESUS IS THE GOD OF THE IMPOSSIBLE! THERE IS NOTHING HE CANNOT DO!

Never give up HOPE! Never stop BELIEVING! Never RELINQUISH!
NO MATTER HOW BAD IT LOOKS, KNOW THIS: THERE IS A LIGHT AT THE END OF THE TUNNEL (His name is Jesus), AND YOU WILL MAKE IT, AND NOT JUST MAKE IT – You are going over the TOP!

Shake yourself - Speak life and not death – arrest your thoughts – PRAISE THE ONE WHO MAKES THE IMPOSSIBLE HAPPEN –
Watch Jesus do His thing!

~Dr Micheal Spencer

July 1

Joseph – The Man of Faith & Victory pt. I

When we think about Joseph we think about his coat of many colors and that he saved the entire nation of Israel and his family. It is not right to look at the END without looking at the process! Joseph was a GREAT man of faith, trust, reliance upon the God that He met in a supernatural experience. Genesis 37:5-11
Where were you when you really had an encounter with Christ? Whenever you have that encounter that changes your entire life, you have to know that the enemy of your soul is coming to try to steal away that seed (John 10:10, The thief does not come except to steal, and to kill, and to destroy. I have come that they may have life, and that they may have it more abundantly.)
Joseph was excited and shared with his brother's and father the God experience, and the dream. The dream was that his brother's and father would all bow to him. The sharing of the dream was that last straw for his brothers that hated him anyway.
Genesis 37:24 When Joseph brought his brother's food while they were tending the flocks, they grabbed him and stripped his coat, and then through him in a pit!
You can imagine the mind of Joseph – God we just hung out and You spoke to me, so I know you are going to get me out of this mess. Then those brother's are going to get it for sure!
Ummm – NOPE – they sold their little brother, who just met with God, to the Midianites, who them sold him to Potiphar (Genesis 37:36)
Can you understand what Joseph must have been thinking? Where are you God? We just had this awesome experience, why did you let this happen to me? I'm alone. I'm scared. I thought you would have delivered me out of the pit, why am I here?
Because Joseph had a relationship with God – because he did not base that on his situations – because he chose to keep the faith – because he continued in fighting the good fight of faith and not giving up & getting mad at God – GOD BLESSED HIM EVEN IN THE HARD PLACE.
Genesis 39:1-4 God blessed Joseph with increase, prosperity, favor and most of all – His Presence. All because Joseph did not lose faith – Faith is our Victory!
It was a dark season. A hard season. A season of losing everything near and dear to him, BUT, he chose to stay close to God. IN YOUR DARK SEASON – YOUR ANSWER DETERMINES YOUR RESULT!
Joseph was in a horrible place, yet, the place did not determine his blessing. The God he trusts determined his blessing and prosperity.

~Dr Micheal Spencer

July 2

Joseph – The Man of Faith & Victory pt. 2

Ok, so, Joseph had a supernatural encounter with God, the real deal!

He gets mugged by his own brother's and thrown into a pit. He then is sold into slavery. He is on his own, no family, no friends, no normal environment. He is then sold again into Potiphar's house.

What did Joseph do? He kept the faith, relied upon his God, didn't give up, didn't blame God, didn't get bitter. **BECAUSE HE KEPT THE FAITH, he was blessed, prospered, rose in authority, received favor.**

GLORY TO GOD, EVERYTHING IS ON THE UPSWING!

Everything is looking better, whewwwww! Ummm, hang on..

Genesis 39:7-8, 12, 17/ **FALSE ACCUSATIONS**- Potiphar's wife wanted Joseph, but he would not have sex with her, so, she got mad and said he tried to rape her. Who is a husband going to believe? Can you imagine Joseph's emotions? God!! Where are you?? This is not true, I didn't do it, I was doing right and NOW THIS!

Joseph was being blessed even in the midst of his great loss of everything he knew. NOW, it gets worse!

Genesis 39:20-21 **Joseph was not just a sold into slavery, now he is thrown into prison!** Hello God? Where are you? I thought that day you spoke to me everything was going to be perfect and it would all go my way. Now look, I want nothing to do with you! This church stuff doesn't work, this faith, this Bible junk isn't working for me, I'm outta here!

Genesis 39:21, 23 This was not the heart of Joseph, he kept the faith, trust and relationship even though it didn't make sense, even though it looked bad, he never took his eyes off his relationship with God.

Because of this – God didn't take him out, He took Joseph through with blessing, favor and prosperity. REMEMBER- HE IS IN PRISON!

Genesis 40 In prison the Pharaoh's butler and baker were thrown. They both had dreams. One would be killed, and the other restored. Joseph interpreted supernaturally the dreams! Don't forget me when you get restored butler.

2 years later, not an hour, not a week, not a month, not a year, 2 years later, he is remembered.

EVERYONE LIKES THE PART OF SAVING EVERYONE – BUT – IF JOSEPH HAD NOT KEPT FAITH FOR VICTORY YOU AND I WOULD NOT BE SAVED.

If you don't keep the faith & victory, how many will not be saved?

~Dr Micheal Spencer

July 3

Alcohol?

"Leaders can't afford to make fools of themselves, gulping wine and swilling beer, Lest, hung over, they don't know right from wrong, and the people who depend on them are hurt. Use wine and beer only as sedatives, to kill the pain and dull the ache Of the terminally ill, for whom life is a living death. Proverbs 31:4-7 MSG

Ok. It's the WORD OF GOD.

Don't drink too much wine. That cheapens your life. Ephesians 5:18 MSG

Oh listen, dear child-become wise; point your life in the right direction. Don't drink too much wine and get drunk; don't eat too much food and get fat. Drunks and gluttons will end up on skid row, in a stupor and dressed in rags. Proverbs 23:19-21 MSG

WINE IS a mocker, strong drink a riotous brawler; and whoever errs or reels because of it is not wise. Proverbs 20:1 AMP

~Pastor Rhonda Spencer

July 4

Too Busy, or Just LAZY?

Matthew 7:13-14 " Enter by the narrow gate; for wide is the gate and broad is the way that leads to destruction, and there are many who go in by it. Because **narrow is the gate and difficult is the way which leads to life, and there are few who find it.**

Well that is not too encouraging Pastor!

Really it is, because without the truth & understanding, then it is like taking a trip without having a map.

Many have not made it because they begin the race, they give their heart to Jesus, they enter into relationship with God, and ......ummmm......yup......that's it.

Church once a month, ok, maybe twice a month (which is the national average), is good enough once you made that prayer.

Relationship is what Jesus is after, not our religious mantra.

Can you imagine getting married and coming home only once or twice a month, and when you are asked where you have been your answer is simply, I've been busy.

Church will not get you to heaven, but Jesus created His house for a purpose. Without His house you cannot grow up and fulfill God's purpose for your life. We MUST have a mindset change about church. It is not about your convenience, it is about your respect to your Heavenly Father, and your spiritual growth.

When we as "BELIEVER'S" get too busy to give God 2 hours of our week to obey Him in corporate worship, then we are too busy, or lazy.

"I'm not lazy, I have things to do on Sunday morning"

So when you need Jesus you expect Him to jump and meet your need, but when He asks you to simply honor Him with 2 hours a week, you are too busy, or lazy......

I'm on a soapbox this morning because many will never make it, or if they do, will never fulfill God's purpose for their lives on this planet. People will be LOST because of selfishness. I don't like church! TOUGH, obey God! I don't like organized religion! TOUGH, do what you are told!

Oh, I know we don't like hearing that as adults, but we don't mind telling that to our children and expecting them to follow through.

Hebrews 10:24-25 And let us consider one another in order to stir up love and good works, not forsaking the assembling of ourselves together, as is the manner of some, but exhorting one another, and so much the more as you see the Day approaching.

HOW ABOUT YOU? Will you obey God?

~Dr Micheal Spencer

July 5

I KNOW YOU!!!!

One of the things we do the quickest is judge people's hearts.
"I know them." "I know who they really are."
At times there might be truth in those statements, but, honestly, truthfully, knowing a person's heart is really only for God.
Ok, let's flip this beast.....
Do we really know our own hearts motivations?
Jeremiah 17:9 "The heart is deceitful above all things, And desperately wicked; Who can know it?
We so quickly want to assume (*and we know what assume means*) we know what others motives are without truthfully finding out our own reasons for doing what we do.
God judges the heart, not the actions.
We as humans usually judge the actions, and not the heart.
One of the scariest things I have ever done was ask God to truly show me my own heart. We think we know why we do what we do, but in reality, we even can deceive ourselves.
Why do we not like so and so?
Why do I do the job I do?
Why are we really offended?
Why do I do the ministry I do?
Why do I go to church?
Why do I wear the clothes I wear?
We are driven by self-motivation, self-preservation, self-gratification, when we are to be motivated as a servant.
We can say we know why, but, without asking God to reveal our hearts, we can easily lie to ourselves to satisfy the flesh and subconscious.

TODAY – ASK GOD TO REVEAL YOUR HEART!
Hang on because it can get ugly when we actually see how impure our motives really are!

~Dr Micheal Spencer

July 6

Shhhhhhhh you're talking too much.

Too much talk leads to sin. Be sensible and keep your mouth shut. Proverbs 10:19 NLT

Know this, my beloved brothers: let every person be quick to hear, slow to speak, slow to anger; for the anger of man does not produce the righteousness of God. James 1:19-20

Even a fool who keeps silent is considered wise; when he closes his lips, he is deemed intelligent.
Proverbs 17:28

Spouting off before listening to the facts is both shameful and foolish. Proverbs 18:13

Let's try not talking so much and most of all paying attention to the words coming out our mouths. Are our words making a fool out of us or even becoming sin?

~Pastor Rhonda Spencer

July 7

ARE YOU SLUGGING ALONG?

One minute slides into the next, then the hour is consumed by the next hour, then the day is whisked away, and all of a sudden, the year is gone.......TIME!
There are two things that never stop:
1. Change
2. Time
That is why the Word says,
Joshua 24:15 And if it seems evil to you to serve the Lord, **choose for yourselves this day whom you will serve**, whether the gods which your fathers served that were on the other side of the River, or the gods of the Amorites, in whose land you dwell. But as for me and my house, we will serve the Lord."

TODAY is the only today you will have, because tomorrow is the next, not the NOW.
What are you doing with the NOW?
Have you chosen to serve Jesus today?
Have you chosen to do His will today?
Have you determined to read the Word today?
Have you decided to pray today?
Have you focused on sharing Jesus today?
OR
Are you just letting today happen?
Choose....Determine.....Decide.....Direct....
Don't let your day run you, let Christ run your day!!!

~Dr Micheal Spencer

July 8

You Got FOOD POISONING!

2 Timothy 4:3-4 For the time will come when they will not endure sound doctrine, but according to their own desires, because they have itching ears, they will heap up for themselves teachers; and they will turn their ears away from the truth, and be turned aside to fables.

We live in a time and era of the church where majority of Christians do not know the Word of God. They have never been taught, or they choose other things of the world over being taught.

Without knowing the Word, without knowing God's principles, it is so easy to be sucked into falsehood and confusion.

There were some parents who had a dinner party at their home as a celebration. They made an amazing spread of food for all their friends and family. There was prime rib, lobster, shrimp, with all the fixings and nobody walked away without saying it was the best meal in years. The parents had a baby that was now scooting around the house on his own. One day the mother turned and the baby had scooted away to the den and was quiet. You and I know that when a child is quiet, it is time to check on them. She went to the den and found the baby behind the chair eating. The baby had found a plate of food from the party that was now about 3 days old. The child ate shrimp, that by this time was very rancid. She didn't get the baby help quick enough and he died of food poisoning.

This happens to Christians all the time. They do not get sound doctrine, they do not learn the Word and then...... some freak comes to town, or some new TV evangelist pops of the network and begins to feed tainted spiritual food. It looks good, might even smell good, but will end up poisoning your spirit and killing you.

KNOW THE WORD, KNOW GOOD DOCTRINE, FEED YOUR SPIRIT, AND YOU WILL LIVE!!

~Dr Micheal Spencer

July 9

YOU OFFENDED ME! Part 1

I've been doing some housekeeping in my personal life, and in doing so, while sharing what God is doing in my life with friends…I have discovered a bacteria infecting our lives in common. **THERE IS A SPIRIT OF OFFENSE IN THE HOUSE.**
I want to call attention to this crafty ploy of the enemy. You see many "mature" Christians can't be tripped up by the big obvious things, so the enemy of our soul has used a masterful technique on the body of Christ, and its called offense.
Maybe its like this: "uh…that pot hole, my car is going to fall apart…don't they understand I can't afford to have to fix my car… if they don't fix that hole I'm just not going to keep coming down that driveway to church…"
"Grrrrrrr … he's parked in my parking spot!"
"She just walked right by me and never said hi…..what did I ever do to her…how rude and she calls herself a Christian?"
"That music is just awful….it's so loud…they'll never be able to keep people with it screeching like that."
"I can't believe she wore *that* to church….this is the house of God!"
I'm not ever going to sit here again…all they do is talk, right out "loud…how rude I can't even concentrate. I'm just going to find another church where it will be better."
HOW AM I DOING SO FAR?
IT'S NOT THE CHURCH THAT'S THE PROBLEM….we feel dry, empty and far from God because, week after week, we go through the motions of church but NOT ACTUALLY GETTING TO WORSHIP, LEARN OR GROW….so for 10 years we feel like the church has failed us, and we need to go somewhere else to get fed…..which will work for a few weeks until you get back into the same old routine of offense!!!!
Mark 4:16-17 AMP And in the same way the ones sown upon stony ground are those who, when they hear the Word, at once receive and accept and welcome it with joy; And they have no real root in themselves, and so they endure for a little while; then when trouble or persecution arises on account of the Word, they immediately are offended (become displeased, indignant, resentful) and they stumble and fall away.
Offenses are hurting YOU! They are destroying YOU! They are making YOU a bitter, nasty, unsavory saint that oozes stank instead of sweet Jesus.
REPENT…… and be healed!!

~Pastor Rhonda Spencer

July 10

YOU OFFENDED ME! Part 2

Being offended does not destroy the other person! It destroys YOU!

The destruction is always felt in many dimensions. The dimension we live in is touched because now we are walking around with hurt feelings, "hurt people, hurt people". It also touches your walk with God. In fact, it doesn't touch it, ***it eats it away***.

Mark 6:3-5 NKJV Is this not the carpenter, the Son of Mary, and brother of James, Joses, Judas, and Simon? And are not His sisters here with us?" So they were offended at Him. But Jesus said to them, "A prophet is not without honor except in his own country, among his own relatives, and in his own house." **Now He could do no mighty work there**, except that He laid His hands on a few sick people & healed them.

DID YOU GET THAT? THEY WERE OFFENDED, AND HE WASN'T ABLE TO DO MIGHTY WORKS THERE.......THEY WERE UNABLE TO EXPERIENCE THE POWER OF GOD.

OFFENSE STOPS THE POWER OF GOD FROM BEING ABLE TO WORK IN OUR LIVES!!!

Mark 4:16-17 AMP And in the same way the ones sown upon stony ground are those who, when they hear the Word, at once receive and accept and welcome it with joy; And they have no real root in themselves, and so they endure for a little while; then when trouble or persecution arises on account of the Word, they immediately are offended (become displeased, indignant, resentful) and they stumble and fall away.

MANY FALL AWAY FROM JESUS BECAUSE OF OFFENSES. SOME BECAUSE OF THE GOSPEL, BUT OTHERS IN THE GOSPEL. **If you are in God's HOME, you will be offended. Father's house is filled with brothers and sisters and everyone hurts each other. Majority of the time it is accidental, yet, I have watched many walk away because they took offense over an accidental statement or action. I have watched people leave Father's home because they took on the offense of another person. All could cost you your eternity with Christ.**

Matthew 24:10 AMP And then many will be offended and repelled and will begin to distrust and desert [Him Whom they ought to trust and obey] and will stumble and fall away and betray one another and pursue one another with hatred.

ONCE THE OFFENSE HAS TAKEN ROOT, NOW THEY START HATING AND DEVOURING. Watch the venom coming out of your mouth, watch the walls that are built, watch how you pull away. Each action screams, OFFENSE!

Today you can be FREE! Confess your sin, REPENT, and get right, Jesus will forgive you and make you clean again.

~Pastor Rhonda Spencer

July 11

How to FIX your Offense

There is one thing for sure that people do not like to talk about. We all expect our sins to be forgiven, but many refuse to forgive others. It is our right to be forgiven, but God forbid if I am expected to forgive that person who offended me!!!
Matthew 6:14-15 " For if you forgive men their trespasses, your heavenly Father will also forgive you. But if you do not forgive men their trespasses, neither will your Father forgive your trespasses.
Simply stated: If you do not forgive others....you cannot go to heaven!
I have a right to be angry! Anger is not a sin (Ephesians 4:26 "Be angry, and do not sin": do not let the sun go down on your wrath,), it is what you allow that anger to become!
Grown up anger from an offense = bitterness, unforgiveness, eternity separated from Jesus.
OK, you had your feelings hurt, someone offended you – **NOW WHAT DO I DO?**
Matthew 18:15-17 "Moreover if your brother sins against you, go and tell him his fault between you and him alone. If he hears you, you have gained your brother. 16 But if he will not hear, take with you one or two more, that 'by the mouth of two or three witnesses every word may be established.' And if he refuses to hear them, tell it to the church. But if he refuses even to hear the church, let him be to you like a heathen and a tax collector.
COME ON, YOU WANT ME TO DO IT THE JESUS WAY?
Matthew 5:23-24 Therefore if you bring your gift to the altar, and there remember that your brother has something against you, leave your gift there before the altar, and go your way. First be reconciled to your brother, and then come and offer your gift.
IT IS YOUR RESPONSIBILITY TO MAKE IT RIGHT, NOT THEIRS
Make it right for your FREEDOM and obedience in Christ. Apply the anointing for your own healing, and Jesus will heal the brokenhearted (Luke 4:18).

~Pastor Rhonda Spencer

July 12

GET ANGRY AT ANXIETY

None of us would just let someone come in our homes and steal from us. We would put up resistance, we would fight, we would call the police, but we would not allow them to continue to come in every day and steal our stuff.
As Christians, we have to get FED UP with the thief!
John 10:10 The thief does not come except to steal, and to kill, and to destroy. I have come that they may have life, and that they may have it more abundantly.
What is he stealing? OUR PEACE.
Anxiety is overtaking the King's kids!
Anxiety, noun, a feeling of worry, nervousness, or unease, typically about an imminent event or something with an uncertain outcome; A Desire to do something, typically accompanied by unease; Panic attacks (just the term says demonic), insomnia, headaches, and many other side effects.

Anxiety begins somewhere...It has a start....Everything, but God, has a beginning.....
What is the beginning that can cut off before its allowed to steal our peace and create the environment of fear and anxiety?
Philippians 4:6-7 **Be anxious for nothing, but in everything by prayer and supplication, with thanksgiving**, let your requests be made known to God; and the peace of God, which surpasses all understanding, will guard your hearts and minds through Christ Jesus.
When anxiety comes, what do I do?
This is your prescription:
1. Take a stand, call the police! Rebuke the devil and call on Jesus!!
2. Address the real situation with the faith that says, God is able, and I trust HIM
3. Then you start to praise, before you see the evidence, praise and never stop!
4. You will then be flooded with a peace that surpasses all understanding!

~Dr Micheal Spencer

July 13

Suffocating in Worry

Isaiah 26:3 You will keep him in perfect peace,
Whose mind is stayed on You, Because he trusts in You.

When we do not control our thoughts, then they run toward the worst scenario's possible. That is human nature, BUT, we do not have that nature any longer.

We have a new nature, a new way of doing things (2 Peter 1:4)

We live inside new laws –

THE LAW OF LIFE IN CHRIST JESUS!

Because we live in a new law, PEACE is our PROMISE, if, we keep our minds in control!

2 Corinthians 10:5, casting down arguments and every high thing that exalts itself against the knowledge of God, bringing every thought into captivity to the obedience of Christ,

A TRUTH that people hate to hear is that remaining in stress and worry are in sin!

The Word is clear that worry is not of God, and definitely not a believer's portion. It suffocates us with worry and anxiety, which then allows FEAR to control our lives. FEAR is the opposite of FAITH.

Philippians 4:6-7 **Be anxious for nothing**, but in everything by prayer and supplication, with thanksgiving, let your requests be made known to God; **and the peace of God**, which surpasses all understanding, will guard your hearts and minds through Christ Jesus.

We like the part that says, the peace of God that surpasses understanding...BUT, how is that happening?

We must choose to fight against worry, fret, anxiety – it is your enemy!

We must choose to focus on prayer – filled with faith and praise!

We must choose to keep our eyes focused on Jesus – not allowing fear to overcome us!

THEN THE PEACE COMES – supernatural relief even in the middle of the storm!

Don't allow the suffocation of worry, anxiety, fear to be part of your life!

Faith will call those things which are not as though they already are – pulling your miracle out of the heavenlies to this natural earth.

~Dr Micheal Spencer

July 14

Make a Lifestyle of Tithing

Bring all the tithes (the whole tenth of your income) into the storehouse, that there may be food in My house, and PROVE ME now by it, says the Lord of hosts, if I will not open the windows of heaven for you and pour you out a blessing, that there shall not be room enough to receive it. And I WILL REBUKE THE DEVOURER [insects and plagues] for your sakes and he shall not destroy the fruits of your ground, neither shall your vine drop its fruit before the time in the field, says the Lord of hosts. And all nations shall call you HAPPY AND BLESSED, for you shall be a LAND OF DELIGHT, says the Lord of hosts.
Malachi 3:10-12 AMP

I stand on the promise of the Almighty God!
Tithe and He will prove himself and rebuke the devourer and you will be called happy and blessed.

~Pastor Rhonda Spencer

July 15

Is YOUR Faith Weak?

Romans 4:19-22 **And not being weak in faith, he did not consider his own body**, already dead (since he was about a hundred years old), and the deadness of Sarah's womb. He did not waver at the promise of God through unbelief, but was strengthened in faith, giving glory to God, and being fully convinced that what He had promised He was also able to perform. **And therefore "it was accounted to him for righteousness."**

I love this portion of Scripture because we can change a few words around and completely show the opposite of faith.

READ THIS TEXT WITH JUST A FEW CHANGES IN IT!

Romans 4:19-22 And *being weak in faith, he did consider his own body, already dead* (since he was about a hundred years old), and the deadness of Sarah's womb. *He did waver at the promise of God through unbelief*, but *was not strengthened in faith*, giving glory to God, and *was not fully convinced* that what He had promised He was also able to perform. And therefore *"it was accounted to him for unrighteousness."*

The two portions are the same except one is filled with doubt, and one is filled with faith, trust.

Strength or weakness of faith is not determined by God, it is determined by us. Faith comes by hearing the Word and learning to trust God by knowing Him. When our faith is weak it is because we are not feeding our faith. We are not getting into the Word, and not getting teaching to feed our spirit.

The only way to waver is to question God's actually ability. When we are wavering we are saying that we are not sure if God is powerful enough to actually handle the situation. He is weak, unable, not supernatural, just weak like a man. When we begin to waver, that should immediately ignite the necessity to grab the Word and start feeding our faith.

Being convinced, is in that growth. After you have proven God, not God proven to you. This means that you have decided to trust Him. He is always trustworthy, and faithful, but we have to choose to believe and be convinced, or doubt begins to take over.

James 1:6-8 But let him ask in faith, with no doubting, for he who doubts is like a wave of the sea driven and tossed by the wind. For let not that man suppose that he will receive anything from the Lord; he is a double- minded man, unstable in all his ways.

DON'T BE DOUBLE-MINDED, FEED YOUR FAITH!!

~Dr Micheal Spencer

July 16

STOP COMPLAINING!! It Doesn't Fix Anything...

Have you ever hung around people that do not have faith?
I can help you identify a person who has no faith.....
THEY ARE ALWAYS COMPLAINING!!!!!!
Everything is going good, but they will still find something to complain about. What is amazing is that nothing is ever accomplished without faith. So their time is throw away. The time is wasted and will accomplish absolutely nothing.

Philippians 2:14
Do all things without complaining and disputing.

Can you imagine if we all stopped complaining and turned that time toward praying in faith?
Can you believe the RESULTS!!

Today stop complaining and produce results through the prayer of faith!

Here is the plan.... when you get around the complainer. Grab their hand and start praying for the situation they are complaining about and they will stop quickly.

~Pastor Rhonda Spencer

July 17

The Battle for PEACE!

And let the peace of God rule in your hearts, to which also you were called in one body; and be thankful. Colossians 3:15 NKJV
The word Rule means to govern, direct, allow to disallow....
There is a battle going on in your flesh, and in the spirit realm to keep you from your Covenant right of PEACE. BUT WHY?
When you are not in peace it means that something is not correct in your life. It is your relationship with Jesus that is speaking to you when you are out of peace.
WHAT WOULD MY RELATIONSHIP BE SAYING?
1. **You might be out of peace because you are not living right.** I have watched people who once walked closely with God begin to wander. Once they began to wander, they struggled being wherever the presence of The Lord was being manifested. They would feel uneasy, uncomfortable, then begin to make excuses to give their flesh some peace by extracting themselves. Thank God the Spirit is the hound of heaven. Today Jesus continue to draw them home to you with the lack of peace and satisfaction.
2. **You might be out of peace because you are out of step with God.** Maybe you have gone before Him, or maybe, you have lagged behind Him. Ask the Holy Spirit where you are out of step with God. You know when you are out of step in your natural relationship, you begin to argue, get over sensitive, complaining.......
3. **You might be allowing your flesh to rule your sight pattern.** The Word says we walk by faith and not by sight. When we walk by sight then we are not walking in faith. God has not told us to deny the facts, but we have been told to declare the TRUTH. If you are allowing your circumstances to govern you, then you will not be living in PEACE, you will always be in fear and anxiety.
4. **Jesus might be trying to get your attention.** He needs to speak with you, but you never slow down enough for you to hear Him.
5. **He might be trying to warn you of some danger that could be in the future.** You might lose your peace, and that is how God speaks to you that some junk is about to hit the fan, and now you need to start praying.
ONE THING IS FOR SURE, if your peace is not present, then the governor of your spirit is off. **STOP!!**
What do I do? What do you do when you don't know what to do, STAND STILL till you know which are is missing, and what needs to happen to get your peace back.

~Dr Micheal Spencer

July 18

I Just Need PEACE!!! What is going on? Part 1

Isaiah 9:6
For unto us a Child is born,
Unto us a Son is given;
And the government will be upon His shoulder.
And His name will be called
Wonderful, Counselor, Mighty God,
Everlasting Father, Prince of Peace.

1) completeness, soundness, welfare, peace
   a) completeness (in number)
   b) safety, soundness (in body)
   c) welfare, health, prosperity
   d) peace, quiet, tranquility, contentment
   e) peace, friendship
   f) of human relationships
2) with God especially in covenant relationship

Peace isn't just a calming - it is a COMPLETENESS, TOTAL, HEALTH OF THE SPIRIT, SOUL & BODY, and even in your FINANCES!!

This whole Scripture is talking about Jesus, and how He is the One who brings peace to our lives. Not outward peace, like with our circumstances, but peace knowing that Father will take good care of us.
If you do not have peace, that means a simple deduction:
Isaiah 26:3, You will keep him in perfect peace, Whose mind is stayed on You, Because he trusts in You.

If you are not in perfect peace, then immediately you know your mind is not under control....

MORE TOMORROW
"You don't understand, that does not work in my situation....."

~Dr Micheal Spencer

July 19

I Just Need PEACE! What is happening? Part 2

Isaiah 26:3 You will keep him in perfect peace,
Whose mind is stayed on You, Because he trusts in You.

When PEACE is lost in a persons life, it is not because it has gone anywhere, but it was surrendered.

1 Timothy 6:12, Fight the good fight of faith, lay hold on eternal life, to which you were also called and have confessed the good confession in the presence of many witnesses.

We are called to fight the good fight of faith, trust and reliance, knowing that God is able to perform the miraculous.

When a person surrenders their peace, immediately they know that they have allowed their flesh (mind) to take control. Wholeness is now gone. Fret, worry, anxiety and stress are now growing in their soul, and Jesus is diminishing.

Pastor, you don't understand my situation. All these things have happened at once and I am overwhelmed. REALLY? Did you just tell me that God's Word is false and God is too weak to give you PEACE in a storm; that God's Word only works for those going through little issues, but not serious, major junk? God's Word is true no matter how much junk is happening, no matter how many attacks come, no matter how much tragedy comes into your life, God's Word is always true!!!

So what does that mean for me?

If you have surrendered your peace it is because your mind is not focused on Him or the Word, but on the situation right in front of you. What power do you really have to change it? So, how much are you accomplishing by worry, stress, fret, and anxiety? Are you now in more control? Truthfully, if you were in control you could have made it NOT happen in the first place. Ultimately your telling the King of Kings, "I do not TRUST YOU"

Get back to the seed store! Get back to the Word of God! What does the Lord say to you about your reality? Your faith will rise the more you stare at Christ rather than the issue. Feed on the Word, find your promises, and arrest your mind.

WHAT KIND OF PEACE?

PERFECT PEACE IS YOURS IF YOU WANT IT!!

~Dr Micheal Spencer

July 20

Don't Cheat on Your Groom!!

Ephesians 5:27 that He might present her to Himself a glorious church, not having spot or wrinkle or any such thing, but that she should be holy and without blemish.

We are the bride of Christ, engaged until His return, and then we are going to become ONE with Christ.

The Jewish custom of marriage was like this:

1. The groom's father made the approval of the choice of the bride. (John 15:16 You did not choose Me, but I chose you and appointed you that you should go and bear fruit, and that your fruit should remain, that whatever you ask the Father in My name He may give you.)
2. The groom made a covenant with the brides father.
   a. Drinking wine to seal the covenant (Ephesians 4:30, And do not grieve the Holy Spirit of God, by whom you were sealed for the day of redemption.)
   b. Paying a price for the bride (1 Corinthians 6:20 For you were bought at a price; therefore glorify God in your body and in your spirit, which are God's.)
   c. Promising to come back to take her (Acts 1:11...This same Jesus, who was taken up from you into heaven, will so come in like manner as you saw Him go into heaven.")
3. The groom prepared a place (John 14:2, In My Father's house are many mansions; if it were not so, I would have told you. I go to prepare a place for you.)
4. The bride waits for his coming / she is keeping herself / preparing herself

Jesus is preparing a place for His bride and is getting ready to come and get His church, the bride.

It was during this waiting time that the bride PREPARED herself for the groom. She was learning how to be a good wife, how to raise the children, how to minister to her soon to be husband.

The church is in this moment. We are waiting for the Groom to come and get His church, the bride. We should be focused on getting ready, not flirting and playing with every other option that is out there, then at the last moment trying to get all ready.

If you were engaged to a person, it was 1 year before the wedding and they were away at a great distance, what would you think if they were going to clubs, partying, messing with other men or woman, and just living their life, not caring about your wedding or being pure for you? You heard they have slept with 5 different people, yet they were your soon to be?

If the bride stays focused, then there will be no time to sell out on your groom. STAY FOCUSED, JESUS COMING, AND IT MIGHT BE TODAY!!

~Dr Micheal Spencer

July 21

I FEEL SO DIRTY…

Have you ever been done with a conversation and you leave feeling like you need a shower?
You were hanging out with your friend, you never noticed it before, but this time when you left you felt dirty. Not because you were playing in the mud...lol, but because that friend was talking so bad, backbiting about another person, that when you left you felt nasty.
There was a person like that in my life at one time. Did you notice I said "was"? This person was always a blessing to me, but every time I would leave their presence I seriously felt like someone just puked all over me. No bath could wash off the feeling of dirt that this person left on me.
I want to clarify: they were a great person, nice and caring, BUT, a massive backbiting gossip.
I had to make a decision I would no longer talk with them. I care for them, would be there if there was a need, but I could no longer be a friend, I could only be an acquaintance.
Romans 1:30-32 backbiters, haters of God, violent, proud, boasters, inventors of evil things, disobedient to parents, undiscerning, untrustworthy, unloving, unforgiving, unmerciful; who, knowing the righteous judgment of God, that those who practice such things are deserving of death, not only do the same but also approve of those who practice them.
Not that we all don't do this, but, there is a difference between a person who does something in stupidity, and a person who practices, lives, the lifestyle. The person who lives this lifestyle is a person you should stay 2 arms lengths away from. Whether they call themselves a Christian, or even if they are family. The only way to not feel dirty is to not be where the dirt is being flung!
2 Timothy 3:1-5 But know this, that in the last days perilous times will come: For men will be lovers of themselves, lovers of money, boasters, proud, blasphemers, disobedient to parents, unthankful, unholy, unloving, unforgiving, slanderers, without self- control, brutal, despisers of good, traitors, headstrong, haughty, lovers of pleasure rather than lovers of God, having a form of godliness but denying its power. And from such people turn away!

~Dr Micheal Spencer

July 22

WHO IS LEAKING ALL OVER YOU?

1 Corinthians 15:33 **Do not be deceived:** "Evil company corrupts good habits."
Evil companionships (communion, associations) corrupt and deprave good manners and morals and character.
1 Corinthians 15:33 AMP
I can handle it! I'm a big boy, or a big girl!
"Don't tell me who I can hang out with, I can make my own decisions!!" The Word of God is so clear on who we can spend time with, and who we cannot.
Every Christian comes to these crossroads on who they should allow in their lives on a daily basis, and those who you should always keep an arms distance away from.
This is even understood in the worldly mindset. Think about addictions. People who get clean have to break contact with their old crew or they will start walking with them, and soon after they will be running with them again.
I watched a man get seriously saved and Jesus was changing his life. This all happened in the winter through spring timetable. Summer came and he normally played softball in the bar league. Booze was his enemy, his struggle of life, so to stay away from it was imperative. I talked with him about being wise and taking the summer to get strong, and not going to the bar league, but continuing with coming to classes about the Word. He chose the league, and never came back. His enemy captured him when he went back into his camp!
Be careful who you spend time with, even if they call themselves Christian. If they are spewing death and doubt, stay away, pray for them from a distance. Get involved with Kingdom business and God's people who will build, encourage and strengthen your life.
STAY FOCUSED!!

~Dr Micheal Spencer

July 23

Daddy's LOVE is UNCONDITIONAL

Romans 8:38-39, For I am persuaded that neither death nor life, nor angels nor principalities nor powers, nor things present nor things to come, nor height nor depth, nor any other created thing, shall be able to separate us from the love of God which is in Christ Jesus our Lord.
UNCONDITIONAL LOVE OF DADDY
God is love–perfect love–unconditional love
He created for love – designed the earth out of love
He formed humans out of love – His image
He rules the universe out of love
Everything Father does is driven out of love
DADDY LOVES YOU & ACCEPTS YOU – flawed.
Father loves us even when we do not want Him.
There was a young boy growing up who was the apple of his parents' eye. As he grew he got in the wrong crowd. He began to drink, dropped out of school, and despised his parents'. One night he staggered into his parents house drunk, and his mom slipped out of bed without her husband waking. When he woke he assumed she was in the kitchen, most likely crying for her son. The husband went looking and found her sitting on the bed of her son, stroking his hair as he was passed out. He asked, "What are you doing?" She responded, "HE WON'T LET ME LOVE HIM WHEN HE IS AWAKE."
God's unconditional love is uncaused.
Human love is determined by earning, standards, conditions.
Good actions, attributes, attractiveness.
Human love is hurtful, wounding, betrayed, conditional.
Father's love is FREE, unprompted, uninfluenced.
There is nothing we can do to cause God to love us!
Nothing you do could ever make God love you more, or less than He did when He created you.
God's love is without motive, except true love!
1 John 4:7, Beloved, let us love one another, for love is of God; and everyone who loves is born of God and knows God.

~Dr Micheal Spencer

July 24

The God Kind of LOVE

God's love is UNCONDITIONAL!
The awesome part is that He lives inside us, and so that same love that is in the Father can now come through us for the people around us!
The personality of the Holy Spirit now resides in our spirit. We have a new nature – the very nature of our Father in heaven.
The greatest character mark of our Daddy is – LOVE!
Love is patient and kind. Love is not jealous or boastful or proud or rude. It does not demand its own way. It is not irritable, and it keeps no record of being wronged. It does not rejoice about injustice but rejoices whenever the truth wins out. Love never gives up, never loses faith, is always hopeful, and endures through every circumstance. 1 Corinthians 13:4-7 NLT
Suffers long – does not look at the moment – but at your "Z". The word used of the man who is wronged, and who easily has the power to avenge himself, but will not do it out of mercy and patience.
Kind – mild in nature – nice
What love is NOT: Not envious – Is envy a small sin? Envy murdered Abel (Genesis 4:3-8). Envy enslaved Joseph (Genesis 37:11, 28). Envy put Jesus on the cross: For he knew that they had handed Him over because of envy (Matthew 27:18). Opposite of envy – does not resent it when someone else is promoted or blessed. Is happy when others excel, even if they do not.
Does not parade itself – Love gives because it loves to give, not out of the sense of praise it can have from showing itself off. It does not shout, "Look at me!"
Is NOT puffed up – Love doesn't get it's head swelled, it focuses on the needs of others. Be the greatest – be the servant.
Does NOT behave rudely – Where there is love, there will be kindness & good manners.
Does NOT seek its own – Paul speaks the same idea in Romans 12:10, "...in honor giving preference to one another." Also, Philippians 2:4 carries the same thought, "Let each of you look out not only for his own interests, but also for the interests of others." This is being like Jesus in a most basic way, being an others-centered person instead of a self-centered person.
Is NOT provoked – We all find it easy to be provoked, to become irritated with those who are just plain annoying. But it is a sin to be provoked, and it isn't loving. Moses was kept from the Promised Land because he became provoked at the people of Israel (Numbers 20:2-11).
Thinks NO evil – Literally, this means "love does not store up the memory of any wrong it has received." Love will put away the hurts of the past instead of clinging to them.
Does NOT rejoice in sin – Love can always stand with and on the truth, because love is pure and good like truth.

~Dr Micheal Spencer

July 25

The Love Verb

Love is patient and kind. Love is not jealous or boastful or
proud 5 or rude. It does not demand its own way. It is not
irritable, and it keeps no record of being wronged. 6 It does
not rejoice about injustice but rejoices whenever the truth
wins out. 7 Love never gives up, never loses faith, is always
hopeful, and endures through every circumstance.
1 Corinthians 13:4-7, NLT

In yesterday's devotions we went through the details of what love does, and what love does not.

Love either does, or it does not.

Love is not a noun, it is a verb, because when you truly love then an action will automatically happen. It is a natural reflex. I am learning jazz guitar right now, and let me tell you, it is a challenge. One of the first things to develop in my skills is called muscle memory. This is when you practice so much that your brain connects with your fingers and without huge contemplation your fingers go where they are supposed to on the fret board. This takes time and practice. After muscle memory is developed it just FLOWS!

LOVE BECOMES A FLOW, WHEN YOU ARREST YOUR FLESH AND ALLOW HIM TO TEACH YOU HIS WAY OF LOVE!

WHAT LOVE DOES:

BEARS ALL THINGS – The word for "bears" can also be translated "covers". Either way, Paul brings an important truth along with 1 Peter 4:8: And above all things have fervent love for one another, for "love will cover a multitude of sins."

BELIEVES ALL THINGS - We never believe a lie, but we never believe evil unless the facts demand it. We choose to believe the best of others.

HOPES ALL THINGS – Love has a confidence in the future, not a pessimism. When hurt, it does not say, "It will be this way for ever, and even get worse." It hopes for the best, and it hopes in God.

~Dr Micheal Spencer

July 26

LOVE your ENEMIES

If all you do is love the lovable, do you expect a bonus? Anybody can do that.
If you simply say hello to those who greet you, do you expect a medal? Any run-of-the-mill sinner does that.
"In a word, what I'm saying is, Grow up. You're kingdom subjects. Now live like it. Live out your God-created identity. Live generously and graciously toward others, the way God lives toward you.
Matthew 5:46-48 MSG

It is so easy to only help and encourage those who we like. The people that irritate, reject, or are nasty mean are easier to ignore than to embrace. When trouble comes their way it is easier to simply say, "they deserved it", rather than reach out to them to bring healing.

Today we will be short, yet, uncomfortable.
Go out of your way today to SHOW the love of Jesus to a person who has been unlovely to you!

That is right, I said, SHOW. Do something, say something, that will encourage, strengthen, build up that individual. This truly shows love like our Father. He loved us when we were still rejecting Him, yet, He never stopped loving.
Be Jesus to someone TODAY!

~Pastor Rhonda Spencer

July 27

LOVE does not Pacify

So many people forget where they have come from. We all came from mess, and we all need to have grace & mercy with each other as we grow. It is too easy to look at others instead of looking in our own yard! We need to mind our own business, and build each other in Jesus.
1. Jesus was brought a woman caught in the very ACT of adultery. Come on now, not a rumor, not an accusation, in the very act! John 8:1-11.
SHE SHOULD HAVE DIED FOR HER SIN
2. Jesus LOVES people!
The church world teaches God is waiting for you to make a mistake or make a poor decision (anyone here ever made a bad decision?). And then He will bash you over the head and throw you in the pit as He sneers and laughs at you in judgment.
People have been kicked out of churches because of certain sins: 1. Divorce 2. Smoking 3. Remarriage
4. The list is HUGE.
Jesus doesn't pacify sin, He desires to restore. He is focused more on restoration than damnation. He loves us and is passionate to bring us into right relationship with our Father.
Many times, as we get older in the Gospel and more refined by the Spirit, we forget where we have come from.
Sin is sin is sin is sin.
1. Romans 3:23, for all have sinned and fall short of the glory of God,
2. Romans 6:23, For the wages of sin is death, but the gift of God is eternal life in Christ Jesus our Lord.
Sin separates, and we all have some junk that we are working through. SADLY, sin's have consequences. Sins are forgiven, but consequences still can come.
GRACE & MERCY!!!!

~Dr Micheal Spencer

July 28

WE ARE NOT FIGHTING

AGAINST FLESH-AND -BLOOD enemies, but against evil rulers and authorities of the unseen world, against mighty powers in this dark world, and against evil spirits in the heavenly places. Therefore, put on every piece of God's armor so you will be able to resist the enemy in the time of evil. Then after the battle you will still be standing firm. Stand your ground. Ephesians 6:12-14 NLT

It's not people that you war against, the enemy of your soul has an assignment on your life to STEAL, KILL and DESTROY. **Stop fighting people in your life and TAKE UP YOUR AUTHORITY**, the unseen enemy of your soul IS POWERLESS against you.

SO STOP YOURSELF before or even mid-argument....at the first sign of offense or bitterness, and **REBUKE THE REAL ENEMY and he will have to flee!**

~Pastor Rhonda Spencer

July 29

Does God Serve You, or, Do You Serve God?

A bond servant is obedient to their master, and a child is obedient to their parent. Both are obedient for a few reasons. One, because they have a healthy awe, respect, fear, and because of love and trust.

Genesis 22:9-14 Then they came to the place of which God had told him. And Abraham built an altar there and placed the wood in order; and he bound Isaac his son and laid him on the altar, upon the wood. And Abraham stretched out his hand and took the knife to slay his son. But the Angel of the Lord called to him from heaven and said, "Abraham, Abraham!" So he said, "Here I am." And He said, "Do not lay your hand on the lad, or do anything to him; for now I know that you fear God, since you have not withheld your son, your only son, from Me." Then Abraham lifted his eyes and looked, and there behind him was a ram caught in a thicket by its horns. So Abraham went and took the ram, and offered it up for a burnt offering instead of his son. And Abraham called the name of the place, The-Lord-Will-Provide; as it is said to this day, "In the Mount of the Lord it shall be provided."

WE ALL WANT AND EXPECT THE JEHOVAH JIREH, BUT, DO WE WANT TO OBEY GOD TO THE EXTENT OF RECEIVING?

How far will you trust God? Any time now God!!!

He built the altar, placed the wood (any time now), bound his son (any time now), laid him on the altar (are you serious! Where are you? Any time now), took the knife and raised it (**HOW FAR WILL YOU TRUST GOD?**)

Abraham believed, and OBEYED God – If he sacrificed him, he knew God would raise him from the dead. He did not know how God was going to pull this off, but Abraham trusted God enough to know that He would

Vs 11-13 **WILL YOU PASS YOUR TEST OF FAITH?**

Verse 14, So Abraham called the name of that place The Lord Will Provide. And it is said to this day, On the mount of the Lord it will be provided.

Obedience produces blessing!!

God does not serve us, we serve HIM.

~Dr Micheal Spencer

July 30

Are You An Idol Worshipper?

Genesis 22:1 Now it came to pass after these things that God tested Abraham, and said to him, "Abraham!" And he said, "Here I am."
God is testing Abraham's trust and faith (tested – prove, put to test)
Job 23:10 , But He knows the way that I take;
When He has tested me, I shall come forth as gold.

God proves our faith, but the only way to truly know what our faith is, is through a trial. Do we trust Him or do we say, "I don't think so". Do we fall back to our Ishmael, or do we remain in faith that God is able to do abundantly above all we can ask or imagine?
Father came through with His promise of the child 25 years after He spoke it. Abraham remained in faith for that, now God is telling him to sacrifice is only son of promise that he waited 25 years to produce.
What will Abraham do?
What will you do? If God asks you to sacrifice everything to simply obey Him? What are you willing to give?
Is God really your God, or just your candy man?
Whatever you are not willing to sacrifice has now taken God's position. Whatever you will not sacrifice for God is now god in your life. If there is another god in your life then you worship an idol.
If Abraham was not willing to obey God, then he would have been loving Isaac more than the God who created Isaac. Worshipping the creation, rather than the Creator.
Be honest with yourself, what are you not willing to sacrifice for God?
If there is something today, lay it on the altar and give it to the Father.

~Dr Micheal Spencer

July 31

What Kind of Fashion Statement Are You Making?
Certain parts are our clothing are more important than others, and accomplish specific purposes.
Ephesians 6:10-18 The Whole Armor of God
Finally, my brethren, be strong in the Lord and in the power of His might. Put on the whole armor of God, that you may be able to stand against the wiles of the devil. For we do not wrestle against flesh and blood, but against principalities, against powers, against the rulers of the darkness of this age, against spiritual hosts of wickedness in the heavenly places. Therefore take up the whole armor of God, that you may be able to withstand in the evil day, and having done all, to stand. Stand therefore, having girded your waist with truth, having put on the breastplate of righteousness, and having shod your feet with the preparation of the gospel of peace; above all, taking the shield of faith with which you will be able to quench all the fiery darts of the wicked one. And take the helmet of salvation, and the sword of the Spirit, which is the word of God; praying always with all prayer and supplication in the Spirit, being watchful to this end with all perseverance and supplication for all the saints—

HAVE YOU NOTICED SOMETHING? You will be naked in the flesh and in the Spirit if YOU do not CLOTHE YOURSELF!
Colossians 3:8-10 But now you yourselves are to put off all these: anger, wrath, malice, blasphemy, filthy language out of your mouth. Do not lie to one another, since you have put off the old man with his deeds, and have put on the new man who is renewed in knowledge according to the image of Him who created him,
WE HAVE A PART in getting dressed every day in the Spirit.
Write these verses out and read them every morning before crossing your doorstep into the battlefield.
MAKE YOUR FASHION STATEMENT!!

~Dr Micheal Spencer

August 1

FEAR of FAILURE

Many people are afraid to live their dreams!
It is such a powerful truth that Jesus gives us purpose and He gives us dreams for our lives. The one thing about our Father is He loves, rejoices to bless His family!
Psalm 35:27, Let those who favor my righteous cause and have pleasure in my uprightness shut for joy and be glad and say continually, "Let the Lord be magnified, Who takes pleasure in the prosperity of His servant." AMP

SO WHY DO SO MANY PEOPLE NOT EVER REACH OUT FOR THEIR DREAMS? WHY DO SO MANY CHOOSE TO LIVE A LIFE THAT IS MEDIOCRE? WHY DO WE ALLOW OUR DREAMS AND VISIONS TO BE BURIED IN THE GROUND WHEN WE DIE?

I am convinced that the most amazing inventions, companies and cures have been buried in the minds of the people being lowered 8 feet down.
SO WHY? PEOPLE ALLOW FEAR TO CONTROL THEIR DESTINY. The fear of what? FAILURE, OR SOMETIMES EVEN SUCCESS. Abram had some fear when leaving his homeland for no known destination- BUT HE MOVED TOWARD IT!
Noah had some fear when he was told to build a boat to save the world - BUT HE MOVED TOWARD IT.
Jonah had some fear when he was told to preach to Nineveh - AND HE RAN FROM IT!
It's all about choice. CHOOSE FEAR AND NEVER ACCOMPLISH GOD'S PLAN FOR YOUR LIFE or CHOOSE FAITH AND STEP OUT ON NOTHING TO LAND ON SOMETHING.
I choose FAITH!

Philippians 4:13 I can do all things through Christ who strengthens me.

RESURRECT YOUR DREAMS THAT GOD PLACED IN YOUR HEART!

~Dr Micheal Spencer

August 2

WHAT DO I DO…Ahhh…HELP!

You are on your way to work, and your car not only breaks, but blows up!
Your spouse looks at you this morning and out of nowhere say, "I want a divorce."
The doctor tells you there is a serious sickness.
Each one of these incidences are real, and have happened to people that I have known over the years. Each one immediately puts an AHHHHHH, in your heart. It almost feels like your heart is going to beat so fast that it will explode. Your mind starts racing, and you begin to feel a panic sweep in. No matter how big a man, or tough a lady, the news about drops you to your knees.
If this is allowed, then you will spiral out of control.
What do you mean allowed?
I said, "if we allow these feelings to own us, then we can not be part of the solution."
We have a plan in case someone catches on fire, STOP, DROP, ROLL!
We also have to have a plan when life comes to us, and it is a fire!
STOP – Do not allow your emotions to overtake you. They will be there, they are real, they are intense, but you can take authority over your thoughts and feelings.
2 Corinthians 10:5 Casting down arguments and every high thing that exalts itself against the knowledge of God, bringing every thought into captivity to the obedience of Christ,
It is not going to help you to allow your thoughts to take control. It is not going to change or help the crisis if you allow fear to grip, and begin to strangle you.
STOP – 1 John 4:18, There is no fear in love; but perfect love casts out fear, because fear involves torment. But he who fears has not been made perfect in love.
Crawl up into Father's lap – Hebrews 4:16, Let us therefore come boldly to the throne of grace, that we may obtain mercy and find grace to help in time of need.
Know this, fear, worry, untethered emotions, freak out, anxiety, none of these FIX or HELP anything.
So let's focus on what will help and have option to fix – His name is Jesus!!

~Dr Micheal Spencer

August 3

The choices you are making right now, today, are HAVING AN EFFECT!

Your choices affect 3 to 4 generations immediately:
Parent, Child, Grandchild, and, if you're a Great-Grandparent, FOUR generations!
Someone told me the other day that their grandfather, who was a pastor, died and that was the last day his wife, children and grandchildren went to church! That day, three generations were taken out and it has changed the course of their lives.
We are not an island to ourselves. Our lives have impact whether it is for good or evil. Make every decision to sow to the spirit and not to the flesh, ensuring that we are sending blessings down through the generations.
Genesis 17:7 NLT "I will confirm my covenant with you and your descendants[a] after you, from generation to generation. This is the everlasting covenant: I will always be your God and the God of your descendants after you.
Exodus 34:7 NLT I lavish unfailing love to a thousand generations. I forgive iniquity, rebellion, and sin. But I do not excuse the guilty. I lay the sins of the parents upon their children and grandchildren; the entire family is affected—even children in the third and fourth generations."
Psalm 103:17-18 NLT But the love of the Lord remains forever with those who fear him. His salvation extends to the children's children of those who are faithful to his covenant, of those who obey his commandments!
Isaiah 44:3-4 For I will pour out water to quench your thirst and to irrigate your parched fields. And I will pour out my Spirit on your descendants, and my blessing on your children. They will thrive like watered grass, like willows on a riverbank.

The choices you are making RIGHT NOW, TODAY, are HAVING AN EFFECT!

~Pastor Rhonda Spencer

August 4

ENCOURAGEMENT FOR YOU

God has expressed His kindness to you. (Ephesians 2:7)
You are a member of God's household. (Ephesians 2:19)
Therefore if anyone is in Christ, he is a new creation.
The old has passed away; behold, the new has come
2 Corinthians 5:17
You are chosen and dearly loved. (Colossians 3:12)
I have called you friends. (John 15:15)
In all these things we are more than conquerors through Him who loved us. For I am sure that neither death, nor life, nor angels nor rulers, nor things present nor things to come, nor powers, nor height, nor depth, nor anything else in all creation, will be able to separate us from the love of God in Christ Jesus our Lord." Romans 8:37-39
And my God will supply your need according to His glorious riches in Christ Jesus. Philippians 4:19
"For I know the thoughts I think toward you, saith the Lord, thoughts of peace, and not of evil, to give you an expected end." Jeremiah 29:11
"The thief comes only to steal and kill and destroy; I came that they may have life, and have it abundantly." John 10:10
You are protected (John 10:28-29)
You are victorious (1 Corinthians 15:57; 1 John 5:4)
"I have told you these things, so that in Me you may have peace. In this world you will have trouble. But take heart! I have overcome the world. John 16:33
"So do not fear, for I am with you; do not be dismayed, for I am your God. I will strengthen you and help you; I will uphold you with my righteous right hand." Isaiah 41:10
You have purpose (Ephesians 1:9, 3:11)
"Fear not, for I have redeemed you; I have called you by name, you are mine." Isaiah 43:1
"...for he who touches you touches the apple of his eye." Zechariah 2:8
If God is for us, who can be against us? Romans 8:31
"The Lord appeared to us saying, "I have loved you with an everlasting love; I have drawn you with loving-kindness." Jeremiah 31:3
BE ENCOURAGED AND HAVE A PRODUCTIVE DAY.

~Pastor Rhonda Spencer

August 5

STOP! Listen

Life is moving and shaking so much and so quickly that it is easy to get engulfed.
Quiet is unheard of, silence is rare.

There is a need to make yourself available to hear from God. There must be moments in our days that just like a radio, we tune in to hear.

The Holy Spirit rarely shouts, he usually speaks quietly, and we are never quiet, we will never hear!

STOP!
Take 15 minutes, and don't even ask for anything, just listen. Jesus wants to speak to you today.

Then He said, "Go out, and stand on the mountain before the Lord." And behold, the Lord passed by, and a great and strong wind tore into the mountains and broke the rocks in pieces before the Lord, but the Lord was not in the wind; and after the wind an earthquake, but the Lord was not in the earthquake; and after the earthquake a fire, but the Lord was not in the fire; and after the fire a **still small voice.** 1 Kings 19:11-12

~Dr Micheal Spencer

August 6

Refuse to be offended today…

IT DOES HAVE RAMIFICATIONS...on your spiritual life, your attitude, your job, your children and your spouse. I WILL NOT BE OFFENDED, I will not rationalize or justify so I can keep ANY offense.

...many will be offended and repelled and will begin to distrust and desert [Him Whom they ought to trust and obey] and will stumble and fall away and betray one another and pursue one another with hatred. Matthew 24:10 AMP

Confess to one another therefore your faults (your slips, your false steps, your offenses, your sins) and pray [also] for one another, that you may be healed and restored [to a spiritual tone of mind and heart]. The earnest (heartfelt, continued) prayer of a righteous man makes tremendous power available [dynamic in its working]. James 5:16 AMP

Good sense makes a man restrain his anger, and it is his glory to overlook a transgression or an offense. Proverbs 19:11 AMP

~Pastor Rhonda Spencer

August 7

Your Ishmael or Isaac pt 1

Genesis 15:4-6 And behold, the word of the Lord came to him, saying, "This one shall not be your heir, but one who will come from your own body shall be your heir." Then He brought him outside and said, "Look now toward heaven, and count the stars if you are able to number them." And He said to him, "So shall your descendants be."And he believed in the Lord, and He accounted it to him for righteousness.
(Reiterated from Gen 12:1-3)
It's not just important learning how to walk by faith, but it is as challenging learning how not to step out of faith.
THE WORD OF THE LORD WAS GIVEN TO ABRAHAM AND IT WAS CLEAR WITH NO QUESTION.
"I'LL HELP GOD DO HIS PROMISE."
Our trust level determines whether we will step in and try to help God, or we will trust that what He's says He will do, especially when it looks impossible.
Abram was about 85 years old when God spoke this Word to Abram, that means his wife Sarah was about 75ish.
It is interesting when we allow ourselves to walk by sight more than trust God
2 Corinthians 5:7, For we walk by faith, not by sight.
When we begin to walk by sight, we then have made the decision that God is not a God of His Word, and that He needs our help.
You know you have stepped out of faith when we start conniving, manipulating, and making things happen from our ability and concepts.
Romans 14:23, But he who doubts is condemned if he eats, because he does not eat from faith; for whatever is not from faith is sin.
Hebrews 11:6, But without faith it is impossible to please Him, for he who comes to God must believe that He is, and that He is a rewarder of those who diligently seek Him.
This walk of faith, this trusting God and taking Him at His Word can be a challenge, especially when we don't see it happening at the pace we want it, or we cannot understand how He will bring it to pass.

~Dr Micheal Spencer

August 8

Ishmael or Isaac pt 2

SARAH DECIDED that she was too old and was barren (her words, not God's Word). She was actually pregnant with the Word, which is the seed, before she saw the promise!
Genesis 16:1-2, Now Sarai, Abram's wife, had borne him no children. And she had an Egyptian maidservant whose name was Hagar. So Sarai said to Abram, "See now, the Lord has restrained me from bearing children. Please, go in to my maid; perhaps I shall obtain children by her." And Abram heeded the voice of Sarai.
Verses 1-2, Sarai is about 76 years old and she has had no children, so she comes up with an idea. Go have sex with my maid and make a child of promise for God.
When you start helping God, you are opening a can of hardship.
Verse 3-5, Abraham was a dog! He knew and did not doubt the promise, but...... his wife was offering, and it seems somewhat pressuring him to make a baby....umm
SURE HONEY, IF YOU WANT ME TO BE WITH HER, WHATEVER TO MAKE YOU HAPPY.... Dog!
Then – jealousy, envy, pain, emotions, hurt
Whenever you step out of His design, there will be pain
ABRAHAM HELD THE WORD AS TRUTH
Romans 4:19-22, 19 And not being weak in faith, he did not consider his own body, already dead (since he was about a hundred years old), and the deadness of Sarah's womb. He did not waver at the promise of God through unbelief, but was strengthened in faith, giving glory to God, and being fully convinced that what He had promised He was also able to perform. And therefore "it was accounted to him for righteousness."
DON'T CONNIVE, MANIPULATE, TAKING IT OUT OF GOD'S HANDS. IF HIS WORD SAYS IT, THEN IT IS MORE ABOUT TIMING THAN LACK OF ABILITY.

~Dr Micheal Spencer

August 9

Enter By the Narrow Gate

for wide is the gate and broad is the way that leads to destruction, and there are many who go in by it. Because narrow is the gate and difficult is the way which leads to life, and there are few who find it. Matthew 7:13, 14 NKJV

He isn't keeping the answer a secret. It's like a maze printed out on paper with many entrances to begin at, and he draws an arrow and says, "Enter here."
NOTHING LIKE BEING GIVEN THE ANSWERS TO THE TEST :). "Enter by the narrow gate".

Oh not the popular way, not the way everyone else is going?

So you have the answer to the test, go the right way now.

~Pastor Rhonda Spencer

August 10

F..L..A..S..H..!!!!!

Have you ever been believing for something, and it just seems like it will never happen?
You have prayed, believed, declared, spoken, stood, and even now still stand, but at times when doubt floods in, you wonder.....WILL IT EVER HAPPEN?

I want to encourage you today NEVER to lose Faith!
It will literally take Jesus a second of time to fulfill your passion and desire.
If we lose our faith, or give up, then it will NEVER happen.
Arrest your mind, arrest your emotions and do not disconnect yourself from your faith believing!
One day my sons and I were driving in the truck in a storm and **F..L..A..S..H..**, lightning hit and shoot the truck. It happened so fast, we were not prepared for how fast it was and the results that came from such power.
Jesus is fast, powerful and loving. Hang on! He will reward you (Hebrews 11:6, He is a rewarder of those who diligently seek Him).
He is into the "suddenlys" – Acts 2:2, And suddenly there came a sound from heaven, as of a rushing mighty wind, and it filled the whole house where they were sitting.

Hang on for the **F..L..A..S..H..**
Do not lose faith.....
Start praying in tongues right now and stir up the gift of God!

~Dr Micheal Spencer

August 11

Are You All Shriveled and Dried Up?

Can you picture your mom, or grandma putting a piece of bread in with the freshly baked cookies as she puts them in the jar?

I used to work at Mr. Donut when I was in high school and after a full shift we usually would have to toss the donuts that were left because they were hard and getting dry. Sometimes they would get so dry we would throw them around like a ball and then try to smash them against a wall. They might even look good, but when you bite them, they are nasty!!

What happens? Why do things get stale?

Why do things dry up, and not stay moist?

Stale is because too much air (environment) dries out the moisture of the product. Moisture is drawn out when left open to the climate, the elements.

This can happen in our relationship with Jesus. If you and I do not keep the moisture in us, then we will get stale, and over time, the dryer you get, then you become HARD.

When you are in the elements of the world all the time and you neglect the House of God, the Word and prayer, then the world sucks the moisture right out of you, and you become stale.

Spiritually this happens to people all the time. People get touched by heaven and get refreshed, but refuse to be consistent in their time in the Word, prayer and the House of God. Then they start getting stale, dry, but over time.......THEY DRY UP AND GET HARD.

Acts 3:19 Repent therefore and be converted, that your sins may be blotted out, so that times of refreshing may come from the presence of the Lord,

Isaiah 55:1-3 "Ho! Everyone who thirsts, Come to the waters; And you who have no money, Come, buy and eat. Yes, come, buy wine and milk without money and without price.
Why do you spend money for what is not bread, and your wages for what does not satisfy? Listen carefully to Me, and eat what is good, and let your soul delight itself in abundance.
Incline your ear, and come to Me. Hear, and your soul shall live; and I will make an everlasting covenant with you—
The sure mercies of David.

~Dr Micheal Spencer

August 12

WHERE ARE YOU... HELLO?

Maybe this happened to you once, or maybe even twice..... You are in the supermarket or department store and you have your children with you. One second your 4 year old is standing next to you as you are looking at the formula for your infant Francis, and the next second you look down and he is gone!
You call his name quietly at first, Dexter, Dexter, come here please.
No response!
You get a tad bit louder as you spin your cart to head back where you came from, DEXTER!!
No response!!
Now, everything has changed as the rush of fear, and FREAK out is upon you and now you are no longer calm,
WHERE IS MY BABY?
There is a sense of helplessness, fear, overwhelming AHHHHHHHH feeling.
Father God has felt this too.
Genesis 3:8-9 And they heard the sound of the Lord God walking in the garden in the cool of the day, and Adam and his wife hid themselves from the presence of the Lord God among the trees of the garden. Then the Lord God called to Adam and said to him, **"Where are you?"**
God physically knew where Adam was, but, now Adam was lost. It wasn't just that Adam was lost in sin, but what Father really lost was the time he spent with Adam and Eve walking in the cool of the garden everyday. Daddy lost, really lost, and missed His time with His family.

Today, Don't make Daddy run around asking where you are. Spend time with Him. He is waiting for you, and wanting to spend time with you today. Jesus made it so that we can have what Adam lost, the time, friendship, relationship with the Father.
WHERE ARE YOU??????

~Dr Micheal Spencer

August 13

Cast Down? Cast It Back!!

Psalms 42:5 NKJV Why are you cast down, O my soul? And why are you disquieted within me? Hope in God, for I shall yet praise Him for the help of His countenance.
Psalm 42:5 MSG Why are you down in the dumps, dear soul? Why are you crying the blues? Fix my eyes on God— soon I'll be praising again. He puts a smile on my face. He's my God.

Sometimes no matter how much you are praying and believing, there are times we begin to get discouraged. It doesn't start with discouragement, it usually begins with just simply getting tired, and that is the foothold (Ephesians 4:27) for the enemy to come in with discouragement.
Galatians 6:9 And let us not grow weary while doing good, for in due season we shall reap if we do not lose heart.
How come we just seem to get so tired, and how can I fix that in my life?
As a Pastor I have heard it so many times that someone has "burned out" in the ministry. This is the same scenario as we are talking above.
Here are some steps to break that cycle in your life
1. Live out of your excess – We should never be so dry in the Spirit that are have to live and give out of our need. You must do devotions every day, get into the Word to feed and water your spirit.
2. 1 Peter 5:7, casting all your care upon Him, for He cares for you. This literally means to throw like a stone. Throw your cares, burden, situation, concerns, cares to Him. I mean, go ahead and do it right now. Literally, throw your cares to Him!!
3. Pray in the Holy Spirit often and always – Jude 1:20, But you, beloved, building yourselves up on your most holy faith, praying in the Holy Spirit,
4. Find a Faith Friend - find someone that will speak life and encouragement to you and your situation, and not doubt. We never need sympathy, we need empathy. Sympathy says how sad it is while empathy says, let's get this thing fixed.
He is waiting to strengthen you today. You do not have to be discouraged, or tired, get your strength from above!

~Dr Micheal Spencer

August 14

Ummm, Like, Put Some Clothes On Please!!

Can you imagine walking out of the house butt naked and just going to work?

You might be sexy for yourself, but the neighborhood is running and screaming like Godzilla is invading....lol

(of course I am only talking about myself, right?).

There are all different types of clothes. Skirts, shirts, pants, suits, in every color shape and design. The clothing that you wear is not only a statement of who you are, but also protects and covers unseemly portions.

As a Christian God has created clothing for us to protect us!

As a Christian, you and I should never leave our houses naked in the flesh or in the Spirit.

Isaiah 61:10 I will greatly rejoice in the Lord, my soul shall be joyful in my God; for He has clothed me with the garments of salvation, He has covered me with the robe of righteousness, as a bridegroom decks himself with ornaments, and as a bride adorns herself with her jewels.

The New Testament talks about our clothing too!

Ephesians 6:10-18 The Whole Armor of God

Finally, my brethren, be strong in the Lord and in the power of His might. Put on the whole armor of God, that you may be able to stand against the wiles of the devil. For we do not wrestle against flesh and blood, but against principalities, against powers, against the rulers of the darkness of this age, against spiritual hosts of wickedness in the heavenly places. Therefore take up the whole armor of God, that you may be able to withstand in the evil day, and having done all, to stand.

Stand therefore, having girded your waist with truth, having put on the breastplate of righteousness, and having shod your feet with the preparation of the gospel of peace; above all, taking the shield of faith with which you will be able to quench all the fiery darts of the wicked one. And take the helmet of salvation, and the sword of the Spirit, which is the word of God; praying always with all prayer and supplication in the Spirit, being watchful to this end with all perseverance and supplication for all the saints—

No more nakedness please!!

~Dr Micheal Spencer

August 15

Do You Believe in Ghost Towns?

John 9:4 I must work the works of Him who sent Me while it is day; the night is coming when no one can work.

Can you imagine back in the gold dust days a booming town. One minute it was nothing but barren ground, with no people, the next minute....EUREKA!!
A mad rush from all over the country to get to that spot where they found gold. That spot of dirt is now a city filled with life and great wealth, families, money, and activity; but, something happened.
The gold was still there, but everyone decided to just hang out at the corner. They didn't look for gold, no more digging, no more prospecting, just sitting around. Soon enough the money runs out and the booming town becomes nothing more than tumbleweeds and a dog running down the center of the road. What happened to make this a ghost town?
THEY STOPPED WORKING! THEY GOT CONTENT.
Jesus said He came to work the works of the Father.
This is interesting to me – the first word works means (labor, exercise, perform), the second word works means (business, industry).
So the verse says:
I MUST LABOR, PERFORM THE INDUSTRY, BUSINESS OF THE FATHER!
Unless the body of Christ decides to go back to work on the Father's business then the local church will become a ghost town.
How many people have you shared Jesus with this week?
How many people have you led to the Lord this year?
How many friends or enemies have you brought to Father's House for a meal?
Stop being a spiritual welfare recipient, and get back to work!

~Dr Micheal Spencer

August 16

Don't Look Back

Genesis 19:17 So it came to pass, when they had brought them outside, that he said, "Escape for your life! Do not look behind you nor stay anywhere in the plain. Escape to the mountains, lest you be destroyed."
Genesis 19:26 But his wife looked back behind him, and she became a pillar of salt.

Lot's wife had a love affair with Sodom, and the lifestyle of the world. It cost her everything in the attempt to grab that old life.
This is one of the saddest moments in ministry. Watching people choose their old life over the life of Christ. I can remember as each soul received Jesus and the joy that covered their face and the peace that flooded their soul. You could see the change in their lives, and they could not wait to be in the presence of Jesus. Their passion for the Word, getting into classes, asking question after question as they grew in relationship.
THEN! THE CROSSROADS......everyone comes to those crossroads. The temptation to go back!
A friend, a job, a party, some sex, a man or a woman......
THE CROSSROADS....
Many choose to go back to their old life. They choose to return to what they hated in the first place. They asked Jesus to take them out of that lifestyle, they ESCAPED, but did not choose to cut ALL the cords. They always left a little door open, just a small one, just enough....
2 Peter 2:22 But it has happened to them according to the true proverb: "A dog returns to his own vomit," and, "a sow, having washed, to her wallowing in the mire."

Do not be like Lot's wife – she lost it all because she did not cut the love of the world. Run all the way to Jesus, and do not look back!

~Dr Micheal Spencer

August 17

WHAT DO YOU BELIEVE?

I have learned how to be content (satisfied to the point where I am not disturbed or disquieted) in whatever state I am. Philippians 4:11 AMP

We can all LEARN to be content in all situations.

"Don't be afraid, I've redeemed you. I've called your name. You're mine. When you're in over your head, I'll be there with you. When you're in rough waters, you will not go down. When you're between a rock and a hard place, it won't be a dead end— Because I am God, your personal God, The Holy of Israel, your Savior. I paid a huge price for you: that's how much I love you! I'd sell off the whole world to get you back, trade the creation just for you. Isaiah 43:1 MSG

WHAT DO YOU BELIEVE ABOUT GOD?
Contentment comes from what you believe.

~Pastor Rhonda Spencer

August 18

GET THE LEAD OUT OF YOUR PANTS!

Genesis 19:15-17 When the morning dawned, the angels urged Lot to hurry, saying, "Arise, take your wife and your two daughters who are here, lest you be consumed in the punishment of the city." **And while he lingered,** the men took hold of his hand, his wife's hand, and the hands of his two daughters, the Lord being merciful to him, and they brought him out and set him outside the city. So it came to pass, when they had brought them outside, that he said, "**Escape for your life! Do not look behind you nor stay anywhere in the plain. Escape to the mountains, lest you be destroyed.**"

Lingering – staying in a place longer than necessary, usually because of a reluctance to leave

Lot was lingering in Sodom. The place where they wanted to gang rape God's angels, a place so corrupt that in all the earth this was the place of judgement. Lot and his family liked, got comfort living in this life.

As a person who has confessed Jesus as LORD, not just Savior, we need to examine our love.

1 John 2:15 Do not love the world or the things in the world. If anyone loves the world, the love of the Father is not in him.

1 Corinthians 6:20 For you were bought at a price; therefore glorify God in your body and in your spirit, which are God's.

1 Peter 2:11 Beloved, I beg you as sojourners and pilgrims, abstain from fleshly lusts which war against the soul,

The devil desires to get you to love the world. What does that mean?

It means that your whole life is enthralled with pleasing yourself and doing your will. God made the earth for us, He wants us to enjoy the planet, He wants us to enjoy life (John 10:10), but not to the place that we REPLACE Him.

When you become too busy to pray, when you have become too busy to read the Word, when you have become to busy to come to the house of God, when you have become too busy for ministry, you automatically know, YOU LOVE THE WORLD MORE THAN JESUS.

Stop lingering, sin, the worlds business, the worldly focus will totally detach you from Christ. We must occupy till He comes, but this is not our home!

GET THE LEAD OUT OF YOUR PANTS AND GET REFOCUSED ON ETERNAL PRINCIPLES!

~Dr Micheal Spencer

August 19

IS YOUR LIFE A JOKE?

Genesis 19:12-14 Then the men said to Lot, "Have you anyone else here? Son- in- law, your sons, your daughters, and whomever you have in the city—take them out of this place! For we will destroy this place, because the outcry against them has grown great before the face of the Lord, and the Lord has sent us to destroy it." So Lot went out and spoke to his sons- in- law, who had married his daughters, and said, "Get up, get out of this place; for the Lord will destroy this city!" But to his sons- in- law he seemed to be joking.

The Lord sent the angels to deliver Lot and his family. God so loves us, that He sent Jesus to do what the angels were sent to Sodom to accomplish.

Jesus desires family, and His passion is to restore us to Himself. God by nature is a deliverer! How does God deliver? All through the Word we see God sending His representative to bring deliverance to His people (angels, Moses, Joseph, the Judges, Jesus....). God sends men and woman with His Word in their mouth.

Isaiah 52:7 How beautiful upon the mountains, Are the feet of him who brings good news,

The major manner in which God brings deliverance with through the mouth and life of another person.

Ours lives and speech either convince people that they need Jesus, OR, they think it is all a joke!

Lot's son-in-laws were warned by Lot of the impending judgement, but because Lot hung out with them, and didn't ever take a stand against the sin, then they thought he was joking. So much so that they never left Sodom, and were destroyed with the city. Their wives left, but they died, and all because their father-in-law lived a life that said NOTHING.

Today, people's eternity is resting upon your living of life, and your speech.

IS YOUR LIFE A JOKE?

ARE THE WORDS YOU SAY ABOUT JUDGEMENT, ETERNITY, A JOKE because your life does not proclaim Christ?

This is not a joke, this is reality. When you share Jesus and salvation, do they laugh because they see no difference in your life than their own?

IT IS TIME TO MAKE A DIFFERENCE AND TO SNATCH PEOPLE FROM JUDGMENT!

~Dr Micheal Spencer

August 20

Homophobic or Sinophobic?

Genesis 13:12-13 Abram dwelt in the land of Canaan, and Lot dwelt in the cities of the plain and pitched his tent even as far as Sodom. But the men of Sodom were exceedingly wicked and sinful against the Lord.

This is what we know so far.

1. God was going to destroy Sodom, but Abraham interceded! **Prayer changes things!**
2. Lot was living in Sodom, and becoming very familiar with the people of the city and their sin. Lot became comfortable with sin, and did not take a stand against, but condoned through silence.
3. God sent the angels to deliver Lot and his family from the destruction of the city.
4. Lot asked the angels to come and stay the night at his house.

Here we go......

But before they retired for the night, all the men of Sodom, young and old, came from all over the city and surrounded the house. They shouted to Lot, "Where are the men who came to spend the night with you? Bring them out to us so we can have sex with them!" Genesis 19:4, 5 NLT

The men of Sodom wanted to gang rape the angels of God!

Homosexuality is a sin, and is the main reason for God destroying Sodom.

Your a homophobic! NO, I am SINOPHOBIC!

Lot got comfortable & accepting of different "lifestyles" of sin. He sat at the city gates with the sinners, which means he hung out with them. We are called to occupy till Jesus comes, but not to settle down. This is not our home!

Lot became accepting of the homosexual lifestyle and did not take a stand until they wanted to rape the angels. The men of the city were ok with Lot until he took a stand against sin.

It is not about "hating" homosexuals, but it is about "hating" sin. Sin is sin is sin, we should take a stand against sin...period! Whether it is lying, stealing killing, or homosexuality, sin is sin, and people need to be free.

If Lot had taken a stand against sin before, he would not have been in this situation now.

We are not promoting homophobia, we are promoting holiness, and purity.

Take a strong stand against sin, take a loving stand with the sinner. We all need Jesus!!

~Dr Micheal Spencer

August 21

"Lot, Your Wife Looks a Little Salty" Part I

Genesis 13:10-13 **And Lot lifted his eyes and saw** all the plain of Jordan, that it was well watered everywhere (before the Lord destroyed Sodom and Gomorrah) like the garden of the Lord, like the land of Egypt as you go toward Zoar. Then Lot chose for himself all the plain of Jordan, and Lot journeyed east. And they separated from each other. Abram dwelt in the land of Canaan, and Lot dwelt in the cities of the plain and pitched his tent even as far as Sodom. But the men of Sodom were exceedingly wicked and sinful against the Lord.

MAKING SIGHT DECISIONS

2 Corinthians 5:7, For we walk by faith, not by sight.

The moment you allow yourself to be governed by sight, then the only senses that you will be making decisions from are your flesh.

Lot made a decision when it was time to separate from Abram according to what he could see, not caring what was really there.

He looked out and saw that the land was good for his animals.

When we make sight decisions then we are limited to only the moment, and success cannot be determined by looking at a snapshot. It is like taking a picture and telling the story from looking at the picture. The only thing you can really do it make up a story. I'm thinking about that movie "What About Bob". If you only had the picture of the family together after his morning interview, you would think that the Doc loved him. The truth of the whole story was that Bob drove him nuts. Bob crashed his vacation and was crazy, BUT, according to the snapshot, it all looked good.

When we make decisions according to sight, then we are trying to create our own story around one moment of sight. The truth of the story that will unfold could be like Lot and his family. Once you make those sight decisions, then you have to accept the consequences of the choice.

Lot made a choice – I WILL PITCH MY TENT AS FAR AS SODOM.

~Dr Micheal Spencer

August 22

"Lot, Your Wife Looks a Little SALTY" Part 2

Genesis 13:10-13 And Lot lifted his eyes and saw all the plain of Jordan, that it was well watered everywhere (before the Lord destroyed Sodom and Gomorrah) like the garden of the Lord, like the land of Egypt as you go toward Zoar. Then Lot chose for himself all the plain of Jordan, and Lot journeyed east. And they separated from each other. Abram dwelt in the land of Canaan, and Lot dwelt in the cities of the plain and pitched his tent even as far as Sodom. But the men of Sodom were exceedingly wicked and sinful against the Lord.

2 Corinthians 6:17 Therefore "Come out from among them And be separate, says the Lord. Do not touch what is unclean, And I will receive you."

GETTING TOO COMFORTABLE?

Let's go through the Word together and see what was happening with Lot and Sodom.

Genesis 18 – Abram was interceding for Sodom. Without the intercessors, the people of prayer, judgment comes sooner.

Genesis 19:1, God sends His team to get you out of the mess! God is in the saving business, it is what He loves to do, BUT, when He is fed up with sin, and no repentance is seen by the people, then judgement comes. **Don't deceive yourself to believe that just because you do not see immediate judgement means that God is cool with your sin.** We must REPENT (turn 180 degrees), to acquire God's forgiveness.

Genesis 6:3 And the Lord said, "My Spirit shall not strive with man forever....

Galatians 6:7 Do not be deceived, God is not mocked; for whatever a man sows, that he will also reap.

Check your life out! What needs to come out?

God has sent His best to drag you from the mess, how will you respond to that gift?

Here is what you do:

1 John 1:9 If we confess our sins, He is faithful and just to forgive us our sins and to cleanse us from all unrighteousness.

~Dr Micheal Spencer

August 23

LUKEWARM

"I know all the things you do, that you are neither hot nor cold. I wish that you were one or the other! But since you are like lukewarm water, neither hot nor cold, I will spit you out of my mouth! Look! I stand at the door and knock. If you hear my voice and open the door, I will come in, and we will share a meal together as friends." Revelation 3:15-16, 20 NLT

Do not put out the Spirit's fire. (1Thessalonians 5:19)

Never be lacking in zeal, but keep your spiritual fervor, serving the Lord. (Romans 12:11)

That is why I would remind you to stir up (rekindle the embers of, fan the flame of, and keep burning) the [gracious] gift of God, [the inner fire] that is in you
2 Timothy 1:6 AMP

Fan the flame and get the fire of God blazing HOT in your life. THIS LUKEWARM STUFF WON'T DO!!! Not one foot in and one foot out. He wants to spit that place right out of His mouth. So whatever you've gotta do, REKINDLE THE FIRE - that is the place where the ALMIGHTY, MIRACLE POWER OF GOD will come and fellowship with your life.

Shout some praise and give thanks to God, worship Him, testify to anyone who will listen of God's goodness, speak in tongues often...RIGHT NOW, go ahead.

Get that fire inside you HOT once again.

~Pastor Rhonda Spencer

August 24

God vs Satan pt. I

When the Word tells us that signs will follow them that believe, we must believe that this is part of our purpose! Mark 16:15, 17-18 And He said to them, "Go into all the world and preach the gospel to every creature. And these signs will follow those who believe: In My name they will cast out demons; they will speak with new tongues; they will take up serpents; and if they drink anything deadly, it will by no means hurt them; they will lay hands on the sick, and they will recover."

1) We are all called to share the Gospel – the Truth – Jesus and His great salvation for the people of this planet.

2) We are told that signs will follow the believers. Every single Christian will have signs following them. WE are POWERFUL people!! Empowered by Jesus to fulfill His purpose of reaching the lost!

3) IN JESUS' NAME - that powerful name of Jesus!! Philippians 2:9-11, Therefore, God elevated him to the place of highest honor and gave him the name above all other names, that at the name of Jesus every knee should bow, in heaven and on earth and under the earth and every tongue confess that Jesus Christ is Lord, to the glory of God the Father.

In Jesus' name every demon is subject to us, even Satan himself. Luke 10:17, When the seventy-two disciples returned, they joyfully reported to him, "Lord, even the demons obey us when we use your name!"

WHAT ARE THE SIGNS THAT WILL BE SHOWING?

You will cast out devils - demon spirits will come out, and off of people so they can be free from the bondage, the prison of Satan.

NO CHRISTIAN SHOULD EVER BE AFRAID OF A DEMON – THEY ARE AFRAID OF YOU!

THEY ARE HOPING THAT CHRISTIANS STAY DUMBED UP AND DO NOT LEARN WHO THEY ARE.

WHEN YOU KNOW WHO YOU ARE, THE DEMONS WILL SHUTTER WHEN YOU PUT YOUR FEET ON THE FLOOR EVERY DAY!

~Dr Micheal Spencer

August 25

God vs Satan pt. 2

There are only 2 main characters in the ETERNAL.
God the Father, and Satan the defeated! This understanding is imperative as we unfold why Wicca, Reiki, witchcraft, Voodoo, psychics, séances, readings are not a God thing, but they are a god thing (notice the BIG "G" and the small "g").
GOD THE FATHER- King of Kings – Rev. 19:16, On his robe at his thigh was written this title: King of all kings and Lord of all lords.
Creator – Genesis 1:1, In the beginning God created the heavens and the earth
All Powerful – Mark 10:27, Jesus looked at them intently and said, "Humanly speaking, it is impossible. But not with God. Everything is possible with God."
All Knowing – 1 John 3:20, Even if we feel guilty, God is greater than our feelings, and he knows everything.
All Present – Jeremiah. 23:24, Can anyone hide from me in a secret place? Am I not everywhere in all the heavens and earth?" says the Lord.
The ONLY TRUE GOD – Isaiah 44:6, "I am the First & the Last; there is no other God.
1 Timothy 6:15-16, which He will manifest in His own time, He who is the blessed and only Potentate, the King of kings and Lord of lords, who alone has immortality, dwelling in unapproachable light, whom no man has seen or can see, to whom be honor and everlasting power. Amen. NKJV
Satan is NOT "God", he is a "g" god....Satan was a created creature – an archangel over worship – Ezekiel 28:13-16
Satan decided he wanted to rebel against the ONLY TRUE God – Isaiah 14:12-15 (I will ascend above God was his declaration)
Satan was cast down for his rebellion – Luke 10:18-20
Satan is completely DEFEATED – Colossians 2:15, In this way, he disarmed the spiritual rulers and authorities. He shamed them publicly by his victory over them on the cross.
Satan is NOT all-knowing – he only knows what he is told, observes or projects.
Satan is NOT all-powerful – he is limited because he is a created being (for a Christian the only power he has is what you give him).
Satan is NOT all-present – he can only be at one place at one time.
Satan IS A LIAR – John 8:44, the father of lies.
THERE IS NO BATTLE BETWEEN GOD THE FATHER & satan, THERE IS no COMPARISON!
THERE IS ONLY ONE TRUE, ALL POWERFUL, SUPREME KING, and it is not Satan.

~Dr Micheal Spencer

August 26

You are VICTORIOUS over the Devil

Matthew11:12 "And from the days of John the Baptist until now the kingdom of heaven suffers violence, and the violent take it by force. NKJV
There is a need for force (taking, plucking, pulling).
The reason for force is because we have an adversary.
1 Peter 5:8 Be sober, be vigilant; because your adversary the devil walks about like a roaring lion, seeking whom he may devour.
The weapons of our warfare are not carnal
2 Corinthians 10:3-5
The reason for force is because of resistance / There is a resistance to the advancement of the purposes of God.
There is a real enemy, but he is defeated. James 4:7 Therefore submit to God. Resist the devil & he will flee from you.
When there is a frontal advancement, there will be adversity to stop that if possible; the normal attacks of the enemy. When you identify these, you and thwart them before they wound you.
Using our circumstance against us is usually the first thing the enemy does to DISTRACT us, and he starts in the MIND.
1) Discouragement 2) Confusion 3) Depression 4) Loss of vision 5) Disorientation 6) Withdrawal 7) Despair 8) Defeat
How to overcome when, not if, the attacks come. With the Word of God . Luke 4:3-12
We need each other:
Colossians 3:16 Let the word of Christ dwell in you richly in all wisdom, teaching and admonishing one another in psalms and hymns and spiritual songs, singing with grace in your hearts to the Lord. NKJV
Hebrews 3:13 but exhort one another daily, while it is called "Today," lest any of you be hardened through the deceitfulness of sin.
1 Corinthians 14:31 For you can all prophesy one by one, that all may learn and all may be encouraged.
Hebrews 10:25 not forsaking the assembling of ourselves together, as is the manner of some, but exhorting one another, and so much the more as you see the Day approaching.
Don't get disconnected from your destiny, get aggressive against the devil!

~Dr Micheal Spencer

August 27

Reiki, Psychics where do they get power?
1 Timothy 4:1, Now the Holy Spirit tells us clearly that in the last times some will turn away from the true faith; they will follow deceptive spirits and teachings that come from demons.
We have got to be clear that there are ONLY two places that generate power from the supernatural, ONLY TWO. So that means we can actually distinguish where the power source is, and distinguish if it is a God thing, or a "g" god thing.
TWO POWER SOURCES
1) God the Father – all-powerful, creator, all-knowing, all-present, unconditional love, restorer, holy, UNDEFEATED, King of Kings, Lord of Lords, the ONE TRUE GOD.
2) Satan – limited, defeated, cannot be everywhere, can only know what he is told, cannot do everything, HATER OF ALL MANKIND.
Angels play a role too, but they are acting out the will of their master, whether God, or Satan.
GOD'S NATURE IS LOVE AND RELATIONSHIP. SATAN'S NATURE IS HATRED AND DESTRUCTION. (John 10:10, Satan's ONLY focus is to steal, kill and destroy)
It is extremely important that we understand this. Satan HATES man - we were created in the image of God (Genesis 1:26), and he despises God and His greatest creation, man. The greatest trophy for the diabolical is the reward of taking one who was made in God's image to the Lake of Fire with him. DO NOT BE DECEIVED, THE DEVIL HATES YOU! If he has to sucker you in with blessing, kindness, reward, then he will do it, but always know, sin is fun but for a season, then you have to pay the piper. Satan plays for keeps, eternal keeps.
Because Satan is NOT the creator, he can only strive to COUNTERFEIT.

~Dr Micheal Spencer

August 28

Reiki, a Counterfeit of the Laying on of Hands Part 1

Because Satan is NOT the creator, he can only strive to COUNTERFEIT. His deception is to come as close as he can to what God has made great and twist, contort, manipulate so that it will look good, but its roots are poison.
One day I was looking to buy a Gibson es-355 guitar. They are the top of the line for the Gibson es series. I found one on a website and it was selling for about $2000 when it really goes for $3500 used. I called and they sent me all the pictures. I also asked for the serial number on the back. The pictures were gorgeous, everything looked right. I decided to check the serial number with Gibson, and guess what I found out? It looked right, had the right name on it, would play, BUT IT WAS A FAKE! The serial number was a FAKE. The maker was a FAKE, a COUNTERFEITER! It was only worth $300
Satan can only COUNTERFEIT!
Satan is a LIAR, and the father of lies (John 8:44).
READ ALL THIS WEEK TO SEE THE FAKES, THE COUNTERFEITS, that are now being accepted by the church, but are at the root EVIL.
Reiki healing is an occult, demoniacally based practice that is counterfeiting a Biblical principle by using demonic powers.
Reiki is a spiritual practice developed by a Japanese Buddhist named Mikao Usui in 1922.
Reiki practitioners believe they are transferring energy through the palms of the hand which bring healing. Reiki calls upon the energy force to release power to physically touch for healing on the inside and on the outside of a person.
The word “Reiki” is made of two Japanese words, “REI” means god’s wisdom or the higher power and “KI” is life force energy. It also translates into mysterious atmosphere and supernatural influence.

~Dr Micheal Spencer

August 29

Reiki, a Counterfeit of the Laying on of Hands Pt 2

There are only two places a person can get power, God the Father or Satan. They are not claiming, or giving glory to the Lord Jesus Christ for the power, they are using another force to accomplish the task. If it is not Jesus, then the only other option is Satan. They are releasing demonic power and energy into a person's life as a spiritualist. God the Father condemns spiritualists. This is an occult, new age, practice.

Deuteronomy 18:9-14, "When you enter the land the Lord your God is giving you, be very careful not to imitate the detestable customs of the nations living there. For example, never sacrifice your son or daughter as a burnt offering. And do not let your people practice fortune-telling, or use sorcery, or interpret omens, or engage in witchcraft,or cast spells, or function as mediums or psychics, or call forth the spirits of the dead. Anyone who does these things is detestable to the Lord. It is because the other nations have done these detestable things that the Lord your God will drive them out ahead of you. But you must be blameless before the Lord your God. The nations you are about to displace consult sorcerers and fortune-tellers, but the Lord your God forbids you to do such things."

Many massage therapists are using Reiki on you, and you do not even know it. Do not allow them to lay hands on you and impart demonic energy. Ask first if they are a Reiki practitioner. Reiki is the counterfeit for the laying on of hands to release the anointing to heal the sick.

Mark 16:18b, They will be able to place their hands on the sick, and they will be healed."

Hebrews 6:1-2, So let us stop going over the basic teachings about Christ again and again. Let us go on instead and become mature in our understanding. Surely we don't need to start again with the fundamental importance of repenting from evil deeds and placing our faith in God. You don't need further instruction about baptisms, the laying on of hands, the resurrection of the dead, and eternal judgment.

It is also based off another religion called Buddhism, which has another god called Buddha, not the ONLY TRUE GOD.

The power is real and is coming from demonic spirits that release satanic energy to produce a result. THESE SPIRITUAL ACTIVITIES ARE NOT FROM GOD!

Pastor, they do good things....why are they bad? Satan will *come nice to sucker you into himself, but in the end there is still only one purpose (John 10:10).*

2 Corinthians. 11:14, But I am not surprised! Even Satan disguises himself as an angel of light.

~Dr Micheal Spencer

August 30

Does God Use Psychics? Pt 1

We have established that there are ONLY two places that power comes from.

1) God the Father – the King of Kings, Creator, One and Only True God.

2) Satan- the defeated, created angel that rebelled, and was made an open show by Jesus (Col. 2:15)

We also know that angels have a role in the supernatural, but that they serve the design of the God, or "god", that they follow. So if psychics claim that God gives them the gift and that they are used of God, then the real question is, "WHICH GOD"?

A psychic is one who reveals information that they could not have to others. CLEAR SIGHT

Psychics also will call themselves mediums, fortune-tellers – Diviners.

Medium-ship is an act where the practitioner attempts to receive messages from spirits of the dead and other spirits that the practitioner believes exists.

They will use different tools to tell your past/present: Tarot Cards, Ouija boards, Crystal balls, Tea leaves, Palm reading, Séance – religion of Spiritualism, it is generally a service to communicate with the dead.

Saul consulted the witch of Endor and a familiar spirit manifested of Samuel – Saul died for doing this – 1 Chronicles 10:13.

When Saul had the psychic call up the dead, a demon who looked like Samuel appeared. This was not Samuel, it was a familiar spirit. When a demon takes on the likeness of a person, we know the demon counterfeits them to gain you.

How do you know it was not my dead relative or friend? When a person dies they either go to heaven or hell. If they are born again – they go straight into the presence of the Lord in heaven (2 Corinthians 5:8). If they are not born again then they are cast right into hell which is the holding tank for the unrighteous, and the next time they will be released will be at the White Throne Judgment in Rev. 20:11-15.

Paul ran across a psychic in Acts 16:16-18. He cast the demon out of her and her power ceased. She was set free from the demon who was giving her information about people.

THIS IS THE COUNTERFEIT OF THE GIFTS OF THE SPIRIT (1 Corinthians 12)

God the Father condemns psychics!!

~Dr Micheal Spencer

August 31

Does God Use Psychics? Pt 2

THIS IS THE COUNTERFEIT OF THE GIFTS OF THE SPIRIT
(1 Corinthians. 12)
God the Father condemns psychics!!
Leviticus 20:6, "I will also turn against those who commit spiritual prostitution by putting their trust in mediums or in those who consult the spirits of the dead. I will cut them off from the community.
Deuteronomy 18:9-14, "When you enter the land the Lord your God is giving you, be very careful not to imitate the detestable customs of the nations living there. For example, never sacrifice your son or daughter as a burnt offering. And do not let your people practice fortune-telling, or use sorcery, or interpret omens, or engage in witchcraft, or cast spells, or function as mediums or psychics, or call forth the spirits of the dead. Anyone who does these things is detestable to the Lord. It is because the other nations have done these detestable things that the Lord your God will drive them out ahead of you. But you must be blameless before the Lord your God. The nations you are about to displace consult sorcerers and fortune-tellers, but the Lord your God forbids you to do such things."
IF GOD THE FATHER CONDEMNS THEM, AND IS NOT THE ONE GIVING THEM THE POWER, THEN THERE IS ONLY ONE OTHER PLACE TO GET THAT POWER – SATAN. Psychics are demoniacally used to counterfeit, to draw people away from Jesus. Psychics are being used by the devil to deceive people and to fulfill his passion of stealing, killing and destroying.
FINAL TRUTH: Psychics are not from God! They are satanically-empowered, not God-empowered. When you open yourself up to psychics you are opening yourself up to be influenced, motivated and possibly possessed, but easily oppressed by a demon spirit. STAY AWAY! Repent if you have gone, and never go back again to the counterfeit.

~Dr Micheal Spencer

September 1

Resuscitate Your Life

It's easy to find success and then flat-line. You feel like you have "attained" or "achieved" some level of success, and at that point you actually flat-line. Flat-lined in medical terminology is crisis/death.

I don't mean to say that I have already achieved these things or that I have already reached perfection. But I press on to possess that perfection for which Christ Jesus first possessed me. Philippians 3:12 NLT

This can happen in our spiritual walk. So, if you have been serving God for any length of time---be careful of feeling like you have "attained" and then become dormant or flat-line!!!! If you have flat-lined, get up early and dig in the Word, get out to every class that you can, get involved with men's or women's ministry. Get active in a ministry ASAP!!! This WILL resuscitate your spiritual life!

I spoke the message as He commanded me, and breath came into their bodies. They all came to life and stood up on their feet - a great army. Then He said to me, "Son of man, these bones represent the people of Israel. They are say9ing, 'We have become old, dry bones - all hope is gone. Our nation is finished.'"
Ezekiel 37:10-11 NLT

The way you live will always honor and please God, and your LIVES WILL PRODUCE EVERY KIND OF GOOD FRUIT. All the while, you will grow as you learn to know God better and better.

We also pray that you will be strengthened with all his glorious power so you will have all the endurance and patience you need. May you be filled with joy always thanking the Father. He has enabled you to share in the inheritance that belongs to his people, who live in the light. For he has rescued us from the kingdom of darkness and transferred us into the Kingdom of his dear Son, who purchased our freedom and forgave our sins. [] Yet now he has reconciled you to himself through the death of Christ in his physical body. As a result, he has brought you into his own presence, and you are holy and blameless as you stand before him without a single fault. But you must continue to believe this truth and stand firmly in it. Don't drift away from the assurance you received when you heard the Good News. The Good News has been preached all over the world, and I, Paul, have been appointed as God's servant to proclaim it. Colossians 1:9-14, 22-23 NLT

~Pastor Rhonda Spencer

September 2

Possession or Oppression

Mark 16:17a, These miraculous signs will accompany those who believe: They will cast out demons in my name....

We have solidified that the only two powers to draw from are God and Satan. We uncovered spiritual activity (Wicca, psychics, Reiki, tarot cards, mediums...) and that they obtain their information from Satan, not the only true God.

Now that we can understand how to look at spiritual activity and discern whether it is from God or Satan, we can get into the difference between a possessed person, and an oppressed person.

SATAN IS A COUNTERFEITER!

The first thing we think about when the word possession is said is a head spinning around backwards, foam coming out of the mouth, a little girl talking in a man's demonic voice....ahhhhhhh!! BUT

Satan did not think up possession, he is not a creator, he is not creative, he is a thief, a counterfeiter of God's GREATNESS!

God the Father is the one who created POSSESSION.

Before we know the Lord our spirit man is dead (Ephesians 2:1, Once you were dead because of your disobedience and your many sins.) You and I were not dead physically, but spiritually dead. When we do not know the Lord as our Savior, then we are dead inside, our spirit is dead in sin.

When you and I give our hearts to the Lord (Romans 10:9-10) everything changes. This is when possession comes in, literally!!

1 Corinthians 6:19, Don't you realize that your body is the temple of the Holy Spirit, who lives in you and was given to you by God? You do not belong to yourself.

Colossians 1:27b, And this is the secret: Christ lives in you. This gives you assurance of sharing his glory.

Literally, not figuratively, the Holy Spirit, God, comes and dwells in your spirit – YOU BECOME POSSESSED BY GOD! You are not God! God comes and lives in you. He dwells inside of you! LITERALLY!

Galatians 2:20, My old self has been crucified with Christ. It is no longer I who live, but Christ lives in me. So I live in this earthly body by trusting in the Son of God, who loved me and gave himself for me.

God the Father created POSSESSION! If you know Jesus as your Savior, you are POSSESSED!

TODAY AS YOU WALK AROUND, AS WE LIVE IN HIM (Acts 17:28), KNOW WITH YOUR KNOWER THAT YOU ARE POSSESSED BY GOD HIMSELF!

Would you act, talk, walk or do differently as you realize that Jesus is literally possessing you?

~Dr Micheal Spencer

September 3

Can a Christian be POSSESSED by a Demon?

The devil is a COUNTERFEITER! Possession was not his idea – it was God the Father's plan to come and live inside man!
There are preachers in Christendom that teach that you can be possessed by Jesus and by a demon at the same time. THAT IS A LIE!
Here is a simple truth: GOD IS A BAD SHARER! God will not share His house with a demonic spirit!
Mark 3:24-27, If a kingdom is divided against itself, that kingdom cannot stand. And if a house is divided against itself, that house cannot stand. And if Satan has risen up against himself, and is divided, he cannot stand, but has an end. No one can enter a strong man's house and plunder his goods, unless he first binds the strong man. And then he will plunder his house. NKJV
God is a jealous God – Exodus 34:15, You must worship no other gods, for the LORD, whose very name is Jealous, is a God who is jealous about his relationship with you.
He is not going to live in you with a demon spirit! A Christian CANNOT be possessed by a demon! A Christian can be OPPRESSED by a demon!
Possession is living inside with ownership. Oppression is a coming upon with influence.
Here are a few demonic spirits that can oppress a Christian:
1. A spirit of fear - 2 Timothy 1:7, For God has not given us a spirit of fear, but of power and of love and of a sound mind. NKJV
2. A spirit of infirmity – Luke 13:16, So ought not this woman, being a daughter of Abraham, whom Satan has bound—think of it—for eighteen years, be loosed from this bond on the Sabbath?"
3. A spirit of depression & suicide – The opposite of depression is joy, a fruit of the Holy Spirit (Galatians 5:20-23). Suicide is the desire of Satan (John 10:10)
The list can become large, but there is great news for a believer:
John 8:36, So if the Son sets you free, you are truly free.
1 John 4:4, But you belong to God, my dear children. You have already won a victory over those people, because the Spirit who lives in you is greater than the spirit who lives in the world.
Romans 8:37, No, despite all these things, overwhelming victory is ours through Christ, who loved us.
Jesus has set you free from any oppressive, controlling spirit that is striving to influence your life. Take authority in the name of Jesus and tell it to get off, and to not return in JESUS' NAME. They know His name. They recognize His name! They fear His name!
Mark 16:17a, These miraculous signs will accompany those who believe: They will cast out demons in my name....

~Dr Micheal Spencer

September 4

In JESUS' Name!

Mar 16:17-20 And these signs shall follow them that believe; In my name shall they cast out devils; they shall speak with new tongues; They shall take up serpents; and if they drink any deadly thing, it shall not hurt them; they shall lay hands on the sick, and they shall recover. So then after the Lord had spoken unto them, he was received up into heaven, and sat on the right hand of God. And they went forth, and preached every where, the Lord working with them, and confirming the word with signs following. Amen.

In the NAME OF JESUS we have authority over the demonic, whether possession or oppression.

In today's life people say the name of Jesus all the time as a swear word. By making it a cuss word the demonic have diminished the name by associating it with meaningless purpose, or only negative reactions.

The demonic are afraid of not just the name, but the powerful One behind the name – JESUS!

Philippians 2:9-11 Therefore God also has highly exalted Him and given Him the name which is above every name, that at the name of Jesus every knee should bow, of those in heaven, and of those on earth, and of those under the earth, and that every tongue should confess that Jesus Christ is Lord, to the glory of God the Father.

John 14:13-14 And whatever you ask in My name, that I will do, that the Father may be glorified in the Son. If you ask anything in My name, I will do it.

Luke 10:17 Then the seventy returned with joy, saying, "Lord, even the demons are subject to us in Your name."

Acts 3:6 Then Peter said, "Silver and gold I do not have, but what I do have I give you: In the name of Jesus Christ of Nazareth, rise up and walk."

Colossians 3:17 And whatever you do in word or deed, do all in the name of the Lord Jesus, giving thanks to God the Father through Him.

TODAY HIS NAME IS NOT A SWEAR WORD!

His name is Jesus! The awesome God!

IN HIS NAME EVERYTHING IS AVAILABLE! IN HIS NAME IS ALL AUTHORITY!

The name is backed up by heaven!

I LOVE THE NAME OF JESUS! Say His name out loud right now – JESUS! You will sense the anointing rise when you say His name!

SAY HIS NAME AGAIN, AND GET READY FOR THE PRESENCE OF THE HOLY SPIRIT.

~Dr Micheal Spencer

September 5

Doubt Your Doubts

1 John 5:4 For whatever is born of God overcomes the world. And this is the victory that has overcome the world—our faith.
James 1:6-8 But let him ask in faith, with no doubting, for he who doubts is like a wave of the sea driven and tossed by the wind. For let not that man suppose that he will receive anything from the Lord; he is a double-minded man, unstable in all his ways.
If FAITH is our Victory, then DOUBT is our defeat! We must hate doubt!
DOUBT YOUR DOUBTS
DOUBT is the road of failure & discouragement. It is the road of unanswered prayers!
UNANSWERED PRAYERS. So many get mad at God for not answering their prayers...Where are you God? Why are you not showing up?
These verses are a key to many unanswered prayers
People will start off in faith believing for what they are asking for, but when they do not get a miracle, and their faith is stretched, that FORK comes to them.
If a person ventures down the path of doubt and unbelief then literally they have stopped God from answering their prayer.
It isn't God who stopped your answer, you stopped your answer!
The Law of Life in Christ Jesus says that God is moved by faith, not by hope, not by need, He is moved by faith.
Doubt is that cancellation notice of faith. It tells God that He is unable to accomplish what He says He is able to do.
The children of Israel:
Hebrews 3:16-19, For who, having heard, rebelled? Indeed, was it not all who came out of Egypt, led by Moses? Now with whom was He angry forty years? Was it not with those who sinned, whose corpses fell in the wilderness? And to whom did He swear that they would not enter His rest, but to those who did not obey? So we see that they could not enter in because of unbelief.
ARREST THE DOUBT THAT IS TRYING TO GRIP YOUR MIND AND STAY IN TRUST!

~Dr Micheal Spencer

September 6

ARE YOU CONFUSED AND LOST? Part 1

Which way to I go, which way do I go?
Spinning round and round, and round and round.....
I am not sure what God wants me to do, I am so confused?
It makes no difference how old you are, or how young you are, if you have no clue then you are just wandering around with no major focus. The difficulty with that is that it is hard to accomplish anything.

Let me help you with your initial direction.
1 Thessalonians 5:16-18 Rejoice always, pray without ceasing, in everything give thanks; for this is the will of God in Christ Jesus for you.

The very first thing – BE A WORSHIPER!!
When you begin to worship, then you are positioning yourself to hear from God. As you worship your spirit becomes more aware because you are focusing your heart and mind on Him, then He can speak to you and you will be listening.

Next time you are at church, don't just sit and watch, get to the front and worship! How? You will learn, it will come natural as you take the steps to touch Him.
MORE TO COME TOMORROW.....

~Dr Micheal Spencer

September 7

ARE YOU CONFUSED AND LOST? Part 2

In part 1 we began talking about the will of God for our lives.
The first thing we spoke about was that the will of God is simple, and not complex.
We established that it is the will of God to REJOICE, to learn how to praise. I would encourage you every Sunday to come to the altar during praise and worship. Every morning you get up, start thanking Jesus for the day ahead. Remember, there is no wrong side of the bed for a Christian. When we place our feet on the ground, hell should shake in fear.
The next step in knowing the will of God is:
1 Thessalonians 5:17-18
pray without ceasing, in everything give thanks; for this is the will of God in Christ Jesus for you.

PRAY WITHOUT CEASING!!
You mean I have to pray all day? How can I do that, I have to work, take care of the family.......
This means that we are in the attitude of prayer all day. That if the Lord wants or needs you to pray you are paying attention to hear His voice and you will be available. Praying in tongues is another way to pray without ceasing. You can talk to Jesus all day, even while you work, and pray in tongues right along with it. The attitude of prayer is so powerful!

So today, we know it is the will of God to rejoice (praise), and pray without ceasing. So start now thanking Him for all He has done in your life, and then just start talking to Him about whatever the Holy Spirit puts on your heart. This is how you do the will of God and learn more about the will of God.

~Dr Micheal Spencer

September 8

ARE YOU CONFUSED AND LOST? Part 3

We have established the will of God in two areas of your life.
1. Praise
2. Prayer
If you are not sure of the will of God for your life, this is where you begin. Every day (without ceasing), you spend time in praise, and prayer.

The next sure will of God for your life is sharing the Gospel.
Mark 16:15,17-18, And He said to them, "Go into all the world and preach the gospel to every creature. And these signs will follow those who believe: In My name they will cast out demons; they will speak with new tongues; they will take up serpents; and if they drink anything deadly, it will by no means hurt them; they will lay hands on the sick, and they will recover."

Share with others that Jesus changed your life, and talk to people about forgiveness and how Jesus gave you a brand new beginning. Talk about the peace of God and how He accepted and loves you for who you are.

HOW HAS JESUS CHANGED YOUR LIFE?
That is simply what you share with others.
Here it is, simply!
1. Praise
2. Prayer
3. Share how Jesus changed your life.

This is the WILL OF GOD for your life.

~Dr Micheal Spencer

September 9

ARE YOU CONFUSED AND LOST? Part 4

There are three things that we know for sure about the will of God.
It is God will to:
1. Praise
2. Pray
3. Share Jesus with others
The next question is about specifics on each person.
Like I said, the will of God is simple.
Psalm 139:14 I will praise You, for I am fearfully and wonderfully made; Marvelous are Your works, And that my soul knows very well.
You are not an accident, and God created you with special gifts and He designed your personality.
I remember as a child saying, "I don't ever want to be a missionary to Africa," and someone retorted, "don't ever say that, God will send you there just because you said that." I was like, nooooooooooo, I don't want to goooooooo!! That is the mentality of many, that God will make you do what you do not enjoy doing. There are times that He does that to teach a humility, but on the large scale, God tweaked you a certain way with likes and dislikes because of His plan for you.
Here it is simple!
What do you like to do? If you do not like children, then you are not called to children's ministry. If you want to be on the worship team, but cannot sing, then that is not your gift. God put desires in our hearts that direct us to our purpose. So here is the first step in the will of God concerning your more specific purpose, WHAT DO YOU ENJOY DOING? Whatever that is, do it (Biblical of course)! If you love teens, get involved with youth groups. If you love the babies, get involved with children's church, if you like mowing, taking care of the property, mow the church lawn. The list will never end, because each person is so different.
WHAT DO YOU LIKE DOING?
Start there today, call the church and get involved.

THIS IS THE WILL OF GOD FOR YOU!

~Dr Micheal Spencer

September 10

Walk in LOVE

If someone says, "I love God," and hates his brother, he is a liar; for he who does not love his brother whom he has seen, how can he love God whom he has not seen? And this commandment we have from Him: that he who loves God must love his brother also.
1 John 4:20, 21 NKJV

And LOVE IS------->
Love endures long and is patient and kind; love never is envious nor boils over with jealousy, is not boastful or vainglorious, does not display itself haughtily. It is not conceited (arrogant and inflated with pride); it is not rude (unmannerly) and does not act unbecomingly. Love (God's love in us) does not insist on its own rights or its own way, for it is not self-seeking; it is not touchy or fretful or resentful; it takes no account of the evil done to it [it pays no attention to a suffered wrong]. Love bears up under anything and everything that comes, is ever ready to believe the best of every person, its hopes are fade-less under all circumstances, and it endures everything [without weakening]. Love never fails [never fades out or becomes obsolete or comes to an end] 1 Corinthians 13:4, 5, 7, 8 AMP

Let's walk in obedience to the Word today and walk in LOVE the Bible way.

~Pastor Rhonda Spencer

September 11

Kill Those Religious Cows

Mark 7:13 Making the word of God of no effect through your tradition which you have handed down. And many such things you do."

Traditions: statements, beliefs that are passed down from generation to generation.
Lies, thoughts, concepts……

We try to write our own religion. We might not say we do that, but how we live declares it. We want to do what we desire and still reap the benefits of Christ's sacrifice. We want to experience the anointing, the presence, the glory of God, yet we want God to adhere to our religion that we have created. The amazing part is that when God doesn't accomplish what we expect, we are actually shocked or upset. We run our religion, with our traditions, and then expect God to fulfill our desires. Doesn't that sound foolish?

God's Word, is God's design for His people. We are not called lord, He is supposed to be called Lord. He is the Master. His is the King. He is God, and doing His will brings forth His results.

Kill some religious cows today in your life. Ask yourself if you are living God's Word, or you are living your own religion and expecting God to follow you.

Don't nullify God's power, anointing, presence and glory by your religion. He desires to give you the BEST, don't cheat yourself.

~Dr Micheal Spencer

September 12

"Stop Eating So Much!" NEVER!!

I have heard people say, "Your life is so surrounded by God, the Bible and Church, it is like you are consumed."
ABSOLUTELY TRUE!!
Shout it out loud right where you are, "I AM CONSUMED"!
One way to lose weight is just to simply push away from the table when you're satisfied. I agree with that when it comes to food, but you can NEVER get enough of Jesus, the Word, or being in the house of God!
NEVER ENOUGH, OR TOO MUCH OF JESUS!
Matthew 22:37-38, Jesus replied, "'You must love the Lord your God with all your heart, all your soul, and all your mind.' 38 This is the first and greatest commandment.
NEVER ENOUGH, OR TOO MUCH OF HIS WORD!
Ezekiel 3:1-3, The voice said to me, "Son of man, eat what I am giving you—eat this scroll! Then go and give its message to the people of Israel." So I opened my mouth, and he fed me the scroll. "Fill your stomach with this," he said. And when I ate it, it tasted as sweet as honey in my mouth.
Jeremiah 15:16, When I discovered your words, I devoured them. They are my joy and my heart's delight, for I bear your name, O Lord God of Heaven's Armies.
Psalm 119:11, I have hidden your word in my heart, that I might not sin against you.
Hebrews 4:12, For the word of God is alive and powerful. It is sharper than the sharpest two-edged sword, cutting between soul and spirit, between joint and marrow. It exposes our innermost thoughts and desires.
NEVER ENOUGH, OR TOO MUCH OF HIS HOUSE!
Psalm 84:10, A single day in your courts is better than a thousand anywhere else! I would rather be a gatekeeper in the house of my God than live the good life in the homes of the wicked.
Psalm 133, How wonderful and pleasant it is when brothers live together in harmony! For harmony is as precious as the anointing oil that was poured over Aaron's head, that ran down his beard and onto the border of his robe. Harmony is as refreshing as the dew from Mount Hermon that falls on the mountains of Zion. And there the Lord has pronounced his blessing, even life everlasting.
Hebrews 10:25, And let us not neglect our meeting together, as some people do, but encourage one another, especially now that the day of his return is drawing near.
WHOMEVER IS SAYING YOU ARE GETTING TOO MUCH OF GOD, HAS TOO LITTLE OF GOD!
NEVER STOP EATING TOO MUCH OF JESUS, HIS WORD, AND HIS HOUSE!
Never push away from the table.

~Dr Micheal Spencer

September 13

Correction: Part I

Hebrews 12:5-13
And you have forgotten the exhortation which speaks to you as to sons: "My son, do not despise the chastening of the Lord, nor be discouraged when you are rebuked by Him; For whom the Lord loves He chastens, and scourges every son whom He receives." If you endure chastening, God deals with you as with sons; for what son is there whom a father does not chasten But if you are without chastening, of which all have become partakers, then you are illegitimate (bastards) and not sons. Furthermore, we have had human fathers who corrected us, and we paid them respect. Shall we not much more readily be in subjection to the Father of spirits and live? For they indeed for a few days chastened us as seemed best to them, but He for our profit, that we may be partakers of His holiness. Now no chastening seems to be joyful for the present, but painful; nevertheless, afterward it yields the peaceable fruit of righteousness to those who have been trained by it. Therefore strengthen the hands which hang down, and the feeble knees, and make straight paths for your feet, so that what is lame may not be dislocated, but rather be healed.

The purpose of correction:
The Father love's and desires to protect you, even from yourself. Protection in your relationship with Jesus. Sin separates us from God. Correction helps us realize the cost of sin.

Our Father is a Jealous God / hungers for our attention and love, and when He sees us straying, He woe's first and if that does not work, then He corrects.

~Dr Micheal Spencer

September 14

Correction: Part 2

These are ways Father God will NOT correct you!!
Pastors and Churches have created a distorted understanding of our Father, so much that His own babies are afraid of Him. Perfect love casts off all fear.
God does not correct through:
1) sickness / many have had tremendous guilt because they felt that someone's sickness or death was because God was punishing them, or someone else because of them.
2) death / God is going to kill you / because you lied/sinned I am going to have to kill you!!
3) Abandonment / can you imagine kicking your children out of the house every time they disobey? This is how the Father in heaven is categorized, no wonder so many don't want to serve Him.
4) Demeaning / Your Dad does not want to tear down, but lift you up – God's plan is to make you successful, not discouraged.
5) Abuse / He does not beat you down / He might spank you to get your attention / but He will never abuse you.
How will Father God correct me?
a) Conviction – John 16: 8 "And when He has come, He will convict the world of sin, and of righteousness, and of judgment:
b) The check in the spirit – That nasty feeling when you choose to do something against His Word
c) His Word – Hebrews 4:12 For the word of God is living and powerful, and sharper than any two-edged sword, piercing even to the division of soul and spirit, and of joints and marrow, and is a discerner of the thoughts and intents of the heart.
d) Ministry Gifts - 2 Timothy 4:2 Preach the word! Be ready in season and out of season. Convince, rebuke, exhort, with all long-suffering and teaching. - The Lord will use your Pastor to correct.
There is no greater concern than not being corrected by our Father when we sin. If you find no conviction in your life, please fall on your face today and ask Jesus to be the Lord of your life.

~Dr Micheal Spencer

September 15

Abram to Abraham – THE JOURNEY pt 1

1 John 5:4 For whatever is born of God overcomes the world. And this is the victory that has overcome the world—our faith.
Hebrews 11:8 By faith Abraham obeyed when he was called to go out to the place which he would receive as an inheritance. And he went out, not knowing where he was going.
I have made you a father of many nations.
Genesis 17:5 No longer shall your name be called Abram, but your name shall be Abraham....
The Promises:
Genesis 12:1-3 Now the Lord had said to Abram: "Get out of your country, From your family, And from your father's house, To a land that I will show you. I will make you a great nation; I will bless you, And make your name great; And you shall be a blessing. I will bless those who bless you,And I will curse him who curses you And in you all the families of the earth shall be blessed."
Everyone loves the promises
In one of Dad Hagin's books, he was sharing that so many people see how successful Rhema Church and Bible College are, and want to be part. He was saying how everyone sees the success, but few see the journey. They were not with him when he was driving from one church to another preaching. One day he was driving to the next church and his car died. He had to walk to his next destination to share the Word.
One day we had a couple come visit His Tabernacle when we were at the Holiday Inn. They said they liked it, but would return once it was bigger. They were not interested in the journey, just in participating with the success.
Abram – exalted father, was his name in the beginning, but for us to see his success and graduation to, Abraham- father of a multitudes, we need to watch his walk of faith.
HERE IT IS TO PONDER TODAY – He obeyed God!
To be able to reach the destination, we MUST be willing to obey God!
Noah did it, and we are here today.
Jesus did it, and we can be saved today.
You did it, and ___________ will be saved from being eternally lost.

~Dr Micheal Spencer

September 16

Abram to Abraham, THE JOURNEY Part 2

Genesis 17:5 No longer shall your name be called Abram, but your name shall be Abraham...
Hebrews 11:8 By faith Abraham obeyed when he was called to go out to the place which he would receive as an inheritance. And he went out, not knowing where he was going.
Everyone loves the destination, but does not want to take the journey!
THE JOURNEY
The journey began when he listened to the Word of God "Get out of your country, from your family, to a land I will show you.
Verse 4 – "So Abram departed as the LORD had spoken to him..."
God did not give him details, just go!
You can never begin your journey of faith, until you OBEY with the first step.
Everyone wants the promises, but few want to take the steps of faith to lay hold of the promises of God.
This prophecy was conditional. If Abram, did not obey, then he would never have become Abraham
The journey was about 800 miles.
We all want the quick results.
We all want the "shazaam"! But without TIME, we will never become who God has called us to be.
Abram, not Abraham, was walking his whole family to a land of promise, but he did not know where that was, he was just obeying God.
Hardship of the trip: It was not just him and his wife; It was all his goods; All his servants; All his animals;
Everything he owned...Providing food –
Cost to obey God; Marching through the heat, some months up to 110 degrees, the nights are cold, Sand storms, Sand fleas and mosquitoes.
It was not a breeze trip, it was a walk of faith and trust
He is still not Abraham – this trust walk was building him into becoming the man called Abraham.
You have not reached the final destination - God is still working on you. Don't stop the walk of faith!

~Dr Micheal Spencer

September 17

FOCUS ON JESUS!

Our lives are so swift when it comes to time. Remember when we were teenagers (or are still), and you just prayed for time to go by quickly?
When my children were in school we prayed together every morning, and they would pray like this, "Lord, let this day go by quickly."
I would say, "you don't want to pray that", but they felt that time was going to slow. Now that age has come upon us, we all want one thing for sure......SLOW DOWN, YOUR GOING TO FAST!!!!
Time is speeding by, situations in life will make time slow up a little, but the majority of the TIME, don't turn around too quickly because 10 years is gone.
Today, right now, STOP!
Take time by the tail, and say STOP!

Let's start our day off in slow mo, focusing on the One who this day revolves around.
Acts 17:28 for in Him we live and move and have our being, as also some of your own poets have said, 'For we are also His offspring. '
Colossians 3:1-2 If then you were raised with Christ, seek those things which are above, where Christ is, sitting at the right hand of God. Set your mind on things above, not on things on the earth.
Hebrews 12:2 looking unto Jesus, the author and finisher of our faith, who for the joy that was set before Him endured the cross, despising the shame, and has sat down at the right hand of the throne of God.

STOP!
TAKE TIME, AND LOOK TO JESUS.
It will be the best time spent today.

~Dr Micheal Spencer

September 18

Noah FEARED the Lord

Hebrews 11:7 By faith Noah, being divinely warned of things not yet seen, moved with godly fear, prepared an ark for the saving of his household, by which he condemned the world and became heir of the righteousness which is according to faith.
Noah walked with God, and knew the Father which produced great faith and trust in the Lord. BUT, there is another portion here we do not want to miss.
NOAH WAS MOVED WITH GODLY FEAR
Proverbs 9:10 "The fear of the Lord is the beginning of wisdom,
And the knowledge of the Holy One is understanding.
This is not the "ahhhhhhh, shutter and hide" fear.
This is respect, honor, awe, with a little healthy fear to spread on the bread.
God is not a man, He is not a dude, God is King, He is Lord, He is our God, He is the Creator. There is nothing weak about Him.
When I was young my dad would ask me to do something and I would, for one main reason: I did not want to get in trouble. I didn't want to get disciplined. I had a healthy fear, respect, for my dad.
Noah had that with God.
The command was crazy. Build an ark 450 ft long, 75 ft wide, 45 ft tall, but yet it never rained before, never mind flood.
Noah obeyed because He trusted God, but he was also moved with respect.
If Father asked him to do something, Noah obeyed.
Do you respect, honor, trust God enough that you would obey Him, even if the request was crazy?
Do you fear God enough to obey?

~Dr Micheal Spencer

September 19

Noah, What If He Gave Up?

1 John 5:4 For whatever is born of God overcomes the world. And this is the victory that has overcome the world—our faith.
Hebrews 11:7 By faith Noah, being divinely warned of things not yet seen, moved with godly fear, prepared an ark for the saving of his household, by which he condemned the world and became heir of the righteousness which is according to faith.
God was sick and tired of the rebellion and evil, He says that He will not always strive with man.
Genesis 6:14, Make yourself an ark of gopher-wood; make rooms in the ark, and cover it inside and outside with pitch.
Not only build an ark, but do it this way: 450 feet long, 75 feet wide, 45 feet tall
That is a CRAZY request!!
So here Noah is being told, not asked ...This is where some people are stuck. God is telling us to do things for eternal purposes, and yet many refuse (tithing, praying, reading the Word, sharing the Gospel).
God does not need your opinion, He demands your obedience
It was going to take 75-100 years to build this ark
What would have happened if he said, "skip this, I have a life, I deserve to have fun, I'll do it when I can find time"
Do Christians today do this or what???? "I'll obey you Jesus, as long as it works in my schedule. That's money out of my pocket."
What would have happened if Noah had given up??
This Christian stuff is not working for me. God didn't do what I asked Him to do. This is too much!!
IT IS TOO HARD TO SERVE GOD!
Noah had to know & trust his God because for 75-100 years he CONTINUED faithfully sawing, hammering and smearing pitch because God told him that a flood was coming. Yet, what is a flood? What if he would have given up on year 48 or on year 62?
What if he had said, "I'm almost 600, give me a break"
WE WOULD NOT BE HERE TODAY
Our decisions of faith and obedience effect generations to come.
NEVER GIVE UP, NEVER STOP, NEVER LOSE FAITH.
He was mocked and laughed at, Noah never gave up
Luke 17:26-27 And as it was in the days of Noah, so shall it be also in the days of the Son of man. They did eat, they drank, they married wives, they were given in marriage, until the day that Noah entered into the ark, and the flood came, and destroyed them all.
NOAH NEVER GAVE UP! DON'T YOU GET LAZY, DON'T YOU GIVE UP! BUILD YOUR FAITH SO THAT, IN THE DIFFICULT DAYS, YOU CAN STAND.

~Dr Micheal Spencer

September 20

The Gospel is NOT AMERICAN

I have been crucified with Christ [that is, in Him I have shared His crucifixion]; it is no longer I who live, but Christ lives in me. The life I now live in the body I live by faith [by adhering to, relying on, and completely trusting] in the Son of God, who loved me and gave Himself up for me. I do not ignore or nullify the [gracious gift of the] grace of God [His amazing, unmerited favor], for if righteousness comes through [observing] the Law, then Christ died needlessly. [His suffering and death would have had no purpose whatsoever.]" Galatians 2:20-21 AMP

But put on the Lord Jesus Christ, and make no provision for the flesh, to fulfill its lusts. Romans 13:14 NKJV

The gospel is NOT AMERICAN (ALL ABOUT ME). Me has been crucified and should no longer be living. If we begin to hear ourselves say "but I", or "what about how I feel or what I want?", then we need to quickly remind ourselves to crucify the "me". It's not about what I want, but all about what God wants. So let's get re-dressed and take off ME and put on CHRIST today. LIVE FOR HIM

~Pastor Rhonda Spencer

September 21

WHOLENESS is YOUR Covenant

The law of sin and death demands that you be hurt in your emotions and mind, and physically you will always have sickness.

Romans 8:2 For the law of the Spirit of life in Christ Jesus has made me free from the law of sin and death.

Glory to God, we have been delivered by the Lord Jesus Christ from the world's rules, to the newness of life in Christ Jesus!! You have the right to be healed and set free from hurts and wounds in every area of your life! Jesus paid for it with His life, don't let the sacrifice go to waste.
1 Peter 2:24 Who Himself bore our sins in His own body on the tree, that we, having died to sins, might live for righteousness—by whose stripes you were healed.
Luke 4:18 "The Spirit of the Lord is upon Me, because
He has anointed Me to preach the gospel to the poor;
He has sent Me to heal the brokenhearted,
To proclaim liberty to the captives
And recovery of sight to the blind,
To set at liberty those who are oppressed;
Psalms 147:3 He heals the brokenhearted
And binds up their wounds.
James 1:21 Therefore lay aside all filthiness and overflow of wickedness, and receive with meekness the implanted word, which is able to save your souls.

The Word of God will SAVE our soul. The soulish realm needs healing from the wounds of every day life. The more you are in the Word, the more healing is released into your soul.
3 John 1:2 Beloved, I pray that you may prosper in all things and be in health, just as your soul prospers.

~Dr Micheal Spencer

September 22

Focused Future

The majority of people on this planet live their lives on accident.
Our purposes and desires get hidden in life! We live life out of reaction rather than living it on purpose.
The problem with that is that life runs past us, then we wake up and we are in the sunset of our timetable on this earth.
What have we accomplished?
What has my life meant?
What legacy did I leave?
What, what, what, what...?
Sadly so many will end up their lives, and have ended up their lives, with these thoughts racing through their minds; BUT YOU DO NOT HAVE TO!

Today-right now-you can FOCUS on purpose! At this moment that you are reading this devotional, a thought, a desire or a dream is welling up inside of you. It might be one that you have carried since you were a child and never allowed to be free. Today, right now, God desires that you DREAM BIG! See what your passions, purposes and desires are and begin to run after them.
Do not allow life to end, and the dream to die with it!
Determine from today on, you will live life with focused direction!

Ephesians 3:20-21, Now to Him who is able to do exceedingly abundantly above all that we ask or think, according to the power that works in us, to Him be glory in the church by Christ Jesus to all generations, forever and ever. Amen.

~Dr Micheal Spencer

September 23

UNLIMITED POTENTIAL

The awesome truth about God the Father is that He wants to MAKE us more successful than we even desire to be! It is amazing when the light-bulb goes on in our hearts and heads that Father God desires to MAKE your name GREAT!
Genesis 12:1-2, Now the Lord had said to Abram:
"Get out of your country, From your family and from your father's house, To a land that I will show you. I will make you a great nation; I will bless you and make your name great; and you shall be a blessing.
Daddy not only is a good God, but He loves to use the word GREAT! He is a Great God, and He desires that His children become GRRRREAT (as Tony the Tiger would say). He spoke to Abraham, and He is speaking to you today. He wants to MAKE your family GREAT! He will bless you! Daddy desires to make your NAME GREAT, and when your name is GREAT, you become a blessing!
Source determines potential – whatever Father God spoke to had the potential to increase. As long as you stay connected to your source, you will always have the ability to increase. When God created the plant, He spoke to the dirt, and as long as the seed stays connected to the source it will flourish.
When God wanted man, He spoke to Himself. As long as we stay connected to the Source we have the ability of the Source, who is God! How much potential does God have? Unlimited. How much potential do we have as long as we stay connected with the Source? Unlimited.
If you want to fly with the eagles, you have to stop hanging with the turkeys.
YOU HAVE UNLIMITED POTENTIAL AS LONG AS YOU STAY CONNECTED WITH THE SOURCE!
Philippians 4:13, For I can do everything through Christ, who gives me strength.

~Dr Micheal Spencer

September 24

Release Your Potential

Since God wants to make us GREAT! (Genesis 12:1-3),
Since God has given us POWER TO BECOME GREAT! (Ephesians 3:20-21),
WHY ARE SO MANY PEOPLE IN SURVIVAL MODE RATHER THAN RELEASING THEIR POTENTIAL IN CHRIST?
That answer is simple. People do not BELIEVE THAT THEY HAVE THE POTENTIAL!
Faith activates, and doubt erases our potential in God.
In yesterday's devotion we talked about staying connected with our SOURCE. Our Source is God the Father, we were created in His image and likeness. God is all powerful, and can do anything. When we stay connected to our Source our potential is also UNLIMITED, until doubt comes in and erases the opportunity for our increase.
The children of Israel were on the threshold of the promise of the promised land. God delivered them from Egypt supernaturally, and now they were at the location of greatness. They sent in 12 spies to check things out, and 10 came back with doubt; only 2 came back in faith that activates. The crowd chose to see and accept the doubt instead of seeing the faith of potential (with God for you, who can be against you? Romans 8:31).
THE CHILDREN OF ISRAEL ERASED THEIR POTENTIAL BY ALLOWING DOUBT IN THE SOURCE TO HAVE A POSITION IN THEIR LIFE!
Hebrews 3:19, So we see that they could not enter in because of unbelief.
It was not stated they could not enter into their promised potential because of inability, or opportunity, they erased their potential because of unbelief in the SOURCE.
Today, right now, do not allow your potential –God's given gift of ability — to slip through your hand of opportunity.
DREAM HUGE, BELIEVE HUGE,
FULFILL YOUR POTENTIAL!

~Dr Micheal Spencer

September 25

How to OVERRIDE Obstacles

When you understand your God-granted POTENTIAL, and then you get a vision to accomplish something GREAT, the obstacles start to become more evident.

When you do not have vision, then obstacles are not really prevalent because you are have no direction in life or ministry.

When you realize your GOD POTENTIAL and get a passion, then you become a dangerous person. When we become dangerous to the devil's domain he will turn up the heat.

In either scenario, there MUST BE AN OVERCOMING, or we will get lost in the sludge of distraction.

The children of Israel did this! When Moses delivered them from Egypt (miracle) they came to the Red Sea. When they came to the Red Sea, instead of remembering how powerful God was to get them out of Egypt, they continued staring at the obstacle. Instead of activating faith to overcome, they sat down and complained. They became engulfed by the obstacle!

Exodus 14:10-12, As Pharaoh approached, the people of Israel looked up and panicked when they saw the Egyptians overtaking them. They cried out to the Lord, and they said to Moses, "Why did you bring us out here to die in the wilderness? Weren't there enough graves for us in Egypt? What have you done to us? Why did you make us leave Egypt? Didn't we tell you this would happen while we were still in Egypt? We said, 'Leave us alone! Let us be slaves to the Egyptians. It's better to be a slave in Egypt than a corpse in the wilderness!'"

Here is what a man with a God encounter, who has an understanding of the God POTENTIAL does:

Exodus 14:13-14, But Moses told the people, "Don't be afraid. Just stand still and watch the Lord rescue you today. The Egyptians you see today will never be seen again. The Lord himself will fight for you. Just stay calm."

When you get engulfed by the obstacle you become a reactionary Christian, and you will always be disengaged from your God POTENTIAL.

When you see the reality BUT know that God's POTENTIAL is best seen in IMPOSSIBLE SITUATIONS, then you will always move FORWARD.

~Dr Micheal Spencer

September 26

Dream MASSIVE!

This is the third day covering the principle of POTENTIAL. If you have just started reading the devotions, I would encourage you to go back and read the last week's worth to help bring today's into a better perspective.
Since you are connected to the SOURCE and your SOURCE is SUPERNATURAL!
Since our SOURCE has given us UNLIMITED POTENTIAL, what is holding you back from excelling?
My willingness to DREAM MASSIVE.
Most are afraid to dream massive because they do not want to be disappointed. The real issue is that you will never be disappointed because you will never believe beyond what you can control. What a sad life, when it consists of only what we can control! What can we really control?
Our SOURCE, God the Father, desires to bless you with unlimited potential if you will only believe. If you never dream massive, you will never receive massive.
So many think that my wife and I are "rich", but truthfully we make a small wage with two people working. "Then how are you able to have what you have?" We KNOW that God has given us unlimited potential and when we activate our faith in Him, the SOURCE, then He blesses us with our desires. God has already prepared everything we need and want in eternity, we just have to tap that UNLIMITED POTENTIAL to obtain it.
What have you always desired to do? What are your passions? What are your MOST MASSIVE DREAMS?
There is NOTHING YOU CANNOT DO, there is NOTHING YOU CANNOT HAVE!
It is time to start tapping into your God-given potential! It is just dormant in heaven until you start calling those things which are not as though they already are!

Ephesians 3:20-21, Now all glory to God, who is able, through his mighty power at work within us, to accomplish infinitely more than we might ask or think. Glory to him in the church and in Christ Jesus through all generations forever and ever! Amen.

~Dr Micheal Spencer

September 27

Don't Drag Your Feet

BE LIKE THOSE WHO STAY THE COURSE with committed faith and get everything promised to them.

When God made His promise to Abram, He backed it to the hilt; putting His own reputation on the line. He said, "I promise that I'll bless you with everything I have - bless and bless and bless!" (Genesis 12:1-3)

Abraham stuck it out and got everything that had been promised to him. When people make promises, they guarantee them by appeal to some authority above them so that if there is any question that they'll make good on the promise, the authority will back them up. When God wanted to guarantee His promises, He gave His Word: a rock solid guarantee. God cannot break His Word. And because His Word cannot change, the promise is, likewise, unchangeable.

We who have run for our very lives to god have every reason to grab the promised hope with both hands and never let go. It's an unbreakable spiritual lifeline, reaching past all appearances right to the very presence of God where Jesus, running ahead of us, has taken up His permanent post as High Priest. Hebrews 6:9-18 MSG

STAY THE COURSE! Don't allow ANYTHING to intercept you or draw you back to the old, empty life.

Don't drag your feet! RUN THE RACE TO WIN!

~Pastor Rhonda Spencer

September 28

GET YOUR BUTT BACK WHERE YOU BELONG!! Part 1

Genesis 12:1-3 Now the Lord had said to Abram: "Get out of your country, from your family and from your father's house, to a land that I will show you. I will make you a great nation; I will bless you and make your name great; and you shall be a blessing. I will bless those who bless you, and I will curse him who curses you; and in you all the families of the earth shall be blessed."

The promise/covenant with Abram was powerful and one that compelled him to journey about 800 miles with all that he had to the land of promise, Canaan!

It is exciting when God's Word speaks to us as believers, His promises are yes and amen! His Word is saturated with the blessing and covenant promises for His children.

YET! LIFE COMES.......DIFFICULT TIMES ARRIVE....... HARDSHIP APPEARS....NOW WHAT?

Genesis 12:10, Now there was a famine in the land, and Abram went down to Egypt to dwell there, for the famine was severe in the land.

We know that God told him to go to Canaan, and in verse 7 God again declares that this is the land He would give to all his descendants. Abram had raised up an altar – all is well and good and God is good all the time!!!

BUT the situations changed, the environment changed

2 Corinthians 5:7, For we walk by faith, not by sight.

We are cool with walking in faith as long as everything is going good!

As long as the reports are favorable, as long as everything is going my way, as long as it all makes sense, as long as I have it all in control, I will remain in faith....lol

ABRAM obeyed, walked in HUGE faith, but now is faced with a reality – famine/lack – and now has to decide, "do I stay in faith and trust that He brought me this far, that the promise He spoke (the Word that I received) is truth, that the Word of God is truth not only in the good, but in the difficult?"

What happens when you leave the promise and go to Egypt?

We will finish this one tomorrow!!!

~Dr Micheal Spencer

September 29

GET YOUR BUTT BACK WHERE YOU BELONG!! Part 2

1 John 5:4 For whatever is born of God overcomes the world. And this is the victory that has overcome the world—our faith.

Genesis 12:1-3 Now the Lord had said to Abram:"Get out of your country, from your family and from your father's house, to a land that I will show you. I will make you a great nation; I will bless you and make your name great; and you shall be a blessing. I will bless those who bless you, and I will curse him who curses you; and in you all the families of the earth shall be blessed.""

Abram left Canaan (the land of promise) because of a great famine, and he headed toward what made all the sense in the world, he headed to Egypt (the world).

Whenever you leave the Word of God, whenever you leave the directive of the King, whenever you leave faith because of circumstances or environments, you will always begin moving out of faith and trust in God.

Genesis 12:10, Now there was a famine in the land, and Abram went down to Egypt to dwell there, for the famine was severe in the land.

Whenever you leave the Word, you only have one more source for your answers, the world. The world is governed by the god of this world. You know you have stepped out of faith (the Word) when worry, fear, and compromise start gripping your life.

When you go to the world, you always end up compromising. Abram starting the lying game...This is not my wife, she is my sister (she must have been hot because she was about 67 years old at this point).

Verse 17 – The Lord plagued Pharaoh because of taking Sarai. Pharaoh responded by sending them home – get out of the world and get back in faith.

STAY IN FAITH – even when the difficult times come, don't run from the Word, run to the Word and stand on it and don't be moved. God is trustworthy, and His Word is truth.

~Dr Micheal Spencer

September 30

Today is a NEW Day!

Lamentations 3:22-24, The faithful love of the Lord never ends! His mercies never cease. Great is his faithfulness; his mercies begin afresh each morning. I say to myself, "The Lord is my inheritance; therefore, I will hope in him!"
TODAY is not entitled "YESTERDAY"!
Yesterday literally means the OTHER, not this.
Today, right now is NEW!
You have NEVER LIVED THIS DAY BEFORE, and we will never have this day again once it becomes yesterday.

Today, right now, know this...
THE FAITHFUL LOVE OF THE LORD NEVER CEASES!
DADDY'S MERCY NEVER ENDS!
HIS MERCIES ARE NEW TODAY, right now!
Shake yourself, splash some water on your face (please take a shower...lol), and know that TODAY IS NEW!
REPENT OF YESTERDAY'S SINS, and know you have a CLEAN SLATE TODAY!
Now that you are bouncing, call someone, text someone, facebook someone, or look them in the eyes today and ENCOURAGE THEM TOO!
1 Thessalonians 5:9-11, For God chose to save us through our Lord Jesus Christ, not to pour out his anger on us. Christ died for us so that, whether we are dead or alive when he returns, we can live with him forever. So encourage each other and build each other up, just as you are already doing.

~Pastor Rhonda Spencer

October 1

STOP STOPPING FOR GOODNESS' SAKE!! Part 1

2 Timothy 4:7-8, I have fought the good fight, I have finished the race, I have kept the faith.
BEING A FINISHER It is so easy to be a starter
You see something fun and it stimulates your interest - so you start it
You meet someone you like and want a relationship – so you start
You want a new job and see one that looks better – so you start
You have a goal to accomplish losing 20lbs and you see a new exercise machine on TV that looks easy and promises great results – so you start
You want to accept Jesus and live for Him – so you start
You see a good church and want your family to know God – so you start
You see a ministry or class that you want to join – so you start
Starting something is EASY, the true test – ARE YOU A FINISHER?
BETWEEN THE BEGINNING & FINISH LINE
Anything is easy to START, but what lies between the start and finish line is why so many never cross it.
Paul – started the race in Acts 9:1-7
You would think that he would swoon the religious and grab the attention of the disciples – and he did all that, but not in the manner you would think.
You would also think it would be easy for Paul
2 Corinthians 11:24-28, From the Jews five times I received forty stripes minus one. Three times I was beaten with rods; once I was stoned; three times I was shipwrecked; a night and a day I have been in the deep; in journeys often, in perils of waters, in perils of robbers, in perils of my own countrymen, in perils of the Gentiles, in perils in the city, in perils in the wilderness, in perils in the sea, in perils among false brethren; in weariness and toil, in sleeplessness often, in hunger and thirst, in fastings often, in cold and nakedness— besides the other things, what comes upon me daily: my deep concern for all the churches.
It was not easy, but he made a choice – HE WOULD FINISH, AND FINISH STRONG! We all want to go lose a few pounds, we all want to go to heaven, we all want to make a difference.
IT IS NOT HOW YOU START, IT IS HOW YOU FINISH!
FINISH STRONG!

~Dr Micheal Spencer

October 2

STOP STOPPING FOR GOODNESS' SAKE Part 2

Anything is easy to START, but what lies between the start and finish line is why so many never cross it.

Jesus – The Savior of our souls!
You would think He would swoop in and just be loved and accepted by everyone for who He is and was....
Rejected by: Nation/Town/Family/Father/You and me.

Garden of Gethsemane
Matthew 26:36-39, Then Jesus came with them to a place called Gethsemane, and said to the disciples, "Sit here while I go and pray over there." And He took with Him Peter and the two sons of Zebedee, and He began to be sorrowful and deeply distressed. Then He said to them, "My soul is exceedingly sorrowful, even to death. Stay here and watch with Me." He went a little farther and fell on His face, and prayed, saying, "O My Father, if it is possible, let this cup pass from Me; nevertheless, not as I will, but as You will."

The Cross
John 19:28-29, After this, Jesus, knowing that all things were now accomplished, that the Scripture might be fulfilled, said, "I thirst!" Now a vessel full of sour wine was sitting there; and they filled a sponge with sour wine, put it on hyssop, and put it to His mouth. So when Jesus had received the sour wine, He said, "It is finished!" And bowing His head, He gave up His spirit.

It was not easy, but he made a choice – HE WOULD FINISH, AND FINISH STRONG!
We all want to go lose a few pounds, we all want to go to heaven, we all want to make a difference
It is not how you START – it is how you FINISH
FINISH STRONG!!!

~Dr Micheal Spencer

October 3

REBELLION in God's House Part I

Today and for the next few days we want to expose rebellion: witchcraft that appears in the church world and hurts, or even splits churches.
Satan HATES the church, because we are the BODY of Jesus on earth. We have been sent as Ambassadors from heaven to share the good news that Jesus will wash away your sin and heal your life. Satan hates good news!
This is how he combats the church. It is the same mindset he used with Adam and Eve, DIVIDE AND CONQUER. His tactics have never changed, yet most are not aware or attentive to guard against the attack or being used in the attack.
We are going to cover 3 types of rebellion that destroy churches, ministries, God's purposes.
The first type of rebellion was seen manifest by Korah. Korah was one of Moses leaders.

THE REBELLION OF KORAH
a) Numbers 16:1-49
b) Korah's statement was that Moses had lost the anointing, and that he wanted his place in the ministry. This is the mighty take over move, just like Lucifer tried with God the Father in heaven.
c) In verse 3 – "what makes you better than us, we can do what you do?"
d) The rebellion in the congregation – people trying to take over the man of Gods position thinking they know how to do it better, and that the man of God needs to learn a few things, and we will teach him. This is what you will find by board run churches, or more denominational churches.
e) Hell swallowed them up

I love Moses because he didn't fight them, he simply let God show who He chose as the leader.
God is NEVER ok with rebellion in His Kingdom.

~Dr Micheal Spencer

October 4

REBELLION in God's House Part 2

Korah and his rebellion cost him and his crew their lives. One thing is for sure, Satan forgets to tell people the price of sin, not just for the person sinning, but for those around them. The cost is expensive, and never just touches one.
The next spirit of rebellion that comes to God's house is seen manifest through Absalom. This is King David's own son!!

THE REBELLION OF ABSALOM
The most dangerous of all of the rebellious spirits because it is always performed by a person close to the man of God.
2 Samuel 15:1-6 This rebellion is so subtle,and damning because Absalom stole the hearts of the people.

We have this in Churches around the U.S. so strong, mainly in denominational churches. If one in the Church does not agree with the Pastor, then let's draw up a petition. The ones in charge go around to their friends and talk devilish talk against the man of God. They steal the hearts of the people away, then the work of God is destroyed.

You will find that most people are striving to seek the things of God. No Church is perfect, yet most do not concentrate on the things that need to mature unless a person with a REBELLIOUS SPIRIT comes and starts sowing with devilish talk against the situation.

The devil hates the household of heaven, and will do whatever he can to destroy so people will not see Jesus face to face.

Guard your hearts and minds through Christ Jesus and His Word.

~Dr Micheal Spencer

October 5

REBELLION in God's House Part 3

We have covered 2 of the three demonic spirits that stir rebellion within the local church, and today we will complete this series with the last.

Rebellion always stirs division, but it can create a unity amongst the haters. Even unity within haters has great power, but the unity will never receive the blessing of God. The enemy knows that every time there is unity within God's kingdom, there will be a great move of the Holy Spirit. So the enemy works hard in creating fires. When the ministry is focusing on putting out all the fires, then it cannot move ahead in unity.

The last spirit of division is the spirit of Jezebel!

THE REBELLION OF JEZEBEL

I Kings 18 / Revelation 2:20

The Jezebel spirit is one of manipulation against the man of God, and the work of God, to get what you desire. The Jezebel in Kings is not the same as this woman, yet they have so much in common.

This is not necessarily a woman, this is the personality of the spirit manifesting through a person of influence at the church. Using sensuality to allure, manipulate and maneuver the people of God to act in the flesh and abandon Christ for sexual pleasure.

I have heard many ministers teach on this spirit, but I have only actually seen this one time, and it was not a fun experience.

Father will always protect His family and house, so unless Jezebel is allowed to run loose and continue the demonic activity, it will be shut down. I learned that is must be done quickly, never slow.

Revelation 2:20-21 Nevertheless I have a few things against you, because you allow that woman Jezebel, who calls herself a prophetess, to teach and seduce My servants to commit sexual immorality and eat things sacrificed to idols. And I gave her time to repent of her sexual immorality, and she did not repent.

~Dr Micheal Spencer

October 6

AVOID DISPUTES AND PRACTICE GENTLENESS

But avoid foolish and ignorant disputes, knowing that they generate strife. And a servant of the Lord must not quarrel but be gentle to all, able to teach, patient,
2 Timothy 2:23, 24 NKJV

Ok today we avoid all disputes and practice gentleness.

Who is wise and understanding among you? Let him show by good conduct that his works are done in the meekness of wisdom. But if you have bitter envy and self-seeking in your hearts, do not boast and lie against the truth. This wisdom does not descend from above, but is earthly, sensual, demonic. For where envy and self-seeking exist, confusion and every evil thing are there. BUT THE WISDOM THAT IS FROM ABOVE is first pure, then peaceable, gentle, willing to yield, full of mercy and good fruits, without partiality and without hypocrisy. Now the fruit of righteousness is sown in peace by those who make peace.
James 3:13-18 NKJV (emphasis mine)

SEEK WISDOM FROM ABOVE TODAY...the Word of God also says if we lack wisdom ask and HE will give it!!! (James 1:5)

~Pastor Rhonda Spencer

October 7

When Is God Ticked OFF?

Zephaniah 1:6, "And I will destroy those who used to worship me but now no longer do. They no longer ask for the Lord's guidance or seek my blessings."

WHY WAS HE SO TICKED OFF?

God was upset over 3 specific things.

1) They no longer worship Me. My people no longer take the time to worship Who I Am. They go along their day, and simply ignore Me. I am no longer an important part of My people's lives. John 4:23-24, But the time is coming—indeed it's here now—when true worshipers will worship the Father in spirit and in truth. The Father is looking for those who will worship him that way. For God is Spirit, so those who worship him must worship in spirit and in truth."

2) They no longer ask for My guidance. The Lord recognized that He was no longer their Lord. He was dislodged from Kingship in their lives, individually and corporately. The children of God no longer wanted His direction, just His salvation. Prov. 3:5-6, Trust in the Lord with all your heart; do not depend on your own understanding. Seek his will in all you do, and he will show you which path to take.

3) They no longer seek after My blessing. The children no longer desired, or looked to God for, His blessing. As a parent we want and love to bless our babies, and God the Father loves to do the same thing. This is showing total independence from God. It is sad when the Creator of the entire universe longs to bless, but the people no longer want, or desire anything from Him. God wants to bless us! He longs to bless us! Seek Him first, and He will bless you! Psalm 35:27, Let them shout for joy and be glad, Who favor my righteous cause; And let them say continually, "Let the Lord be magnified, Who has pleasure in the prosperity of His servant."

Our initial thought is, "I thought He would be mad at the sin thing." YES! What we are seeing here really is one sin, it is the sin of taking God from utmost importance in our lives, and relegating Him to wanting Him when we need something.

God is a jealous God!

Worship Him, be guided by Him, and seek His blessings!

~Dr Micheal Spencer

October 8

YOU ARE NOT STUCK Part 1

One of the worst things to feel is the lack of HOPE!
When there is no hope the devil comes through that door and starts seeding death. Death in our circumstance. Death in our lives. God is not the One who is the killer.
John 10:10 Jesus came to bring HOPE, JOY, PEACE, STRENGTH, SALVATION, HEALING, FREEDOM!
John 21:3-9, Simon Peter said, "I'm going fishing." "We'll come, too," they all said. So they went out in the boat, but they caught nothing all night. At dawn Jesus was standing on the beach, but the disciples couldn't see who he was. He called out, "Fellows, have you caught any fish?" "No," they replied. Then he said, "Throw out your net on the right-hand side of the boat, and you'll get some!" So they did, and they couldn't haul in the net because there were so many fish in it. Then the disciple Jesus loved said to Peter, "It's the Lord!" When Simon Peter heard that it was the Lord, he put on his tunic (for he had stripped for work), jumped into the water, and headed to shore. The others stayed with the boat and pulled the loaded net to the shore, for they were only about a hundred yards from shore. When they got there, they found breakfast waiting for them—fish cooking over a charcoal fire, and some bread.
The disciples walked with Jesus for 3 years. They saw Him die a horrific death. After the resurrection they saw him once where He appeared and showed Himself (doubting Thomas experience).
BUT, They must have lost HOPE, because Peter said, "I'm going fishing."
When people lose HOPE, they go back to where they came from. The old lifestyle, the old friends, the old sins, the old fruitless, unfulfilling life they initially left because there was nothing there but a void. Why do people go backwards? Why do people return to where they came from when hope is lost? Because it is familiar, and they can handle and accept what it seems they can control.
TODAY, YOU KNOW YOU HAVE LOST HOPE IF YOU ARE STARTING TO GRAVITATE BACK TO YOUR OLD LIFESTYLE AWAY FROM JESUS!
STOP! Do not move another step back. We are going to see Jesus refuel your hope, and faith! You are going to have a fresh fire shut up in your bones.

~Dr Micheal Spencer

October 9

YOU ARE NOT STUCK Part 2

One of the worst things to feel is the lack of HOPE!
John 10:10 Jesus came to bring HOPE, JOY, PEACE, STRENGTH, SALVATION, HEALING, FREEDOM!
John 21:3-9 Simon Peter said, "I'm going fishing."
"We'll come, too," they all said. So they went out in the boat, but they caught nothing all night. At dawn Jesus was standing on the beach, but the disciples couldn't see who he was. He called out, "Fellows, have you caught any fish?" "No," they replied. Then he said, "Throw out your net on the right-hand side of the boat, and you'll get some!" So they did, and they couldn't haul in the net because there were so many fish in it. Then the disciple Jesus loved said to Peter, "It's the Lord!" When Simon Peter heard that it was the Lord, he put on his tunic (for he had stripped for work), jumped into the water, and headed to shore. The others stayed with the boat and pulled the loaded net to the shore, for they were only about a hundred yards from shore. When they got there, they found breakfast waiting for them—fish cooking over a charcoal fire and some bread.
The disciples walked with JESUS for 3 years, and gave up everything to obey and become fishers of men! They knew Jesus was the Messiah! He opened blind eyes, deaf ears, and even raised the dead. THEN, He died on the tree, crucified. The disciples were confused, thinking that Jesus was coming to build an earthly kingdom, now He is dead. After 3 days Jesus is raised from the dead, and He even appears to them (the doubting Thomas moment). Jesus didn't stay, He disappeared again!
WHERE ARE YOU JESUS? I GAVE UP EVERYTHING FOR YOU, AND NOW I CANNOT SEE YOU, FEEL YOU, WHERE ARE YOU?
Have you ever said that?
Peter simply said, "I'm going fishing", and the rest of the disciples said, "We'll come too."
PEOPLE WHO LOSE HOPE, GO BACK TO WHAT THEY CAME OUT OF. Why go back? You left there for a reason, because there was not a life there that you really wanted, yet people who seem to lose hope head back to their old life. It is what they think they can control.
After fishing ALL night, they caught NOTHING! Hopeless, tired, fishless, ready to simply go home, the disciples saw a man standing on the bank of the shore.
DID YOU GET WHAT YOU WERE LOOKING FOR FROM THE OLD LIFE, GUYS (did you catch any fish)? They retorted, "NO!" Jesus said, "Throw your nets to the other side." Jesus is never far away, and when you need Him He is there. JESUS IS THE ANSWER, not the old life!
STOP GOING BACK AND DABBLING WITH THE OLD LIFE WHEN YOU GET DISCOURAGED AND WHEN YOU FEEL HOPELESS.
Call to Him! Jesus is always close.

~Dr Micheal Spencer

October 10

Get Unstuck by JESUS!

You are not stuck in your situation!!
John 21:3-6
Simon Peter said, "I'm going fishing.""We'll come, too," they all said. So they went out in the boat, but they caught nothing all night. At dawn Jesus was standing on the beach, but the disciples couldn't see who he was. He called out, "Fellows, have you caught any fish?" "No," they replied. Then he said, "Throw out your net on the right-hand side of the boat, and you'll get some!" So they did, and they couldn't haul in the net because there were so many fish in it.
JESUS WAS THE ANSWER TO THEIR EMPTY NETS!
JESUS WAS THE ANSWER FOR THEIR HOPELESS HEARTS!
JESUS IS THE ANSWER FOR EVERY ONE OF YOUR SITUATIONS! He is close, watching, and ready to get you unstuck from your situation. He is attentive to your smallest needs, even your hungry stomach. When Jesus showed up on the shore and told them to throw their net to the other side, it brought in a massive harvest of fish. The really cool part that we seem to miss is that He had a fire and food cooking for the men who fished all night long. He cares for every need!! YOU ARE NOT STUCK!

JESUS IS THE ANSWER
- In the name of Jesus we are saved – Romans 10:9-10; Acts 4:12
- In the name of Jesus we are healed – Acts 3:6; Mark 16:17-18 / Jesus' name is bigger than cancer, sickness or disease!
- In the name of Jesus we are delivered – Mark 16:17-18; Luke 10:17
- In the name of Jesus cities are changed – Acts 8:5-8 / Samaria
- In the name of Jesus, financial needs are met – tither / Matthew 17:27 – money in fish
- In the name of Jesus are all our answers!

DO NOT GIVE UP HOPE!
CALL ON JESUS, HE IS REALLY CLOSE PREPARING YOUR BLESSING!

~Dr Micheal Spencer

October 11

It Is NOT The EVENT! Part I

My wife hated driving long distances with me! When I got in the vehicle, I fueled up, and I was ready to go, go, go, go, go! I did not like to stop for pee breaks, and I did not want to stop for food. I have a destination, a place to be, and we were going to get there as quickly as possible. It was really bad one time when we drove in August of 1995 from GA to NY, with 3 babies in the van (all under the age of 5), and we only stopped for gas, and one time to eat. AHHHHHHHHHH!

We have all heard it said that you need to enjoy the flowers on the way......

It's the trip, and not the destination......

It is not the EVENT, it is the JOURNEY....

Ladies, you are not exempt either!

Having performed so many weddings, I have found that the event of the wedding day many times muddles up the journey. When the bride gets engulfed in the wedding day planning to consumption, her entire life revolves about making it perfect. It is sad when it is over because sometimes the brides go into a mini-depression because it was anticlimactic.

When we think about Noah, we think about the ark.

When we think of Moses, we think of the burning bush.

When we think about Elisha, we think of the miracles.

When we think of Peter, it is his preaching on the day of Pentecost.

WE FORGET THAT THEY HAD TO LIVE EVERYDAY, NOT JUST ON THE DAY OF THE EVENTS!

Noah had to build the boat for about 100 years, while he was being mocked!

Moses spent 40 years in the desert.

Elisha followed Elijah around and washed his feet.

Peter: he simply had a serious case of foot-mouth disease.

DO NOT GET DISCOURAGED BETWEEN EVENTS – it is the everyday plowing, seeding, watering, and pulling weeds, that makes the harvest available.

Hebrews 12:1-2, Therefore we also, since we are surrounded by so great a cloud of witnesses, let us lay aside every weight, and the sin which so easily ensnares us, and let us run with endurance the race that is set before us, looking unto Jesus, the author and finisher of our faith, who for the joy that was set before Him endured the cross, despising the shame, and has sat down at the right hand of the throne of God.

~Dr Micheal Spencer

October 12

It Is NOT The EVENT! Part 2

So many are so passionate about getting the next HIGH. They need to get pumped up, get the next sensation, the next prophecy, the next dance, and the next event. In all of this searching for the NEXT thing, they completely miss the journey of maturity.

Moses was schooled in Egyptian education and culture, but he was not Egyptian, he was a Jew. When he saw the slave being beaten by the guard he felt that an event would make him a deliverer. Sadly, the event made him a murderer, and not only was he now rejected by Pharaoh's courts, but his own people did not see the event as making him into anything.

People are not MADE in the event or the experience, people are MADE in the journey of everyday living. Moses was MADE on the backside of the desert, tending sheep. This is where God developed his character and matured his manhood. It's where Moses developed a daily relationship with the living God. It is in those desert places that God hones us, and gets those things out of our lives that will destroy us, or make us unusable, or disqualified for His kingdom. What a gracious God that He deals with our weaknesses in private on the journey, rather than throwing us out in public to deal with them in front of everyone. After 40 years in the desert Moses was then ready for the events that would come from his journey. These events would have destroyed Moses without the maturing, making, spanking, loving relationship with His God.

God called Moses His friend.

James 2:23, And the Scripture was fulfilled which says, "Abraham believed God, and it was accounted to him for righteousness." And he was called the friend of God.

Do not despise the backside of the desert in your life!

It is the grace of God!

Allow Jesus to train you in the journey, and you will be ready when the event comes. If you strive for the events, then the journey is lost, and the event will only be another high, with no substance.

James 1:2-4, Dear brothers and sisters, when troubles come your way, consider it an opportunity for great joy. For you know that when your faith is tested, your endurance has a chance to grow. So let it grow, for when your endurance is fully developed, you will be perfect and complete, needing nothing.

~Dr Micheal Spencer

October 13

Why Was I So Stupid?

Have you ever done anything stupid before?

I want to give you a hint, Jesus knew you were going to do it BEFORE He created you.
It is not that He created you to do stupid things, but He planned your life knowing you would.

THIS IS A BIG WHEW!!
That means God has not given up on you!
That means His plans are still in motion!
That means you have only just begun!

David, the greatest king of Israel, God knew about Bathsheba before He created David, and said he was a man after His own heart.
"Does this mean I can do whatever I want and get away with it? God has to forgive me so I will sin whenever I want!"
Ummmm....forgiveness wasn't cheap!
It is a matter of the heart!
Whose heart do you have?

But God removed Saul and replaced him with David, a man about whom God said, 'I have found David son of Jesse, a man after my own heart. He will do everything I want him to do.' Acts 13:22 NLT

~Dr Micheal Spencer

October 14

DON'T KNOW WHAT TO PRAY???

Likewise the Spirit also helps in our weaknesses. For we do not know what we should pray for as we ought, but the Spirit Himself makes intercession for us with groanings which cannot be uttered.
Romans 8:26 NKJV

I love this, we don't always know what to pray....but the spirit does. PRAY IN THE SPIRIT OFTEN.

So too the [Holy] Spirit comes to our aid and bears us up in our weakness; for we do not know what prayer to offer nor how to offer it worthily as we ought, but the Spirit Himself goes to meet our supplication and pleads in our behalf with unspeakable yearnings and groanings too deep for utterance. And He Who searches the hearts of men knows what is in the mind of the [Holy] Spirit [what His intent is], because the Spirit intercedes and pleads [before God] in behalf of the saints according to and in harmony with God's will. We are assured and know that [God being a partner in their labor] all things work together and are [fitting into a plan] for good to and for those who love God and are called according to [His] design and purpose.
Romans 8:26-28 AMP

Pray in the spirit often. The Holy Spirit will strengthen you and knows what you need to pray for. Partnering with God, we are assured that all things will work together for good.

~Pastor Rhonda Spencer

October 15

WHO is Leading WHOM?

Matthew 4:18-22 And Jesus, walking by the Sea of Galilee, saw two brothers, Simon called Peter, and Andrew his brother, casting a net into the sea; for they were fishermen. Then He said to them, "Follow Me, and I will make you fishers of men." They immediately left their nets and followed Him. Going on from there, He saw two other brothers, James the son of Zebedee, and John his brother, in the boat with Zebedee their father, mending their nets. He called them, and immediately they left the boat and their father, and followed Him.

FOLLOW ME This statement at first sounds really easy, a simple thought, but let's look at what this actually means. Jesus literally walked up to these businessmen, who were working their livelihood, and said, come now!

It wasn't, "Hey guys, you want to come help me with the ministry?" Jesus told them with clarity, and strength to COME NOW!

Many times in American Christianity we have the mindset that we are doing God a favor by coming to church, or helping in a ministry. That we are "following Him" because we do not want to go to the Lake of Fire. That would be a good reason, but we forget that Jesus is looking for relationship, but also for DISCIPLES.

Jesus has called us to follow Him, not for Him to follow us.

Romans 8:14 These are the children of God who are led by the Spirit of God.

We are led by Him. He is our leader.

He is our LORD; we are not our own lord and Jesus is just the guy who keeps us from the Lake of Fire.

IMMEDIATELY – This means exactly that – they got right up and went.

Peter and Andrew left their business.

They did not abandon their business – we see Peter go back to his business after Jesus' death.

They were successful business people, and their companies still ran while they followed Jesus.

John and James left their father sitting on the pier to follow Jesus.

You have to make decisions when you follow the Lord.

IS JESUS FIRST?

~Dr Micheal Spencer

October 16

Art Project?

When I was in art class as a teen, they were teaching us about the potter's wheel. They showed us that the clay first had to be kneaded, and all the hard pieces had to be removed. Then after the clay was worked, it was ready for the potter's wheel.
I was not, and am not, an artist. They told us to make something for our mothers, so I decided to make my mom a creamer thing for coffee. I took the clay, plopped it on the wheel, wet my hands, and meticulously butchered the poor piece of clay. Instead of making a masterpiece, my creamer thing flopped flat, it was just sad! My mom acted happy, she even kept it. But from the work of my hands, I know it was not pretty, or even usable. She kept it as a trinket on the shelf, but never, ever, put creamer in it!
BUT when a master artist takes the clay, molds the clay and fires the clay, it is not just a piece of clay, but it turns into a masterpiece! When we try to make ourselves, we become a flop! FOLLOW JESUS, AND HE WILL MAKE YOU....
Matthew 4:18-22 And Jesus, walking by the Sea of Galilee, saw two brothers, Simon called Peter, and Andrew his brother, casting a net into the sea; for they were fishermen. Then He said to them, "Follow Me, and I will make you fishers of men." They immediately left their nets and followed Him. Going on from there, He saw two other brothers, James the son of Zebedee, and John his brother, in the boat with Zebedee their father, mending their nets. He called them, and immediately they left the boat and their father, and followed Him.
Isaiah 64:8, But now, O Lord, You are our Father; We are the clay, and You our potter; And all we are the work of Your hand.
Ephesians 2:10, For we are His workmanship, created in Christ Jesus for good works, which God prepared beforehand that we should walk in them.
If you and I are following Jesus rather than making Him follow us, then He can MAKE us!
He has a plan for you! You are not an accident!
STAY ON THE POTTER'S WHEEL! STOP MAKING JESUS FOLLOW YOU. ALLOW HIM TO LEAD AND BE LORD OF YOUR LIFE!

~Dr Micheal Spencer

October 17

SUPERHUMAN

For this I labor [unto weariness], striving with all the superhuman energy which He so mightily enkindles and works within me. Colossians 1:29 AMP

We have SUPERHUMAN energy from God!!!!!
WOO-HOO!

May He grant you out of the rich treasury of His glory to be strengthened and reinforced with mighty power in the inner man by the [Holy] Spirit [Himself indwelling your innermost being and personality].
Ephesians 3:16 AMP

Be reinforced today. Gos is infusing you with superhuman energy.

~Pastor Rhonda Spencer

October 18

They PUSHED The BUTTON!

What if all the threats from North Korea were REAL? What would happen if we knew that in 48 hours they would push the button, and the world as we know it would absolutely change forever?
If we all knew we had 48 hours to share Jesus with as many of our family, friends, and even a stranger, would we really know how to bring them to the cross where they would know, beyond a shadow of a doubt, that they would go to heaven.
Would you know HOW to share your FAITH with someone?

1 Peter 3:15, Instead, you must worship Christ as Lord of your life. And if someone asks about your Christian hope, always be ready to explain it.

IF WE ONLY HAD 48 HOURS, WOULD YOU KNOW HOW TO LEAD PEOPLE TO SALVATION?

Ephesians 5:16, Redeeming the time, because the days are evil.
Proverbs 11:30, The fruit of the righteous is a tree of life; and he that winneth souls is wise.

~Dr Micheal Spencer

October 19

How to Lead Someone to the Lord

Matthew 4:18-20, And Jesus, walking by the Sea of Galilee, saw two brothers, Simon called Peter, and Andrew his brother, casting a net into the sea; for they were fishermen. Then He said to them, "Follow Me, and I will make you fishers of men." They immediately left their nets and followed Him.
POLE, BAIT, CATCH We have the pole! We have the bait!
Romans 1:16, For I am not ashamed of the gospel of Christ, for it is the power of God to salvation for everyone who believes, for the Jew first and also for the Greek.
Jesus died. Jesus rose from the dead. He is coming back to take us home. Jesus will forgive you of your sins and restore the relationship with God.
Ephesians 2:8-9, For by grace you have been saved through faith, and that not of yourselves; it is the gift of God, not of works, lest anyone should boast.
Jesus said it BEST!
John 14:6, Jesus said to him, "I am the way, the truth, and the life. No one comes to the Father except through Me."
Share the Word with the "Romans Road"!
Romans 3:23 – All have sinned. That means everyone.
Romans 6:23 – The wages of sin is death, BUT, the gift of God is eternal life through Jesus.
Romans 10:13, For "Whoever calls on the name of the Lord shall be saved."
ASK: "Not that it would happen, BUT, if you passed today, do you know if you would be going to heaven?"
If they say yes, then, "When you stand before God and He asked you why He should let you in, what would you say?"
If they say it's because of salvation in Jesus – awesome!
If they say,"I am a good person", "I go to church", "I believe in God",
Then say, "Repeat after me,
"Dear Jesus, I ask you to forgive me of my sins. I believe that you are the Son of God, and that you died and rose again. I receive you as my Savior, and give you my whole life. Thank you for coming into my life. Amen!"

Follow up with them. Bring them to church

~Dr Micheal Spencer

October 20

Do NOT Jump In The POND

Matthew 4:18-20, And Jesus, walking by the Sea of Galilee, saw two brothers, Simon called Peter, and Andrew his brother, casting a net into the sea; for they were fishermen. Then He said to them, "Follow Me, and I will make you fishers of men." They immediately left their nets and followed Him.

Jesus called us to FOLLOW HIM!
1) This means He knows where He, and WE are going. He is not lost. Psalm 37:23, The Lord directs the steps of the godly. He delights in every detail of their lives.
2) When we FOLLOW HIM, not Him following us, then He will begin to MAKE US.
Now that we are following Him, He is making us fishers of men. That means He has given us each a pond, a lake, or even an ocean to fish out of. We are all responsible to FISH! Luke 19:10, For the Son of Man came to seek and save those who are lost.
Here are some things not to do at your pond.
1) Don't eat the bait (if you are eating the worms, you will have none to put on the hook). Do not keep the Gospel to yourself.
2) Do not keep the bait in the can (which means, nobody knows your a Christian, keeping Jesus all to yourself). If you were arrested today for being a Christian, would there be enough evidence to convict you?
3) Do not jump in the pond (which means, do not jump in the same water and think you are going to catch them). Sinners know how a Christian should live, yet some Christians think that drinking a beer, cussing or going to a party will give them opportunity to reach the fish. I am so sorry to tell you this, BUT the fish know, if you are the fisherman, that you do not belong where they are. Why would they want what you have, when you are swimming in the same cesspool?
2 Corinthians 6:17, Therefore, come out from among unbelievers, and separate yourselves from them, says the Lord. Don't touch their filthy things, and I will welcome you.
LET'S BE WISE, GODLY, ANOINTED, FISHER-PEOPLE FOR JESUS.

~Dr Micheal Spencer

October 21

Negative Words Pollute the Anointing in Your Life

It's crazy how a mind (that is untrained) will automatically speak, and think, critically and negatively.
Ecclesiastes 10:1 DEAD FLIES (such a little thing) cause the ointment of the perfumer to putrefy [and[send forth a vile odor.
Proverbs 10:31-32 MSG A good person's mouth is a clear fountain of wisdom; a foul mouth is a stagnant swamp. The speech of a good person clears the air; the words of the wicked pollute it.
Titus 3:1-2 AMP Remind people to be subject to rulers and authorities, to be obedient, to be ready and willing to do good, to slander or abuse no one, to be kind and conciliatory and gentle, showing unqualified consideration and courtesy toward everyone.
Proverbs 25:26 MSG A good person who gives in to a bad person is a muddied spring, a polluted well.
James 3:10,11,14,15 Out of the same mouth come forth blessing and cursing. These things, my brethren, ought not to be so. Does a fountain send forth [simultaneously] from the same opening fresh water and bitter? But if you have bitter jealousy (envy) and contention (rivalry, selfish ambition) in your hearts, do not pride yourselves on it and thus be in defiance of and false to the Truth. This [superficial] wisdom is not such as comes down from above, but is earthly, unspiritual (animal), even devilish (demoniacal).
Mark 7:20-23 NLT And then he added, "It is what comes from inside that defiles you. For from within, out of a person's heart, come evil thoughts, sexual immorality, theft, murder, adultery, greed, wickedness, deceit, lustful desires, envy, slander, pride, and foolishness. All these vile things come from within; they are what defile you."
Philippians 4:8 AMP For the rest, brethren, whatever is true, whatever is worthy of reverence and is honorable and seemly, whatever is just, whatever is pure, whatever is lovely and lovable, whatever is kind and winsome and gracious, if there is any virtue and excellence, if there is anything worthy of praise, think on and weigh and take account of these things [fix your minds on them].
Ephesians 4:29,31,32Let no corrupt word proceed out of your mouth, but what is good for necessary edification, that it may impart grace to the hearers.[] Let all bitterness, wrath, anger, clamor, and evil speaking be put away from you, with all malice. And be kind to one another, tenderhearted, forgiving one another, even as God in Christ forgave you.
Rid yourself of pollution in the anointing of your life and stop negativity from coming out of your mouth.

~Pastor Rhonda Spencer

October 22

Get Over Here!

Matthew 4:18-22 And Jesus, walking by the Sea of Galilee, saw two brothers, Simon called Peter, and Andrew his brother, casting a net into the sea; for they were fishermen. Then He said to them, "Follow Me, and I will make you fishers of men." They immediately left their nets and followed Him. Going on from there, He saw two other brothers, James the son of Zebedee, and John his brother, in the boat with Zebedee their father, mending their nets. He called them, and immediately they left the boat and their father, and followed Him.

FOLLOW ME

This means that Jesus knew where He was going!

There are two things you can be extremely confident in: that Jesus will never lead you astray, and He knows what makes His Father happy.

So when He says FOLLOW ME, He is saying, "If you let me lead you, I will make you successful."

Proverbs 3:5-6 AMPC, Lean on, trust in, and be confident in the Lord with all your heart and mind and do not rely on your own insight or understanding. In all your ways know, recognize, and acknowledge Him, and He will direct and make straight and plain your paths.

I WILL MAKE YOU

I will make you – the word MAKE is a verb – action. Making isn't creating – creating is instant, making takes time. Everyone likes the event of salvation, but few stay to the journey, which is what MAKES you a great man and woman of God. If you are not going to participate with the journey, you will never be made.

Jesus wants to MOLD US, MAKE US, MATURE US, EMPOWER US, EQUIP US for success.

We MUST ALLOW Him to make us. If we are having Him follow us instead of us following Him, then He cannot MAKE us anything!

Jeremiah 29:11, For I know the thoughts that I think toward you, says the Lord, thoughts of peace and not of evil, to give you a future and a hope.

~Dr Micheal Spencer

October 23

THERE IS POWER IN THE NAME OF JESUS

Therefore God also has highly exalted Him and given Him the name which is above every name, that at the name of Jesus every knee should bow, of those in heaven, and of those on earth, and of those under the earth, Philippians 2:9, 10 NKJV

I DECLARE THE NAME OF JESUS OVER EVERY AREA OF MY LIFE...JESUS. JESUS. JESUS!!!! I love causing everything to have to bow in submission to Him. JESUSSSSS!
JESUS
JESUS
There's STILL power in the name of Jesus!!
JESUS
JESUS
JESUS!!!!!

~Pastor Rhonda Spencer

October 24

Oops or OH YEA?

Jeremiah 29:11
For I know the thoughts that I think toward you, says the Lord, thoughts of peace and not of evil, to give you a future and a hope.

You were not an oops!
You are in the thoughts, and passion of the Creator!

So many struggle with low self-esteem. The world, people, and worse, they themselves are saying they are worthless, and have no purpose.

DO NOT BELIEVE THE LIE!
Father God thinks thoughts about you!
YOU ARE ON HIS MIND & HEART!
The thoughts are not hatred, evil, or disgust, His thoughts are for you, and to enjoy Him, and to live in what Jesus paid for on the cross.

DADDY WANTS TO GIVE YOU A HUGE FUTURE WITH ETERNAL VALUE!

Your thoughts will try to condemn you out of the promises – tell your mind to obey the Word of God!

~Dr Micheal Spencer

October 25

I want THEM to change! Part 1

RENEW MY MIND
Psalm 51:10 Create in me a clean heart, O God & renew a steadfast spirit within me.
Isaiah 40:31 But those who wait on the LORD shall renew their strength; they shall mount up with wings like eagles, They shall run and not be weary, They shall walk and not faint.
Romans 12:2 And do not be conformed to this world, but be transformed by the renewing of your mind, that you may prove what is that good and acceptable and perfect will of God.
2 Corinthians 4:16 Therefore we do not lose heart. Even though our outward man is perishing, yet the inward man is being renewed day by day.
Ephesians 4:23 and be renewed in the spirit of your mind,
Hebrews 12:11-13 Now no chastening seems to be joyful for the present, but painful; nevertheless, afterward it yields the peaceable fruit of righteousness to those who have been trained by it. Therefore strengthen the hands which hang down, and the feeble knees, and make straight paths for your feet, so that what is lame may not be dislocated, but rather be healed.

The renewing of your mind: It is natural human tendency to be satisfied with mediocrity. We'd love to learn and do and be many things but never make the efforts to actually make it happen. We are satisfied with mediocrity, because change takes effort. We refuse to change for the better.
1 Peter 1:13 Therefore, prepare your minds for action; be self-controlled; set your hope fully on the grace to be given you when Jesus Christ is revealed.

So what is hindering our spiritual renewal? Is it not our laziness? We don't like the way we live, and we want things to change. We want our environment to change; we want other people to change. Yet, we just don't want ourselves to change, because that requires a strong determination and significant efforts. We want to stay mediocre because of laziness. Sometimes we know that we ought to change, but we still choose not to change.

~Dr Micheal Spencer

October 26

I want THEM to change! Part 2

This kind of laziness is exemplified by the attitudes of a dieter. They know that they should make the determination to go on a diet to stop this unhealthy cycle, but they don't or they quit very quickly. When we see our friends in such situations (and it is much easier to see it in our friends), we get frustrated about their attitude, wondering why they just would not make the changes as they should. Yet, are we not often making similar choices by refusing to change?

It is natural human tendency to sin, and to counter this tendency would require some significant efforts. The renewing of our minds means to struggle against this sin. The "mind" needs to be changed. That is, our attitudes, our will, and our frame of mind must be renewed in accordance with our knowledge of God's truth. We are to make the determination to change for the better. It is pitiable enough for us to be satisfied with a mediocre appreciation of God's grace, but it is detrimental for us to be satisfied with a mediocre spirituality.

We cannot choose to be halfway between the world and the Kingdom of God. This halfway point is spiritual mediocrity. If we are satisfied with being spiritually mediocre, then we would eventually become spiritually dead. Just like our biological body's renewal is necessary, so our spiritual renewal necessary. We often fail to realize that we have the ability to change spiritually for the better. We tend to think of our personalities, inborn or shaped by environment, as unchangeable factors in the Christian life. Indeed, the totally depraved individual has no ability to change in accordance with God's will. However, when we were born again by the Spirit of Christ, we were given the ability to change anything that needs to be changed in our minds, for in 1 Corinthians 2:12-16, Paul says that we have the "mind" of Christ, as we are filled by the Holy Spirit (2:12). The ability to renew our minds is thus a gift given to Christians.

~Dr Micheal Spencer

October 27

I want THEM to change! Part 3

When we are lazy, we refuse to "renew" our minds, and as a result we cease to be transformed. Transformation may only occur by the renewing of our minds, as Paul so clearly puts it in the passage. The result is that our sinful nature remains in us and becomes magnified. If we refuse to be renewed, then sin will start to corrupt us.

As a biological concept, metabolism designates the "renewing" of our body by the innate chemical reactions that ultimately cause old cells to replace new cells. Every seven years or so, we have a body consisting of a completely different set of cells. We get new hair (2-7 years), new skin(3-7 weeks), and new nails (3- 7 months). This process of biological renewal is crucial in sustaining our life. Without this renewal, the body would die in a very short time. In the same way, we must be continually renewed in our minds, or else our new life may very soon die away.

Much like a Christians, the "mind" is often described as being continually renewed.

Ephesians 4:23-24 And be constantly renewed in the spirit of your mind [having a fresh mental and spiritual attitude], And put on the new nature (the regenerate self) created in God's image, [Godlike] in true righteousness and holiness.

Many Christians lose their faith and stop going to church when they face trials or temptations, and find the end of their lives in spiritual ruins. This will happen to us as well, if we do not continue to be renewed. We don't think it discouraging or negative that we shower daily? Much in the same we need to renew our mind daily. We get dressed daily—put on the mind of Christ daily.

Ephesians 6:11 Put on the full armor of God so that you can take your stand against the devil's schemes.

Ephesians 6:13 Therefore put on the full armor of God, so that when the day of evil comes, you may be able to stand your ground, and after you have done everything, to stand.

Colossians 3:10 and have put on the new self, which is being renewed in knowledge in the image of its Creator.

~Dr Micheal Spencer

October 28

Friendship or Not?

It is very interesting that so many hang on to something that is so dangerous! WHAT DO YOU MEAN BY THAT PASTOR?
How many of you would willfully eat poison? How many of you would allow someone else to feed you poison, and you knew it?
YET, we allow people to infuse their words and actions into our lives and use the excuse that they are our friends.
1 Corinthians 15:33, Do not be so deceived and misled! Evil companionships (communion, associations) corrupt & deprave good manners/morals/character.
There comes a time when we have to look at those who are around us and make choices as to whether they are people who should be feeding us. Nobody tells me what to do! That is a lie. You are who you hang with! We live in a real world, and we're told to occupy till He comes, so we are always going to be around people who do not know the Lord and live for their master, the devil. BUT, we do have the choice as to the level of influence we allow them to have in our lives.
BE CAREFUL WHO YOU ALLOW TO INFLUENCE YOUR LIFE!
If you find, when you are around certain people, that sin seems to rise to the occasion, then most likely those people should be your acquaintances, but not your friends.
OH BE CAREFUL LITTLE EYES WHAT YOU SEE, OH BE CAREFUL LITTLE FEET WHERE YOU GO, OH BE CAREFUL LITTLE MOUTH WHAT YOU SAY..FOR THE FATHER UP ABOVE IS LOOKING DOWN IN LOVE, OH BE CAREFUL LITTLE SOUL WHERE YOU GO...
Proverbs 4:14-15, Enter not into the path of the wicked, and go not in the way of evil men. Avoid it, do not go on it; turn from it and pass on. **IF THEY ARE INFLUENCING YOU MORE THAN YOU ARE INFLUENCING THEM, THEN CHANGE FRIENDS...**
1 Corinthians 6:14-17, Do not be unequally yoked with unbelievers [do not make mismated alliances with them or come under a different yoke with them, inconsistent with your faith]. For what partnership have right living and right standing with God with iniquity and lawlessness? Or how can light have fellowship with darkness? What harmony can there be between Christ and Belial [the devil]? Or what has a believer in common with an unbeliever? What agreement [can there be between] a temple of God and idols? For we are the temple of the living God; even as God said, I will dwell in and with and among them and will walk in and with and among them, and I will be their God, and they shall be My people. So, come out from among [unbelievers], and separate (sever) yourselves from them, says the Lord, and touch not [any] unclean thing; then I will receive you kindly and treat you with favor.

~Dr Micheal Spencer

October 29

Why Are You Talking About ME?

Here is what is interesting about us as humans, we like to categorize in our heads what is a worse sin!!
"Murder is worse than.....At least I never sinned that bad..... They have a real testimony, because they were really bad!!"
Say this with me, **"sin is sin is sin is sin"**, go ahead and say it out loud again please, **"sin is sin is sin is sin."** What does sin do?
IT SEPARATES US FROM GOD! So different sins might have different consequences, but all sin does the same thing, it breaks down our relationship with Jesus.
Murder, homosexuality, adultery, drunkenness, stealing, the list goes on of sins that people esteem less or greater, but today let us think about one that most people do, and say, "well at least I am not as bad as them."
Romans 1:28-32, And so, since they did not see fit to acknowledge God or approve of Him or consider Him worth the knowing, God gave them over to a base and condemned mind to do things not proper or decent but loathsome, Until they were filled (permeated and saturated) with every kind of unrighteousness, iniquity, grasping and covetous greed, and malice. [They were] full of envy and jealousy, murder, strife, deceit and treachery, ill will and cruel ways. [They were] secret backbiters and gossipers, Slanderers, hateful to and hating God, full of insolence, arrogance, [and] boasting; inventors of new forms of evil, disobedient and undutiful to parents. [They were] without understanding, conscienceless and faithless, heartless and loveless [and] merciless. Though they are fully aware of God's righteous decree that those who do such things deserve to die, they not only do them themselves but approve and applaud others who practice them.

BACKBITING, GOSSIP, SLANDER, the sins of your tongue are just as EVIL as sin we deem as HORRIFIC!
Instead of talking about others' faults, shortcomings, and sins, talk about you needing to mow your lawn, or better yet, talk to that person about the LOVE OF JESUS THAT WILL FORGIVE, CHANGE AND EMPOWER THAT PERSON FOR GREATNESS!
STOP TALKING ABOUT OTHER PEOPLE!!!!
START TALKING TO OTHER PEOPLE ABOUT JESUS!!

~Dr Micheal Spencer

October 30

Friendship or Not?

Matthew 7:3-5, "And why worry about a speck in your friend's eye when you have a log in your own? How can you think of saying to your friend, 'Let me help you get rid of that speck in your eye,' when you can't see past the log in your own eye? Hypocrite! First get rid of the log in your own eye; then you will see well enough to deal with the speck in your friend's eye.

Here is an easy fact to swallow, if someone is always picking on others about the junk in their lives, they are striving to hide from their own!
It is so easy to find the faults of other's, but when it comes time to dealing with ourselves, it is so much easier to focus on others.
WHY IS IT SO HARD TO DEAL WITH OUR OWN JUNK?
When we actually start looking at ourselves, we can easily see things that are very ugly. Maybe nobody even knows about them, maybe you have been able to hide the junk, but the truth is, it is still there!
When we allow the Holy Spirit to get in and show us our own issues, then He can start the healing, or the transition from bondage to freedom. When we keep pointing at others stuff to keep our own from coming up, we actually keep ourselves in bondage.

TODAY, DON'T WORRY ABOUT SOMEONE ELSE'S ISSUES – YOU AND I HAVE ENOUGH OF OUR OWN TO DEAL WITH!!
If you are going to need grace someday, you better be one that gives it!!

~Dr Micheal Spencer

October 31

YOU HAVE A PLACE

I love so much being a part of the family of God. Have you ever felt you didn't belong, that you have no place?

YOU ARE A CHILD OF THE MOST HIGH GOD AND YOU BELONG IN HIS FAMILY.

Galatians 4:6-7 MSG
You can tell for sure that you are now fully adopted as his own children because God sent the Spirit of his Son into our lives crying out, "Papa! Father!" Doesn't that privilege of intimate conversation with God make it plain that you are not a slave, but a child? And if you are a child, you're also an heir, with complete access to the inheritance.

~Pastor Rhonda Spencer

November 1

A Smile Day!

Proverbs 17:22, A happy heart is good medicine and a cheerful mind works healing, but a broken spirit dries up the bones.

Ok, today is a day of action. I like doing these days with you because they are fun, but also it keeps us in a thanksgiving mode in our hearts.
The Word of God says that a happy heart is just like medicine, and a cheerful mind brings healing!
BUT
I don't feel happy!
I got up on the wrong side of the bed!
This is a bad day!
Blah, blah, blah, blah.......

Psalm 118:24, This is the day the Lord has made; we will rejoice and be glad in it.

"I don't want to be FAKE!"
You are not being fake when you choose to rejoice even when trouble is troubling you. You are making a decision to rejoice in God who is the deliverer from trouble. You are choosing to fix your eyes on Jesus, the author and finisher of your faith. You are choosing to not live in the flesh. You are choosing to be a blessing today rather than a walking, moping, sad sack that nobody wants to be near.
TODAY, WALK AROUND AND SMILE AT EVERYONE! IF THEY ARE SMILING, SMILE AT THEM. IF THEY ARE NOT SMILING, SMILE AT THEM AND LET THEM KNOW IT IS A GREAT DAY!
IF THE OFFICE, WORK or HOME IS GETTING STRESSFUL, INTENSE and OVERWHELMING,
SMILE AND DECLARE IT IS A GREAT DAY
(Jesus is with you).
Tell me how people react. It is so rare that people today get to experience a SMILE!

~Dr Micheal Spencer

November 2

ONE STEP FURTHER!

Ok! Yesterday we smiled at everyone. Wasn't it interesting to see how people do not know how to react to others smiling? The thief, the devil, is doing his work by stealing merry hearts, which is a medicine. People are miserable, nasty, angry, and they do not even know why.
BUT
We are the CHURCH! The body of Jesus, His ambassadors, and we have the joy of the Lord that is our strength, and our merry hearts will not only medicate us, but we are going to spread the medicine on everyone we see! Give people that vitamin boost of joy, and happiness!
Proverbs 17:22, A happy heart is good medicine and a cheerful mind works healing, but a broken spirit dries up the bones.
OK!
Today, let's take it a step further......
While you are walking around smiling wherever you go, compliment someone about something. If it is a lady, ladies, tell her she has nice shoes. Men, do not compliment her shoes!
Men compliment the men, ladies compliment the ladies, please.......
Men, you can compliment his truck, or his work ethic.
So we are smiling all day again, now we are finding someone to compliment. You will be blown away on their responses. They will smile, and say thank you, and they will think about that all day.
WORDS ARE POWERFUL! Share words of life today!
Proverbs 18:21, Death and life are in the power of the tongue, and they who indulge in it shall eat the fruit of it [for death or life].
Ephesians 4:29, Let no foul or polluting language, nor evil word nor unwholesome or worthless talk [ever] come out of your mouth, but only such [speech] as is good and beneficial to the spiritual progress of others, as is fitting to the need and the occasion, that it may be a blessing and give grace (God's favor) to those who hear it.

~Dr Micheal Spencer

November 3

WHAT DOES THE EVIDENCE SAY?

But the fruit of the [Holy] Spirit [the work which His presence within accomplishes] is love, joy (gladness), peace, patience (an even temper, forbearance), kindness, goodness (benevolence), faithfulness, Gentleness (meekness, humility), self-control (self-restraint, continence). Galatians 5:22-23 AMPC

Take yourself (no one else) through this checklist. Is the Holy Spirit (God) evident in me? If so, His presence in us will produce these things.

REMEMBER, THIS IS FOR YOU! DON'T THINK ABOUT WHAT OTHERS DO!

We say we are Christians (Christ followers), but what does our fruit say?

THE GOOD NEWS IS THAT HE IS FAITHFUL AND JUST TO FORGIVE US AND HE THROWS OUR SIN AS FAR AS THE EAST IS FROM THE WEST.
HIS MERCY IS NEW EVERY MORNING.

Produce the fruit of the Holy Spirit, let the evidence prove who you are.

~Pastor Rhonda Spencer

November 4

Why are you so NEGATIVE?

Have you ever noticed that some people, maybe even ourselves, can be so negative?
The moment something happens, the first thought is........
That first thought is actually a measuring stick for your faith and trust in God.
Is the first thought, "This is horrible and there is no hope", or is your first thought, "This is horrible, but God is able to get me through, and over the top"?
How you think allows faith to rise, or faith to be stripped away from your life.
What can worry do for you? How will it help to allow NEGATIVE thoughts to flood and overtake you? Is there even one answer, or accomplishment provided when we allow worry and stress to control our lives?
Matthew 6:25-27, "That is why I tell you not to worry about everyday life—whether you have enough food and drink, or enough clothes to wear. Isn't life more than food, and your body more than clothing? Look at the birds. They don't plant or harvest or store food in barns, for your heavenly Father feeds them. And aren't you far more valuable to him than they are? Can all your worries add a single moment to your life?
STOP! ARREST YOUR THOUGHTS!
PRAY! PRAYER MOVES GOD, NOT WORRY OR STRESS!
1 Peter 5:7, Give all your worries and cares to God, for he cares about you.
Matthew 17:20, "You don't have enough faith," Jesus told them. "I tell you the truth, if you had faith even as small as a mustard seed, you could say to this mountain, 'Move from here to there,' and it would move. Nothing would be impossible."
ARREST YOUR THOUGHTS, AIM YOUR FAITH, RECEIVE YOUR ANSWER!
Worrying & thinking negative thoughts accomplish NOTHING but death.

~Dr Micheal Spencer

November 5

BLOODSHED

It makes for a good guy movie...

Just think of Him Who endured from sinners such grievous opposition and bitter hostility against Himself [reckon up and consider it all in comparison with your trials], so that you may not grow weary or exhausted, losing heart and relaxing and fainting in your minds. You have not yet struggled and fought agonizingly against sin, nor have you yet resisted and withstood to the point of pouring out your [own] blood.
Hebrews 12:3-4 AMPC

Compare your toughest struggle to this verse.
Have you had to shed blood to endure?

Think about those who have gone before us, and even today, whose very lives are on the line for serving Jesus, and use that as inspiration.

You, too, can go farther and keep pressing on without losing heart.

~Pastor Rhonda Spencer

November 6

What to do with PROPHECY

I Thessalonians 5:20, Do not despise prophecies.
Prophecy is very important to our lives. It is God speaking to us through a man or a woman.
In the Old Testament prophecy held a different place than in the New Testament. In the Old Testament the people could not hear the voice of God for themselves, so they had to rely upon prophecy to get direction. It is important to realize that ,in the Old Testament, they did not have the Holy Spirit living inside of them, and they did not have the right to have a personal relationship with God like we do today.
Since Jesus died on the cross, and the curtain in the Holy of Holies was torn in two (Matthew 27:51), we now have access into the most holy place to meet with our God through the blood of Jesus (Hebrews 4:16).
NOW, TODAY, prophecy takes a different place in a believer. We are not led by prophecy, we are led by the Holy Spirit. Romans 8:14, For as many as are led by the Spirit of God, these are sons of God.
Prophecy is EXTREMELY important for confirming what the Holy Spirit has already directed you to do. It is God speaking and telling you that you are hearing correctly. Whew, I like that!
What if someone prophesies something that I have never heard before? Great question! I call it the "back pocket theory." What that means is, if someone speaks over your life and you have never heard it, put it in your back pocket and do not throw it away. If it is the leading of the Lord then it will come to fruition. No worries, rest assured, God's words to us will always come true.
One time ,three prophesies were spoken within one week about His Tabernacle (our church). We started speaking what the Lord spoke and confirmed. We declared it, thanked Jesus for it, and prepared for what the Lord had spoken through the prophetic words! Do not let them die, speak them out loud and call them into existence. It is exciting to watch the Father speak, and then unfold His desires for our lives individually, and corporately.
ONE LAST NOTE....prophecy always lines up with the written Word of God, it will NEVER contradict!

~Dr Micheal Spencer

November 7

You Do Not Have That LUXURY!

IF QUITTING IS ACTUALLY AN OPTION, THEN YOU DO NOT EVEN HAVE THE LUXURY OF THINKING ABOUT IT!

Ephesians 6:13-14a, Therefore take up the whole armor of God, that you may be able to withstand in the evil day, and having done all, to stand. Stand therefore...

Quitting, running is NEVER, (or should NEVER be) an option. The moment you begin running you very rarely will ever stop. People run all the time, they run from their emotions, situations, jobs, marriage, ministry, love...... The list does not cease!

You must determine in your heart and mind that you will never QUIT!

QUITTING OR RUNNING IS NEVER AN OPTION! Until you make that decision, when a difficult season comes in your life, you will run, quit, give up, move on, look somewhere else.

The devil looks for this weakness. What do I mean by that? Satan does not know the future, but he knows our past. He knows what, and where our breaking point is, and when he sees us becoming dangerous for the Lord, he will start pushing you to that point of GIVING UP. If he can get you to surrender, bow, to your situation, he knows you will never really, ever, be a serious problem because he knows he can make you QUIT.

DETERMINE IN YOUR HEART!
MAKE A DECISION!
QUITTING IS NEVER AN OPTION!

I might fall, but I am getting back up! Falling is not failing. Falling, and not getting back up again, is failure.

GET UP, STAND FIRM, AND AFTER YOU HAVE DONE ALL TO STAND, STAND THEREFORE!

~Dr Micheal Spencer

November 8

Thoughts of Quitting

Yesterday we talked about how the **ONLY PEOPLE WHO HAVE THE LUXURY TO THINK ABOUT QUITTING ARE THOSE WHO NEVER WILL.**

So what about the rest of the population?

Learning to own our thoughts, rather than our thoughts owning us is an important skill. I have heard people say, "I cannot control what I am thinking." I would say without any reservation that is not true!

2 Corinthians 10:5, We destroy every proud obstacle that keeps people from knowing God. We capture their rebellious thoughts and teach them to obey Christ.

We will either control our thoughts, or they will control US.

When discouragement comes, hard times hit, expectations are shorted and hearts are hurt, the natural reaction is to shrink back and lick our wounds. There is a time for that, but that time must be shortened, or we will allow the wound to create fear in our minds and thoughts, which will then cause the reaction of giving up.

Psalm 34:18, The Lord is close to the brokenhearted; he rescues those whose spirits are crushed.

Here is what you do when the feelings and emotions of quitting come to your thoughts.

1) 1 Peter 5:7, Give all your worries and cares to God, for he cares about you.

2) Ask for the wisdom in how to fix it. James 1:5, If you need wisdom, ask our generous God, and he will give it to you. He will not rebuke you for asking.

3) Tell your mind to come into subjection, and start thinking the Word, and not your problem. This is not avoidance, this is focusing on the One who has the answer, and knows the future.

4) Start to worship; thanking Jesus that He is working on your behalf! Philippians 4:6-9, Don't worry about anything; instead, pray about everything. Tell God what you need, and thank him for all he has done. Then you will experience God's peace, which exceeds anything we can understand. His peace will guard your hearts and minds as you live in Christ Jesus. And now, dear brothers and sisters, one final thing. Fix your thoughts on what is true, and honorable, and right, and pure, and lovely, and admirable. Think about things that are excellent and worthy of praise. Keep putting into practice all you learned and received from me—everything you heard from me and saw me doing. Then the God of peace will be with you.

QUITTING CAN ONLY HAPPEN WHEN WE TAKE OUR EYES OFF OF JESUS, AND PUT THEM ON THE SITUATION!

STOP ALLOWING YOUR SITUATIONS & CIRCUMSTANCES TO CONTROL YOU!

YOU CONTROL YOUR MIND, WHICH AFFECTS YOUR EMOTIONS, WHICH DETERMINES YOUR OUTWARD ACTION!

~Dr Micheal Spencer

November 9

I BELIEVE. I BELIEVE. I BELIEVE.
NOTHING IS IMPOSSIBLE WITH GOD!

Yea, though I walk through the valley of the shadow of death, I will fear no evil; For You are with me; Your rod and Your staff, they comfort me. Psalm 23:4 NKJV

When you pass through the waters, I will be with you;
And through the rivers, they shall not overflow you.
When you walk through the fire, you shall not be burned, Nor shall the flame scorch you. Isaiah 43:2 NKJV

I believe if you go into the lion's den,
YOU WILL NOT BE EATEN.
I believe if you have to cross the Red Sea, THE WATERS WILL OPEN UP AND YOU CAN WALK ON DRY LAND.
I believe if you get thrown in the fiery furnace,
YOU WILL COME OUT UNBURNED,
NOT EVEN SMELLING LIKE SMOKE.
I believe NO DEADLY THING SHALL HARM YOU!

I see the mighty hand of God daily moving powerfully.

You may be sitting there saying, "I want to see that."
If we never believe and step out in faith, we will never see these things in our daily lives. WE NEED AN INCREASE OF FAITH IN THE FAMILY OF GOD!!!

HOW?
Romans 10:17 So then faith comes by hearing, and hearing by the word of God.

You increase your faith by increasing your hearing of the Word of God. Be willing and desirous to hear. Every day, get into the Word. Take every class you can. Every time the Word is taught, be present!

Get hungry for hearing the Word...More than just on Sunday. You want more faith, more of God, more miracles, more action, more boldness...it comes from hearing the Word!

~Pastor Rhonda Spencer

November 10

The Season is LIFE!

Life is so interesting!
So many HATE life, others strive to ESCAPE life, still others MEDICATE LIFE, and all because they cannot CONTROL life.
My heart cries out for those who are owned by some substance that shatters the opportunity to GROW & ENJOY TRUE LIFE!
John 10:10, The thief does not come except to steal, and to kill, and to destroy. I have come that they may have life, and that they may have it more abundantly.
Jesus did not come so we might just SURVIVE, but so we would have LIFE, and life MORE ABUNDANTLY!
BUT
"You do not understand how bad my life is!"
I might not understand your life in detail, but I know One who does, and He is the One who promised ABUNDANT life (Hebrews 4:15).
Today, start enjoying the seasons! Yes, there are times when it will feel like someone punched your lights out, but, GET UP! Failure is not falling. Failure is not getting back on your feet and moving forward. Failure is turning to substances to medicate (drugs, booze, sex....) so you stop experiencing life.
ABUNDANT LIFE DOES NOT MEAN HARDSHIP WILL NOT BE A PART OF OUR LIVES, IT MEANS WE ARE MORE THAN CONQUERERS, AND WE ARE GOING OVER THE TOP!
Today, stop whining about your life, your environment or your surroundings. Instead, listen for the birds singing, look at the flowers pushing through the ground or the half moon in the sky.
LIFE WILL MOVE ON WITHOUT YOU, OR, YOU CAN MOVE LIFE TO ABUNDANCE!

~Dr Micheal Spencer

November 11

Be careful little mouth what you say!

The words of our mouths are logged in the heavens.
I call it
GOD ABUSE: Verbal slaying of ones character & nature by the words that are spoken.
What we speak is what we believe.
Job was only restored when he repented of the things he spoke against the Father in chapter 42.
We see the same principle here in Malachi 3:13-18 MSG
God says, "You have spoken hard, rude words to me [] "When you said, 'It doesn't pay to serve God. What do we ever get out of it? When we did what he said & went around with long faces, serious about God-of-the-Angel-Armies, what difference did it make? Those who take life into their own hands are the lucky ones. They break all the rules & get ahead anyway. They push God to the limit and get by with it.'" Then those whose lives honored God got together & talked it over. God saw what they were doing and listened in. A book was opened in God's presence & minutes were taken of the meeting, with the names of the God-fearers written down, all the names of those who honored God's name. God-of-the-Angel-Armies said, "They're mine, all mine. They'll get special treatment when I go into action. I treat them with the same consideration & kindness that parents give the child who honors them. Once more you'll see the difference it makes between being a person who does the right thing & one who doesn't, between serving God & not serving him.

Watch your mouth, guard your lips, and speak life and not death to your life & blessing.
Maybe today you need to repent & make it right with the Father.

~Dr Micheal Spencer

November 12

Is There Any Greater Compliment?

Matthew 25:23
His lord said to him, 'Well done, good and faithful servant; you have been faithful over a few things, I will make you ruler over many things. Enter into the joy of your lord. '

Today we are celebrating the life a great woman of God. Her name is Paulette Mayes. The name does not define the person, the person defines the name! Faithful, caring, loving, consistent are the very nature and character of her friend and Savior Jesus, and these attributes can also describe Paulette. Never preached behind a pulpit, most of her labor for the kingdom was quiet and never seen by others, yet she defined her Jesus through her example.
Is there a greater compliment than for others who actually know you to define you with the attributes of the Master? I say not!
Thank you Jesus for having her invest into your people. Many children are serving Christ, and many adults have been invested into, now it's time to sit at His feet, drink from the cup in His hand, no longer seeing dimly, He is clear.

What will your testimony be after you take your last breath? How will you define your name? We only get one shot while on this planet. Live it strong.

Revelation 12:11
And they overcame him by the blood of the Lamb and by the word of their testimony, and they did not love their lives to the death.

~Dr Micheal Spencer & Pastor Rhonda Spencer

November 13

What's in your Piggy Bank?

Luke 6:45, A good man out of the good treasure of his heart brings forth good; and an evil man out of the evil treasure of his heart brings forth evil. For out of the abundance of the heart his mouth speaks

It is a strange reality when you actually have studied the Word, and come to the understanding how powerful our words are when we speak them!

Proverbs 18:21, Death and life are in the power of the tongue,And those who love it will eat its fruit.

THOUGHTS DETERMINE OUR WORDS!
Our hearts hold as a bank what we actually believe, and what we deposit, is what is held in the bank.
If you deposit the Word of God, when you go to withdraw, the Word of God will come out.
If you deposit the world's mindset, or the fleshly mindset, then when you speak there is only one thing to withdraw, the world and flesh!
There is only one sure foundation!
It is not religion.
It is not a church.
It is not a minister.
It is the Word of God – it is our
ONLY SURE FOUNDATION.

What are you depositing?
Have you been in the Word today?
Talk with Jesus today, He is waiting to talk with you.

~Dr Micheal Spencer

November 14

Is it always about you? CONSIDER OTHERS
Let Each Esteem Others Better Than Himself

"Let nothing be done through selfish ambition or conceit, but in lowliness of mind **let each esteem others better than himself.** Let each of you look out not only for his own interests, but also for the interests of others." Philippians 2:3,4
"For whoever exalts himself will be humbled, and he who humbles himself will be exalted." Luke 14:11
"For where envy and self-seeking exist, confusion and every evil thing are there." James 3:16
"Love suffers long and is kind; love does not envy; love does not parade itself, is not puffed up; does not behave rudely, does not seek its own, is not provoked, thinks no evil." 1 Corinthians 13:4,5
"But I say to you who hear: Love your enemies, do good to those who hate you, bless those who curse you, and pray for those who spitefully use you. To him who strikes you on the one cheek, offer the other also. And from him who takes away your cloak, do not withhold your tunic either."(Luke 6:27-29)

**Whoever Compels You to Go One Mile,
Go With Him Two**

"And whoever compels you to go one mile, go with him two. Give to him who asks you, and from him who wants to borrow from you do not turn away." Matthew 5:41,42
"...Your Father in heaven ... makes His sun rise on the evil and on the good, and sends rain on the just and on the unjust. For if you love those who love you, what reward have you? Do not even the tax collectors do the same?" Matthew 5:45,46

Behave Like a Christian

Let love be without hypocrisy. Abhor what is evil. Cling to what is good. Be kindly affectionate to one another with brotherly love, in honor giving preference to one another; not lagging in diligence, fervent in spirit, serving the Lord; Romans 12:9-11

~Dr Micheal Spencer & Pastor Rhonda Spencer

November 15

Is it always about you? CONSIDER OTHERS Part 2

Behave Like a Christian

"Bless those who persecute you; bless and do not curse. Rejoice with those who rejoice, and weep with those who weep. Be of the same mind toward one another. Do not set your mind on high things, but associate with the humble. Do not be wise in your own opinion. Repay no one evil for evil. Have regard for good things in the sight of all men. If it is possible, as much as depends on you, live peaceably with all men. Beloved, do not avenge yourselves, but rather give place to wrath; for it is written, 'Vengeance is Mine, I will repay,' says the Lord.

Therefore 'If your enemy is hungry, feed him; If he is thirsty, give him a drink; For in so doing you will heap coals of fire on his head.' Do not be overcome by evil, but overcome evil with good." Romans 12:14-21

Even the Son of Man Did Not Come to Be Served

"Let this mind be in you which was also in Christ Jesus, who, being in the form of God, did not consider it robbery to be equal with God, but made Himself of no reputation, taking the form of a bond-servant, and coming in the likeness of men. And being found in appearance as a man, He humbled Himself and became obedient to the point of death, even the death of the cross. Therefore God also has highly exalted Him and given Him the name which is above every name."Philippians 2:5-9

"For even the Son of Man did not come to be served, but to serve, and to give His life a ransom for many." Mark 10:45

Christ Our Pattern

I speak not by commandment, but I am testing the sincerity of your love by the diligence of others. For you know the grace of our Lord Jesus Christ, that though He was rich, yet for your sakes He became poor, that you through His poverty might become rich. And in this I give advice: It is to your advantage not only to be doing what you began and were desiring to do a year ago; but now you also must complete the doing of it; that as there was a readiness to desire it, so there also may be a completion out of what you have. For if there is first a willing mind, it is accepted according to what one has, and not according to what he does not have. For I do not mean that others should be eased and you burdened; but by an equality, that now at this time your abundance may supply their lack, that their abundance also may supply your lack—that there may be equality. As it is written, "He who gathered much had nothing left over, and he who gathered little had no lack." 2 Corinthians 8:8-15

~Pastor Rhonda Spencer

November 16

Is it always about you? CONSIDER OTHERS Part 3

Christ Our Pattern
Let no one seek his own, but each one the other's well-being. 1 Corinthians 10:24
Give, and it will be given to you: good measure, pressed down, shaken together, and running over will be put into your bosom. For with the same measure that you use, it will be measured back to you." Luke 6:38
Take Up the Cross and Follow Him
When He had called the people to Himself, with His disciples also, He said to them, "Whoever desires to come after Me, let him deny himself, and take up his cross, and follow Me. For whoever desires to save his life will lose it, but whoever loses his life for My sake and the gospel's will save it. Mark 8:34-35
Don't be stuck-up and think you're better than everyone else. Proverbs 30:13 MSG

This "considering" is definitely doable! It doesn't require our personal opinions or estimation of "others." Consider kings for instance. Whether noble or ignoble, protocol requires kings be treated as kings.
To non-believers this seems absurd, but for disciples it is doable, even in considering the unGodly.

Just as Jesus tells us to "love" our enemies with His divine "Agape" love, Paul is exhorting us to be humble ourselves, and to esteem God's opinion of "others," whom He no doubt sees more value in than we may be seeing in them at the moment. To Jesus, they are worth dying for. He's not saying we are not important. But we appreciate His estimation of these "others." Then, as we practice showing this preferential "Agape" love to others, we will find we can do so even to those we find difficult to love. If we'll practice considering them more than we focus consideration on our selves, blessings will follow.

If we persevere in this, we'll also wind up liking a lot more people than we expect.

~Pastor Rhonda Spencer

November 17

Who's house do you dwell in?

Behave Like a Christian

At night we lay our heads down in our home, with our bed, and our pillow. We get up in the morning and shower in our bathroom,and eat our food out of our refrigerator. Our home has been tailored to our family.

Ephesians 2:19
19 Now, therefore, you are no longer strangers and foreigners, but fellow citizens with the saints and members of the household of God.

Just a reminder not to get to homey here on this earth because we are part of the household of our Daddy in heaven. This world and it's worldly system is not what directs, teaches, feeds, clothes or comforts us. We are on work assignment!

~Dr Micheal Spencer

November 18

YOU are NOT GOD! Part I

The wisest, and most cunning tactic of the devil in this process of dislocating us from our mission as individuals, and as a local church, is to get us to be a Christ-less Christianity.
- It is to get us to where we no longer need God, except to get to heaven.
- We run our own lives, we handle our own problems, we handle our own finances and we handle our own purpose. We do not need God except to get to heaven.

Genesis 1:26-28 Then God said, "Let Us make man in Our image, according to Our likeness; let them have dominion over the fish of the sea, over the birds of the air, and over the cattle, over all the earth and over every creeping thing that creeps on the earth." So God created man in His own image; in the image of God He created him; male and female He created them. Then God blessed them, and God said to them, "Be fruitful and multiply; fill the earth and subdue it; have dominion over the fish of the sea, over the birds of the air, and over every living thing that moves on the earth.

AN ACT OF TREASON: The greatest crime that can be committed in any nation is the act of treason.
o It is the ultimate act of betrayal.
o It carries a penalty of death.
o The fall of man was not just a personal act of disobedience, but was essentially an act of treason.

~Dr Micheal Spencer

November 19

YOU are NOT GOD! Part 2

AN ACT OF TREASON:

• How was what Adam did considered an act of treason?

• The act of disobedience that Adam and Eve both exercised, was that of declaring independence from the Kingdom of God.

• Through the act of independence he severed, not only his dominion as a representative of the Kingdom of God, but also his relationship with the Holy Spirit. "Adam became an ambassador without portfolio, an envoy without official status, a citizen without a country, a king without a kingdom, a ruler without a dominion." Munroe

INDEPENDENCE – Freedom from control; self-sufficiency; self governed; self-ruled; self determined. Many Christians base their dependence on God only through their salvation, (that means Jesus as their Savior) but God desires also to be their Lord.

He desires to be YOUR Lord.

Proverbs 3:5-6 "Trust in the Lord with all of your heart and lean not unto your own understanding in all your ways acknowledge him and he will direct your path"

Hebrews 12:2 "...looking unto Jesus, the author and finisher of our faith..."

Colossians 3:1-2 "If then you were raised with Christ, seek those things which are above, where Christ is sitting at the right hand of God. First you set your mind on things above, not on things on the earth."

We are not called to be our own god!
There is only ONE! He leads, we follow.

~Dr Micheal Spencer

November 20

Nothing's Happening?!?!?!

Spending time with Jesus, and in the Word, may appear to be doing nothing, but actually you are participating in battles that are going on in spiritual realms. You are waging war - not with weapons of the world, but with heavenly weapons which have divine power to demolish strongholds. YOU ARE CLEARING THE GROUND OF EVERY OBSTRUCTION AND BUILDING LIVES OF OBEDIENCE INTO MATURITY!!!

What you cannot see is more real than what you can see.

The world is unprincipled. It's dog-eat-dog out there. The world doesn't fight fair. But we don't live or fight our battles that way - never have and never will. The tools of our trade aren't for marketing or manipulation, they are for demolishing that entire, massively corrupt culture. We use our powerful God-tools for smashing warped philosophies, tearing down barriers erected against the truth of God and for fitting every loose thought, emotion and impulse into the structure of life shaped by Christ. Our tools are ready at-hand for CLEARING THE GROUND OF EVERY OBSTRUCTION AND BUILDING LIVES OF OBEDIENCE INTO MATURITY.
(2 Corinthians 10:3-6 MSG)

~Pastor Rhonda Spencer

November 21

We are called the LIGHT of the world!

We are the ones that shine Jesus Christ through the LIGHT of His life living through us, or we are the dim lighthouse that allows ships to crash on the rocks without warning because they could not see the LIGHT clearly.

Matthew 5:16 NKJV, Let your light so shine before men, that they may see your good works and glorify your Father in heaven.

Matthew 5:14-16 MSG, Here's another way to put it: You're here to be light, bringing out the God-colors in the world. God is not a secret to be kept. We're going public with this, as public as a city on a hill. If I make you light-bearers, you don't think I'm going to hide you under a bucket, do you? I'm putting you on a light stand. Now that I've put you there on a hilltop, on a light stand—shine! Keep open house; be generous with your lives. By opening up to others, you'll prompt people to open up with God, this generous Father in heaven.

IF THE CHURCH IS DIM, then those in darkness will despise the LIGHT. They will not just not be interested in Jesus because the church is dim, but they will despise the message of Jesus. When those who say they believe do not live the TRUTH then those watching are disgusted by the message knowing it is false, because the lights are dim.

THE MORE YOU PLAY WITH DARKNESS, THE DIMMER YOU BECOME, AND THE LESS YOU CAN SEE. THEN YOU, TOO, ARE SWALLOWED UP IN THE DARKNESS – BLINDED AGAIN!

Come on Christian! Stop playing in the darkness! Stop thinking that you can live and play in darkness and that the LIGHT is still shining.

DO NOT BECOME BLIND AGAIN!

OTHERS NEED THE LIGHT TO SEE THEIR WAY OUT OF DARKNESS AND YOU ARE THE ONLY LIGHTHOUSE THEY MAY EVER SEE.

~Dr Micheal Spencer

November 22

I CAN DO WHATEVER I WANT

It is strange that we expect the favor and blessing of God, but still want to live OUR life, and do OUR thing. Blessings come out of OBEDIENCE.

YOU ARE LIVING FROM THE SEEDS OF WORDS AND ACTIONS YOU ALREADY PLANTED.

"Do not be deceived: God is not mocked, for whatever one sows, that will he also reap. For the one who sows to his own flesh will from the flesh reap corruption, but the one who sows to the Spirit will from the Spirit reap eternal life. And let us not grow weary of doing good, for in due season we will reap, if we do not give up".
-Galatians 6:7-9

So, yes, you can do what you want;
but is that *really* what you want?

~Pastor Rhonda Spencer

November 23

LEAVE NO ROOM

Ephesians 4:27AMP Leave no [such] room or foothold for the devil [give no opportunity to him].

Proverbs 4:23 Keep your heart with all diligence, For out of it spring the issues of life.

Psalm 119:101 I have restrained my feet from every evil way, That I may keep Your word.

Proverbs 22:3 A prudent man foresees evil and hides himself, But the simple pass on and are punished.

1 Peter 5:8 Be sober, be vigilant; because your adversary the devil walks about like a roaring lion, seeking whom he may devour.
2 Timothy 4:5 But you be watchful in all things...

Remember the saying "if you give him an inch; he'll take a mile"? This is true of the one who desires to steal, kill and destroy you. If you leave even a little crack; he's in and he's reeking havoc!!!

LEAVE NO ROOM FOR HIM. Serve him an eviction notice in any areas he has crept in. He does NOT stay to just that area, he makes himself at home.

~Pastor Rhonda Spencer

November 24

The BEMA SEAT of Judgment Part 1

We have all heard people say, "Don't judge me"
The truth is, someday we will all be judged. We will all have to give an account.
If you have accepted Jesus as your Savior, and your sins are washed away, then you will go before the Bema Seat (Judgment Seat) and be judged for your words and your works.
If you do not know Jesus as your Savior you will go before the White Throne Judgment and because your name is not written in the Book of Life, you will be cast into the Lake of Fire.
2 Corinthians. 5:10, For we must all appear before the judgment seat of Christ, that each one may receive the things done in the body, according to what he has done, whether good or bad.

So let's make sure that everyone understands CLEARLY.
If you have accepted Jesus, and are living for Him, then you will be judged at the Judgment Seat (BEMA) of Christ, but not for your sins because they have already been forgiven. If you are at this judgment then you are 100% going to heaven.
If you have not accepted Jesus, and you are not living for Him, then you will be at the White Throne judgment. You will be judged for refusing the sacrifice for your sins, and your name will not be written in the Book of Life. If you are at this judgment you are 100% going to be thrown in the Lake of Fire, and there will be no second opportunity.

NOW THAT WE HAVE THESE TWO CLEAR – Which one are you going to if, at this very moment, the trumpet of God sounds or you draw your last breath?

~Dr Micheal Spencer

November 25

The BEMA SEAT of Judgment Part 2

THIS IS HOW IT WILL HAPPEN:
The Trumpet of God will sound, the dead in Christ will rise first, then we who are alive and remain shall be caught up in the air. 1 Thessalonians 4:16-18
It is called the RAPTURE OF THE CHURCH.
Before we get to heaven, we will be judged.
We will not be judged in heaven, but in the "air".
There are no tears in heaven. There will be tears and regret when we are judged, so it cannot happen in heaven.
Jesus will be the judge over the Christians.
John 5:22, For the Father judges no one, but has committed all judgment to the Son,
Who is judged?
Only the blood washed Christian will be at this judgment.
What are you judged for?
As a Christian your sins are washed away, therefore, you cannot be judged for them. The One that is judging you, is the One who took all your sins upon His body.
So, if we are not judged for our sins, what *are* we judged for?
JUDGED FOR THE THINGS DONE IN THE BODY, or, what you've done here on earth while serving HIM.
We will not be judged in mass, but as an individuals.
He will take each person, and reveal to them personally.

1. What they did do (good, or bad – bad not meaning sin, but worthless).
2. What they could have done.
3. Their words – were they life or death?

We will stand before Jesus, who knows all our motivations, desires, and thoughts. He will take our works and test them for worth. Why we did them....
1 Corinthians 3:11-15, For no other foundation can anyone lay than that which is laid, which is Jesus Christ. Now if anyone builds on this foundation with gold, silver, precious stones, wood, hay, straw, each one's work will become clear; for the Day will declare it, because it will be revealed by fire; and the fire will test each one's work, of what sort it is. If anyone's work which he has built on it endures, he will receive a reward. If anyone's work is burned, he will suffer loss; but he himself will be saved, yet so as through fire.

~Dr Micheal Spencer

November 26

Rewards of The BEMA SEAT

2 Corinthians. 5:10 For we must all appear before the judgment seat of Christ, that each one may receive the things done in the body, according to what he has done, whether good or bad.
Matthew6:18-20 "Do not lay up for yourselves treasures on earth, where moth and rust destroy and where thieves break in and steal; 20 but lay up for yourselves treasures in heaven, where neither moth nor rust destroys and where thieves do not break in and steal.
The exciting part of the Bema Seat (Judgment Seat) of Christ is that we will be able to show Jesus how much we love Him through our passion to please Him.
The works we will be judged for are not to be done out of fear, but out of LOVE. Because we love Him, we desire to please Him. Because we love Jesus, we desire to do His will.
That is what Jesus did with Father, and that is why we do what we do for Him.
There are crowns to be earned. The crowns that will be given at the Bema Seat are earned crowns. The Greek word for the crowns is stephonos, they are the crowns earned in the Grecian time when they would run a race and win.
Paul said that he ran the race to win!
2 Timothy 4:7, I have fought the good fight, I have finished the race, I have kept the faith.
Crowns will be given to those whose works come through the fire; that are done with the right heart and not the wrong motivations.
Crown of Rejoicing – this is for the soul winners (1 Thessalonians 2:19)
Crown of Life – those who endure trials (James 1:12)
Incorruptible crown – for those who mastered their flesh (1 Corinthians 9:25)
Crown of Righteousness – those who love His appearing (2 Timothy 4:8)
Crown of Glory – those who feed the saints (1 Peter 5:4)
Revelation 4:10a, the twenty-four elders fall down before Him who sits on the throne and worship Him who lives forever and ever, and cast their crowns before the throne..
STORE UP YOUR TREASURE IN HEAVEN, NOT ON THIS PASSING, TEMPORARY EARTH.

~Dr Micheal Spencer

November 27

WHITE THRONE JUDGMENT

There are two judgments:

1. **Bema** – for the Christian, they will not be judged for their sin, but for their words and works. If you are at this judgment you are going to heaven.

2. **White Throne** – This is for the sinners, those who chose to reject the blood of Jesus. If you are at this judgment you are going to the Lake of Fire.

Revelation 20:11-15 Then I saw a great white throne and Him who sat on it, from whose face the earth and the heaven fled away. And there was found no place for them. And I saw the dead, small and great, standing before God, and books were opened. And another book was opened, which is the Book of Life. And the dead were judged according to their works, by the things which were written in the books. The sea gave up the dead who were in it, and Death and Hades delivered up the dead who were in them. And they were judged, each one according to his works. Then Death and Hades were cast into the lake of fire. This is the second death. And anyone not found written in the Book of Life was cast into the lake of fire.

THIS IS HOW IT WILL HAPPEN

John saw that those who were in hell.

The rich, The poor, The nationalities, The young, The old: All who never accepted Jesus, or those who rejected Christ will be at this judgment. Christians will NOT be at this judgment (they were judged at the Bema Seat).

Individually they are judged.

As the individual stands before the RIGHTEOUS JUDGE.

Two books: Book of Works / Book of Life

1.The sinner will be judged out of the book of works.

2.Their name will not be written in the book of life.

They will be cast into the Lake of Fire – the second death.

Hell has some reprieve – it vomited up to have the sinner stand in the presence of God one last time.

The Lake of Fire has NO REPRIEVE – eternal, never ending, constant.

LOVE SOMEONE ENOUGH TODAY TO SHARE JESUS WITH THEM – SNATCH THEM FROM SATAN'S HANDS!!

~Dr Micheal Spencer

November 28

23 Minutes in Eternity Part I

We been discussing the 2 judgments.
The Bema Seat (Judgment Seat) is for the Christians – you will not be judged for your sin (Jesus washed them away), but you will be judged for your words & works.
The White Throne Judgment is for the sinners – at this judgment the sinner's life will be read from the Book. It will show choices of the rejection of the blood of Jesus. The individual's name will not be written in the Book of Life, and they will be cast into the Lake of Fire.
Just a reminder, Hell is the holding tank for the sinners until this judgment.
Here is a description from a man who had a vision of hell (Bill Weise).
1. The Cell that he was dropped into in the vision was
15 ft high / 10 ft wide / 15 ft. deep
2. Proverbs 7:27 – "Chambers of death in hell"
3. He had the same looking body as on earth,
yet he felt extremely weak.
4. He realized that he was not alone in the cell, there were 2 demons and they were 10-13 ft tall. They smelled like rotten meat or decaying flesh, like sulfur, but intensified to the level of toxicity. He felt the hatred from these demons, and was paralyzed with fear and panic. Each demon had the likeness of a reptile, but with human form, and they were screaming blasphemous language against God and how much they hated Him.
5. They turned their attention toward him and he felt trapped, helpless, total fear, defenseless. He wanted to run but there was no strength to run. (Psalm 88:4 – I am counted with those who go down to the pit; I am like a man who has no strength.)
6. Two more demons came into the cell, and they all started tormenting him and throwing him into the walls. He was overwhelmed with the sense of physical pain and it would not go away! He wanted to die, but death is not an option. He pleaded for mercy, but there was no mercy.
7. He dragged himself out of the cell. The ground was bare, rock, no life, no green, just wasteland. The screams of massive amounts of tormented of people filled his ears; the screams of terror and pain, the stench of death, no escape, no death could be obtained.
THIS IS FOR ETERNITY!
~Dr Micheal Spencer

November 29

23 Minutes in Eternity Part 2

Bill looked to the left, and saw flames that were from a pit about 10 miles away! It was a RAGING INFERNO! The heat from this place left him parched, yet there was no way to quench his thirst (Luke 16:23). The air itself was so thin, gasping for the next breath was an exhausting task.
The pit of flames was becoming more visible, more describable. When he could understand what was happening, he could see the pit filled with people screaming, scratching to escape as their flesh literally was burning yet not being consumed. The fear never ceases! The pain is never relieved! There is NO peace! There is NO hope of freedom! There is NO rest!
The most painful thought that rushed through his mind was realizing he would NEVER see his wife again, and that he could not warn her about this dreadful, horrible, tormenting place. The thoughts of knowing you will never get out, you will never sleep, you will never have peace, you will never speak to another human; this is just you, being alone for the rest of eternity!
WHAT A HORRIBLE REALITY FOR PEOPLE WHO AT THIS MOMENT ARE IN THIS PLACE. THEY ARE STILL WAITING FOR THE FINAL JUDGMENT.

Please tell someone TODAY!!! Reality is NOT JUST 23 Minutes it is for all of ETERNITY.

At least tell them about Jesus, and His love for them. They will decide for themselves, but give them a chance........

~Dr Micheal Spencer

November 30

FLOP or FIXED

The Bema Seat, (Judgment Seat) of Christ.
This is the judgment for the Christian.
2 Corinthians 5:9-10, Therefore we make it our aim, whether present or absent, to be well pleasing to Him. For we must all appear before the judgment seat of Christ, that each one may receive the things done in the body, according to what he has done, whether good or bad.
One of the harsh realities of being a preacher is that many people like the Word when it is preached. After service you hear the, "wow Pastor, that was an awesome Word from the Lord," BUT, that is not what encourages a preacher of the Word. The Pastor is really excited when they see that the Word being preached is starting to be lived by the saints.
Today, right now, we are either allowing that Word to transform us or it is just another sermon preached by another preacher in a church.
Romans 12:1-2, I beseech you therefore, brethren, by the mercies of God, that you present your bodies a living sacrifice, holy, acceptable to God, which is your reasonable service. And do not be conformed to this world, but be transformed by the renewing of your mind, that you may prove what is that good and acceptable and perfect will of God.
TODAY! RIGHT NOW! APPLY THE WORD!
Do not allow the Word to be a FLOP, but allow it to FIX our hearts and minds on the will and purpose of Jesus.
ARE YOU LIVING LIKE TODAY COULD BE YOUR LAST? ARE YOU LIVING LIKE THE PERSON NEXT TO YOU COULD BE LIVING THEIR LAST DAY?
SHARE JESUS WITH SOMEONE TODAY!!!!

~Dr Micheal Spencer

December 1

You're Called to Champion!

God has not called you to run the race and lose; He has called you to be a champion!

1 Corinthians 9:24-27 Don't you realize that in a race everyone runs, but only one person gets the prize? So run to win! All athletes are disciplined in their training. They do it to win a prize that will fade away, but we do it for an eternal prize. So I run with purpose in every step. I am not just shadowboxing. I discipline my body like an athlete, training it to do what it should. Otherwise, I fear that after preaching to others I myself might be disqualified.

This is not a RAT race, unless you are a RAT!
This is a race to know and fulfill God's purposes for your life, and our life as a church.
Paul makes the declaration that we are to run this race to win, not just make it close to the end. We are running to achieve a prize, and not one made with hands. The world runs the rat race to obtain temporary things. They strive after money, fame, stuff, love and worth from others. But all that will come up short; not just in this life, but in the life to come.
We, the team of Jesus, are running the race to obtain the greatest thing: to hear our Father say "Well done my good and faithful servant."

So, which race are you in today?
What finish line is in front of you?
If you died today, what would be your prize?

~Dr Micheal Spencer

December 2

You CAN Hear God's Voice

Consider the following scriptures:

John 10:27 My sheep hear My voice and I know them. They follow Me.

John 14:26 But the Helper, the Holy Spirit, whom the Father will send in My name, He will teach you all things, and bring to your remembrance all things that I said to you.

John 16:13 However, when He, the Spirit of truth, has come, He will guide you into all truth; for He will not speak on His own authority, but whatever He hears He will speak; and He will tell you things to come.

Just imagine the Lord sitting in Heaven and thinking of you. Did you know He really does this?

Scripture is full of the Lord telling us He is thinking of us all the time.

Look at Psalm 139:17 NIV which says "How precious to me are your thoughts,God! How vast is the sum of them!"
Also consider Jeremiah 29:11 NIV which says "'For I know the plans ("thoughts" in the KJV) I have for you,' declares the Lord, 'plans to prosper you and not to harm you, plans to give you hope and a future.'"

Matthew 7:7 tells us to "ask and receive".
Revelation 3:20 says He is waiting to talk to us.

Become convinced **that you can hear His voice.**

~Pastor Rhonda Spencer

December 3

YOU Cannot Fail!

I have great news for you today!
No matter how difficult the situation you are going through,
No matter how bad it looks,
No matter what other people are saying,
You are not just going to make it – YOU CANNOT FAIL WITH JESUS ON YOUR SIDE!

Philippians 4:13, I can do all things through Christ who strengthens me.
Romans 8:31, What then shall we say to these things? If God is for us, who can be against us?
Romans 8:37, Yet in all these things we are more than conquerors through Him who loved us.

With Jesus on your side, how can you lose?
Luke 1:37, For with God nothing will be impossible.

Get your head up saint of God! You are already on the winning side! You have this thing. Do not hide in a corner, do not whimper or whine.
You are MORE THAN A CONQUEROR!
You are AN OVERCOMER!
You are VICTORIOUS!
Do not allow Satan to steal the TRUTH from you!
LIVE IN VICTORY TODAY!

Revelation 12:11, And they overcame him by the blood of the Lamb and by the word of their testimony, and they did not love their lives to the death.

~Dr Micheal Spencer

December 4

The Devil Is Under Your Feet

Have you felt at times like fear is gripping you? Have you felt like all hell is coming against you, and that you might not make it?

I have great news for you TODAY!
Ephesians 1:20-22 AMP Which He exerted in Christ when He raised Him from the dead and seated Him at His [own] right hand in the heavenly [places], Far above all rule and authority and power and dominion and every name that is named [above every title that can be conferred], not only in this age and in this world, but also in the age and the world which are to come. And He has put all things under His feet and has appointed Him the universal and supreme Head of the church [a headship exercised throughout the church],

JESUS HAS BEEN RAISED TO SUPREME VICTORY!!
Death is conquered.
Sin is conquered.
Satan is conquered.
Sickness is conquered.
Fear is conquered.
JESUS HAS COMPLETE VICTORY!
That means you do too.....
Yet amid all these things we are more than conquerors and gain a surpassing victory through Him Who loved us. Romans 8:37 AMP
You are MORE THAN A CONQUERER, not a survivor! TODAY REMIND THE DEVIL OF YOUR TRUE PLACE WITH CHRIST, and where Satan really is.... UNDER YOUR FEET!

~Dr Micheal Spencer

December 5

Healing Your BROKEN HEART

It does not matter if you are a muscle-bound man, or a petite little woman, we all have feelings, and they can get wounded. I have watched men that are beasts break down and cry like little boys when their hearts have been broken. I have also watched some petite little "Barbie" girls not break down but turn the other direction, and that is bitter.

We are all going to have hurts in our lives.

It was never the plan of God! God did not create us to have to experience rejection, betrayal and emotional wounds. But because of the fall of man, our innocence was lost and sin entered in. Since the fall of man our hearts can be harshly wounded. The great part is that God has a plan! He does not want us crushed by rejection, or demolished because of betrayal or loss. He wants us HEALED, WHOLE, and HEALTHY. Father has provided that for us through Jesus.

Isaiah 53:4-5 AMPC, Surely He has borne our griefs (sicknesses, weaknesses, and distresses) and carried our sorrows and pains [of punishment], yet we [ignorantly] considered Him stricken, smitten, and afflicted by God [as if with leprosy]. But He was wounded for our transgressions, He was bruised for our guilt and iniquities; the chastisement [needful to obtain] peace and well-being for us was upon Him, and with the stripes [that wounded] Him we are healed and made whole.

Jesus paid the price for your broken heart to be healed on the cross. The doctors cannot do surgery, the drugs will only mask and cover, but Jesus can heal you so it does not hurt again!

Psalm 34:18, The Lord is close to the brokenhearted; he rescues those whose spirits are crushed.

Psalm 147:3, He heals the brokenhearted And binds up their wounds.

Luke 4:18, "The Spirit of the Lord is upon Me, Because He has anointed Me To preach the gospel to the poor; He has sent Me to heal the brokenhearted, To proclaim liberty to the captives And recovery of sight to the blind, To set at liberty those who are oppressed; **OK! THIS IS WHAT WE DO NEXT!**

1) Tell Jesus what you are feeling inside. It is ok to cry, He is there listening and waiting to start the process of healing you. You must be honest!

2) Ask Him to start the healing process in your heart.

3) Say this out loud, "Jesus, I receive your healing in my heart, today I choose to be healed and not wounded."

4) Get ready, it has begun, you will start to see a change **already because you have invited the HEALER TO START HIS LOVING WORK IN YOUR LIFE!**

~Dr Micheal Spencer

December 6

It Takes Maturity to Encourage

Romans 15: 1-6 MSG
1-2 Those of us who are strong and able in the faith need to step in and lend a hand to those who falter, and not just do what is most convenient for us. Strength is for service, not status. Each one of us needs to look after the good of the people around us, asking ourselves, "How can I help?"
3-6That's exactly what Jesus did. He didn't make it easy for himself by avoiding people's troubles, but waded right in and helped out. "I took on the troubles of the troubled," is the way Scripture puts it. Even if it was written in Scripture long ago, you can be sure it's written for us. God wants the combination of his steady, constant calling and warm, personal counsel in Scripture to come to characterize us, keeping us alert for whatever he will do next. May our dependably steady and warmly personal God develop maturity in you so that you get along with each other as well as Jesus gets along with us all. Then we'll be a choir—not our voices only, but our very lives singing in harmony in a stunning anthem to the God and Father of our Master Jesus.

1 Thessalonians 5:14-15 NASB
We urge you, brethren, admonish the unruly, encourage the fainthearted, help the weak, be patient with everyone. See that no one repays another with evil for evil, but always seek after that which is good for one another and for all people.

If you claim to be strong and able in the faith, you will be characterized by your service to others. This is a true sign of maturity. No, you can't remain a baby forever. It's a disturbing picture to see an adult in diapers, drinking a bottle and crying.

Move up to maturity.

~Pastor Rhonda Spencer

December 7

INTENSE Love

Come on, we have all seen intense people! It is like their face is about to EXPLODE....lol.
I think we forget how much our Daddy loves us. I think, at times, the words just become words to our minds.
Today I want you to HEAR this verse about your Father, as it pertains to YOU!!
BEFORE YOU READ THIS, PRAY THIS OUT LOUD:
"Holy Spirit, please open the eyes of my understanding as I read the living Word today. Make this ALIVE to me, and reveal to me the INTENSE LOVE my Father has for me."

But God–so rich is He in His mercy! Because of and in order to satisfy the great and wonderful and intense love with which He loved us, Even when we were dead (slain) by [our own] shortcomings and trespasses, He made us alive together in fellowship and in union with Christ; [He gave us the very life of Christ Himself, the same new life with which He quickened Him, for] it is by grace (His favor and mercy which you did not deserve) that you are saved (delivered from judgment and made partakers of Christ's salvation). And He raised us up together with Him and made us sit down together [giving us joint seating with Him] in the heavenly sphere [by virtue of our being] in Christ Jesus (the Messiah, the Anointed One). He did this that He might clearly demonstrate through the ages to come the immeasurable (limitless, surpassing) riches of His free grace (His unmerited favor) in [His] kindness and goodness of heart toward us in Christ Jesus.
Ephesians 2:4-7 AMP

- Intense love.
- He made us alive in relationship.
- He raised us up to sit in heavenly places.
- His kindness, and goodness of heart toward YOU!

TODAY YOU ARE INTENSELY LOVED – RECEIVE HIS LOVE TODAY, THEN PASS IT ON!
And as you go, preach, saying, The kingdom of heaven is at hand! Cure the sick, raise the dead, cleanse the lepers, drive out demons. Freely (without pay) you have received, freely (without charge) give. (Matthew 10:7, 8 AMP)
~Dr Micheal Spencer

December 8

SCREAMS FROM ETERNITY!

2 Corinthians 4:18 while we do not look at the things which are seen, but at the things which are not seen. For the things which are seen are temporary, but the things which are not seen are eternal.
Luke 16:27, 28 AMP And [the man] said, "Then, father, I beseech you to send him to my father's house– For I have five brothers–so that he may give [solemn] testimony and warn them, lest they too come into this place of torment."
The church has forgotten that this is not a game, and that eternity is for keeps.
Satan is striving to keep the BODY of Jesus powerless, not by hurting us, but by keeping us so self-absorbed that we only meet the needs of ME, and not of Thee.
We forget the cries from the eternal!
"HELP ME........."
"PLEASE MOM, PLEASE DAD, SAVE ME...."
"Tell my babies they don't have to come here......"
"I WANT ANOTHER CHANCE, I'LL DO IT RIGHT THIS TIME....."
All those cries, screams, pleading are REAL, not fake!
WE HAVE THE ANSWER!
WE HAVE BEEN SENT WITH THE GOSPEL TO SAVE THEM.
Stop being so saturated with self. It is the plan and plot of Satan that they perish, and we never throw them a life vest.
ARISE CHURCH!!
And from the days of John the Baptist until the present time, the kingdom of heaven has endured violent assault, and violent men seize it by force [as a precious prize--a share in the heavenly kingdom is sought with most ardent zeal and intense exertion]. Matthew 11:12 AMP
WHO TODAY WILL JESUS SEND YOU TO SHARE HIS LOVE AND SALVATION WITH?
Pay attention!!

~Dr Micheal Spencer

December 9

The Letter From Hell Part I

John 11:25-26 Jesus said to her, " I am the resurrection and the life. He who believes in Me, though he may die, he shall live. And whoever lives and believes in Me shall never die. Do you believe this?"

Jesus is the only way to heaven, and when you receive Him as your Savior, you have activated your eternal salvation through His blood.

John 11:44 And he who had died came out bound hand and foot with graveclothes, and his face was wrapped with a cloth. Jesus said to them, " Loose him, and let him go."
Many Christians receive The Lord, but never take off the grave clothes.
"What do you mean?"
The grave clothes represented who they were (dead in their sins). The grave clothes reeked of death, sins that separated them from Christ. The grave clothes represented bondage, or the choice to live the old life before Christ.
Jesus said, "LOOSE HIM". That means that Jesus never planned for us to be saved, yet still live the old life.

2 Corinthians 6:17 Therefore "Come out from among them And be separate, says the Lord. Do not touch what is unclean, And I will receive you."
Today, shred your old sinful clothing. Decide that you refuse to live like the old you, because you are a new creation, new creature, new person, old things have passed away!!
BE THE TESTIMONY THIS WEEK THAT JESUS IS ALIVE – In YOU!!

~Dr Micheal Spencer

December 10

The Letter From Hell Part 2

John 11:25-26 Jesus said to her, "I am the resurrection and the life. He who believes in Me, though he may die, he shall live. And whoever lives and believes in Me shall never die. Do you believe this?" Jesus is the only way to heaven, and when you receive Him as your Savior, you have activated your eternal salvation through His blood.
John 11:44 And he who had died came out bound hand and foot with graveclothes, and his face was wrapped with a cloth. Jesus said to them, "Loose him, and let him go."

As Christians we have been called to do what Jesus did, and MORE!
John 14:12 "Most assuredly, I say to you, he who believes in Me, the works that I do he will do also; and greater works than these he will do, because I go to My Father.
We are called to loose people from the graveclothes by bringing them to the One who can set them free. We have the answer! We have what they need! We are the people who carry the truth that will make them free.
Jesus could have easily said, "Sorry I got here late, he is dead, so that is just the way it is."
NO!
Jesus called Lazarus from his grave.
THEN, they took off his GRAVECLOTHES.
Help someone today, be the answer today, share Jesus today!
DON'T LET YOUR FAMILY, FRIENDS, ENEMIES STAY IN THE GRAVE!
DON'T GET A LETTER FROM HELL SAYING YOU NEVER CARED ENOUGH TO TELL THEM.

~Dr Micheal Spencer

December 11

GRAVE TENDING

So don't you see that we don't owe this old do-it-yourself life one red cent. There's nothing in it for us, nothing at all. The best thing to do is give it a decent burial and get on with your new life. God's Spirit beckons. There are things to do and places to go!
This resurrection life you received from God is not a timid, grave-tending life. It's adventurously expectant, greeting God with a childlike "What's next, Papa?" God's Spirit touches our spirits and confirms who we are. Romans 8:12-17 MSG

There is nothing in that old life for you. Stop considering it, thinking about it and, for your sake, stop going back and visiting it! It's done nothing for you and you owe it nothing. Bury it and don't tend to its grave.

Get on with the new life and enjoy the adventure of supernatural life today.

~Pastor Rhonda Spencer

December 12

What Report Will You bring to Your Situations Today?

"There are giants in the land?" OR "We are well able?"
Caleb quieted the people before Moses, and said, Let us go up at once and possess it; WE ARE WELL ABLE TO CONQUER IT. But his fellow scouts said, We are not able to go up against the people [of Canaan], for they are stronger than we are. So they brought the Israelites an evil report of the land which they had scouted out, saying, The land through which we went to spy it out is a land that devours its inhabitants. And all the people that we saw in it are men of great stature. There we saw the Nephilim [or giants], the sons of Anak, who come from the giants; and we were in our own sight as grasshoppers, and so we were in their sight. Numbers 13:30-33 AMP
AND ALL the congregation cried out with a loud voice, and [they] wept that night. All the Israelites grumbled and deplored their situation, accusing Moses and Aaron, to whom the whole congregation said, Would that we had died in Egypt! Or that we had died in this wilderness! Why does the Lord bring us to this land to fall by the sword? Our wives and little ones will be a prey. Is it not better for us to return to Egypt? And they said one to another, Let us choose a captain and return to Egypt. Then Moses and Aaron fell on their faces before all the assembly of Israelites. And Joshua son of Nun and Caleb son of Jephunneh, who were among the scouts who had searched the land, rent their clothes, And they said to all the company of Israelites, The land through which we passed as scouts is an exceedingly good land. If the Lord delights in us, then He will bring us into this land and give it to us, a land flowing with milk and honey. Only do not rebel against the Lord, neither fear the people of the land, for they are bread for us. Their defense and the shadow [of protection] is removed from over them, but the Lord is with us. Fear them not. But all the congregation said to stone [Joshua and Caleb] with stones. But the glory of the Lord appeared at the Tent of Meeting before all the Israelites. And the Lord said to Moses, How long will this people provoke (spurn, despise) Me? And how long will it be before they believe Me [trusting in, relying on, clinging to Me], for all the signs which I have performed among them? Numbers 14:1-11 AMP

I SAY: WE ARE WELL ABLE!!!!!!

~Pastor Rhonda Spencer

December 13

FEELING DRY!

Sometimes in our walk with God we come to growth plates where we do not FEEL Him as much as we used to. We begin to question, "where is He?", or, "have I missed something?", or an even more dangerous thought: "this is not working for me".
If you have checked your life and it is in order, then you might be going through a growth plate.
What do you mean?
There comes a time in our spiritual growth that we learn to walk not as much by feelings, or sensations, but we learn to walk by faith. We learn that even if I do not FEEL something, I still know because the Word says it to be truth.
This is a growth plate in your maturity in Jesus.
Another growth plate you will come to is learn how to stir yourself up in the Spirit, and not having to rely on everyone else.
2 Timothy 1:6, Therefore I remind you to stir up the gift of God which is in you through the laying on of my hands.
1 Samuel 30:6 AMP David was greatly distressed, for the men spoke of stoning him because the souls of them all were bitterly grieved, each man for his sons and daughters. But David encouraged and strengthened himself in the Lord his God.
Timothy says to pray in tongues to stir yourself up, "but if I am not filled with the Spirit and speak with other tongues YET, what do I do?" Speak the Word, sing a worship song, start talking to Daddy.
Within each of these growth plates is the challenge of walking away from Jesus. We must determine that walking away or taking a break is not an option. I will go THROUGH, not around my schooling in the Spirit.
LET'S GROW TODAY IN OUR RELATIONSHIP WITH JESUS.

~Dr Micheal Spencer

December 14

HAVE YOU EVER BEEN TO THE PLACE WHERE YOU DO NOT KNOW WHAT TO DO?

You think that one option is the best and then another option comes into play. **WHICH WAY DO I GO?**
I remember when Jesus was teaching me this lesson. I was offered a church in Ohio and, WOW, it looked good! I was thinking it was God then another church called and wanted us to pastor them. Both churches looked good and I was confused because I did not know which one Jesus desired me to pastor.
WHAT DO YOU DO WHEN YOU DON'T KNOW WHAT TO DO? *STAND STILL*
I did nothing with both, except pray. When you are not sure, don't make any decisions.
I prayed and the Lord told me to take neither. When I explained it to the first church, they were not happy with me at all. I later found out that the second church had intense internal division and they eventually split.
I THANK YOU, JESUS, THAT I DID NOTHING UNTIL I HEARD FROM YOU!
In fact, if I had chosen either of those churches I would have never launched His Tabernacle Family Church.
So, how did I make the decisions?
WITH THE PEACE OF GOD.

Colossians 3:15 And let the peace that comes from Christ rule in your hearts.

Allow the peace of God to govern your heart. When there is no peace, then you do not move forward. When Jesus gives you peace, even if it doesn't look right, move forward.
BE GOVERNED BY THE PEACE OF GOD THAT DIRECTS YOUR LIFE!

WHAT DO YOU DO WHEN YOU DO NOT KNOW WHAT TO DO?
NOTHING WITHOUT PEACE IN YOUR HEART.

~Dr Micheal Spencer

December 15

WHAT? CHRIST DETHRONED?

You will not worship what you have dethroned.

We must get our eyes off the things of this world and SEEK CHRIST FIRST. Keeping our eyes fixed on the things of this world will dethrone God from His rightful place in our lives. Without even noticing it, we will no longer worship Him.

"So don't worry about these things, saying, 'What will we eat? What will we drink? What will we wear?' These things dominate the thoughts of unbelievers, but your heavenly Father already knows all your needs. Seek the Kingdom of God above all else, and live righteously, and he will give you everything you need." Matthew 6:31-33 NLT

WHATEVER WE PURSUE BECOMES OUR PURPOSE, what we live for, what drives us. Rather than taking the time and putting in the effort to SEEK CHRIST FIRST (who is so worthy of our praise and honor), we get distracted and chase the empty things of this world.

Put Christ back on the throne of your life, pursue Him, run after Him, focus on Him AND HE WILL GIVE YOU EVERYTHING YOU NEED!

~Pastor Rhonda Spencer

December 16

DOUBLE-MINDED

The word was coined by James – it means a person with 2 minds. Have you ever gone to a fast food place and the person in front of you cannot make up their mind what to order? They change their order 2 or 3 times before they finally decide, as the crowd behind them begins to grow. Driving down the road and the car in front of you starts off the ramp and then swerves back hard at you to get back on the highway. They're double-minded, undecided what their decision is going to be.

Double-minded people always head back to safety when trouble comes – they grasp for the control they used to possess.

If Abram was double-minded he would have headed back to his home town.

If Noah was double-minded he would have stopped building the ark.

If Joseph was double-minded he would have rotted in a foreign prison.

Daniel would have been lunch meat.

The 3 Hebrew boys would have burned.

If Jesus was double-minded then He would not have gotten on the cross.

If Lot's wife was double-mined....oh yea, she was, and she died.

If Adam and Eve were double-minded...oh yea, they were.

If Demas was double-minded... oh yea, he walked away.

We have the mind of Christ. (1 Corinthians 2:16)

If you are feeling UNSTABLE – it is because you have not decided that God's Word is premiere, and your foundation!

Until you decide and become single-minded your life will constantly be shifting according to CNN, FOX, gossip, even real life.

You must have a foundation, or you will never be stable.

FAITH IS OUR VICTORY –
THE WORD IS TRUE...PERIOD!

~Dr Micheal Spencer

December 17

YUM, THAT WAS GOOD

So many Christians are hungry for many other things other than Jesus.
Have you ever just craved a food so badly that nothing else hit the spot; BUT the moment this food hit your taste buds you said, “that is what I have been wanting all along”.
Jesus desires us to want Him that much.
The great part about that is you and I do not need to create that craving, we just need to ask Him to put it there. We have to ask, to receive, knock for it to be opened, seek, and we will find. We do have a part, but He creates that hunger when we make the step of faith.
Matthew 5:6 Blessed are those who hunger and thirst for righteousness, for they shall be filled.
God puts the hunger in the heart.
Psalms 42:1-2 As the deer pants for the water brooks, So pants my soul for You, O God. My soul thirsts for God, for the living God. When shall I come and appear before God?
2 Chronicles 7:14-16 If My people who are called by My name will humble themselves, and pray and seek My face, and turn from their wicked ways, then I will hear from heaven, and will forgive their sin and heal their land. Now My eyes will be open and My ears attentive to prayer made in this place. For now I have chosen and sanctified this house, that My name may be there forever; and My eyes and My heart will be there perpetually.
Ask Jesus now to put a fresh hunger in your heart for spending time with Him. He wants you more than you could ever desire Him. He is after you!!
There are a couple of books I would encourage you to purchase to fan the flame of your desire:
“The God Chaser” by Tommy Tinney and
“Crazy Love” by Francis Chan.
Feed and Grow!

~Dr Micheal Spencer

December 18

IT'S TOO HARD

Sometimes we hear in our own heads,
"YOU WILL NEVER MAKE IT" or "IT'S TOO HARD".

SHOUT IT OUT LOUD WITH ME THIS MORNING
"Devil, Mind, YOU ARE A LIAR
IN THE NAME OF JESUS, **SHUT UP!**"

I refuse to be discouraged.
Do not listen to the whispers of your mind or that foul devil.
LISTEN TO THE WORD OF GOD! Let me say it this way:
"LISTEN TO THE WORDS OF YOUR FATHER":
Romans 8:31 NLT What shall we say about such wonderful things as these? If God is for us, who can ever be against us?
Philippians 4:13 NLT For I can do everything through Christ, who gives me strength.
Matthew 17:20 NKJV So Jesus said to them, "Because of your unbelief; for assuredly, I say to you, if you have faith as a mustard seed, you will say to this mountain, 'Move from here to there,' and it will move; and **nothing will be impossible** for you.
Romans 7:21-25 NLT I have discovered this principle of life—that when I want to do what is right, I inevitably do what is wrong. I love God's law with all my heart. But there is another power within me that is at war with my mind. This power makes me a slave to the sin that is still within me. Oh, what a miserable person I am! Who will free me from this life that is dominated by sin and death? **Thank God! The answer is in Jesus Christ our Lord.**

SAY THIS WITH ME:
I CANNOT FAIL!
I AM MORE THAN AN OVERCOMER.
I CAN DO ANYTHING THROUGH CHRIST JESUS.
MIND, COME INTO SUBJECTION.
I REBUKE YOU DEVIL.
I AM GOING ALL THE WAY WITH JESUS!

ROMANS 8:37 No, despite all these things, overwhelming victory is ours through Christ, who loved us.

~Dr Micheal Spencer

December 19

BE AN ENCOURAGER

It is so rare today to have someone in our lives who actually believes in and encourages us. The majority of us are surrounded with people who complain, mumble, grumble, whine, whimper, dig, use daggers...

HOW MANY PEOPLE DO YOU KNOW WHO ARE ENCOURAGERS?
Jesus believed in people that were unrefined and unbridled. He believed in them, even when they were foolish or in sin.
ARE YOU ONE OF THEM?
Proverbs 16:24 NLT Kind words are like honey, sweet to the soul and healthy for the body.
1 Thessalonians 5:11 NLT So encourage each other and build each other up, just as you are already doing.
Hebrews 10:25 NLT And let us not neglect our meeting together, as some people do, but encourage one another, especially now that the day of his return is drawing near.
Hebrews 3:13 NIV But encourage one another daily, as long as it is called "Today," so that none of you may be hardened by sin's deceitfulness.
HERE IS YOUR HOMEWORK
Be an encourager for every person you come in contact with for the next three days.
HOW? Within the first 30 seconds, compliment something about them. Take that second and let them know how you appreciate their character, their clothing or something positive about them.
WATCH their face, it will change!
People just need others to believe in them and speak kind words. Change the atmosphere of your life and those around you today.
BE AN ENCOURAGER!

~Dr Micheal Spencer

December 20

The GREATEST Commandment

LOVE is the greatest commandment of the Kingdom of the King!
Everything that is manifested is generated by LOVE, even judgement.
Salvation came because of LOVE!
Faith even works through LOVE!
We MUST INCREASE IN LOVE!
Insist on walking in the commandment of LOVE.
John 13:34-35 A new commandment I give to you, that you love one another; as I have loved you, that you also love one another. By this all will know that you are My disciples, if you have love for one another."

We have a debt – THE DEBT OF LOVE
We are responsible to love Him.
It's the love of God that shows the world that God is alive, and that comes through us.
Matthew 5:46-48 For if you love those who love you, what reward have you? Do not even the tax collectors do the same? And if you greet your brethren only, what do you do more than others? Do not even the tax collectors do so? Therefore you shall be perfect, just as your Father in heaven is perfect.
You have to walk in love even with the haters.
HOW DID GOD LOVE?
John 3:16 – God gave
Even if I dole out all that I have [to the poor in providing] food, and if I surrender my body to be burned or in order that I may glory , but have not love (God's love in me), I gain nothing. 1 Corinthians 13:3 AMP
There is profit to love.
How do you get perfected in love? PRACTICE

SHOW CHRIST'S LOVE TODAY – throw a life-saver to a person lost in darkness!

~Dr Micheal Spencer

December 21

Is all well? "It is well with my soul" Part I

We are so blessed and daily enjoy the blessings of God. Whether it be having a roof over our head or food to eat, or having it all: cars, houses, dishwasher, washing machine, dryer, toys, entertainment, TVs, DVRs, fast food, designer shoes, handbags, clothes. We are so used to living in the blessings of God that when any trial or mountain comes our way we have become "soft", unable to still say: "whatever my lot, you have taught me to say, it is well with my soul". Whether feast or famine, God is still God and our trust should never waver.

Read this story and learn to say, no matter your circumstances, IT IS WELL WITH MY SOUL..

HYMN HISTORY: "It is Well With My Soul" This hymn was written by a Chicago lawyer, Horatio G. Spafford. You might think to write a worship song titled, 'It is well with my soul', you would indeed have to be a rich, successful Chicago lawyer. But the words, "When sorrows like sea billows roll ... It is well with my soul", were not written during the happiest period of Spafford's life. On the contrary, they came from a man who had suffered almost unimaginable personal tragedy. Horatio G. Spafford and his wife, Anna, were pretty well-known in 1860's Chicago. And this was not just because of Horatio's legal career and business endeavors. The Spaffords were also prominent supporters and close friends of D.L. Moody, the famous preacher. In 1870, however, things started to go wrong. The Spaffords' only son was killed by scarlet fever at the age of four. A year later, it was fire rather than fever that struck. Horatio had invested heavily in real estate on the shores of Lake Michigan. In 1871, every one of these holdings was wiped out by the great Chicago Fire.
This man, a man who knew pain and tragedy, is the author of the great hymn IT IS WELL WITH MY SOUL.
When peace like a river, attendeth my way, When sorrows like sea billows roll; Whatever my lot, Thou hast taught me to say, It is well, it is well with my soul. Though Satan should buffet, though trials should come, Let this blest assurance control, That Christ hath regarded my helpless estate, And hath shed His own blood for my soul! It is well ... with my soul!
It is well, it is well, with my soul.

~Pastor Rhonda Spencer

December 22

Is all well? "It is well with my soul" Part 2

Read the rest of this story and learn to say, no matter your circumstances, IT IS WELL WITH MY SOUL..
Aware of the toll that these disasters had taken on the family, Horatio decided to take his wife and four daughters on a holiday to England. And, not only did they need the rest — D.L. Moody needed the help. He was traveling around Britain on one of his great evangelistic campaigns. Horatio and Anna planned to join Moody in late 1873. And so, the Spaffords traveled to New York in November, from where they were to catch the French steamer 'Ville de Havre' across the Atlantic. Yet just before they set sail, a last-minute business development forced Horatio to delay. Not wanting to ruin the family holiday, Spafford persuaded his family to go as planned. He would follow on later. With this decided, Anna and her four daughters sailed East to Europe while Spafford returned West to Chicago. Just nine days later, Spafford received a telegram from his wife in Wales. It read: "Saved alone." On November 2nd 1873, the 'Ville de Havre' had collided with 'The Lochearn', an English vessel. It sank in only 12 minutes, claiming the lives of 226 people. Anna Spafford had stood bravely on the deck, with her daughters Annie, Maggie, Bessie and Tanetta clinging desperately to her. Her last memory had been of her baby being torn violently from her arms by the force of the waters. Anna was only saved from the fate of her daughters by a plank which floated beneath her unconscious body and propped her up. When the survivors of the wreck had been rescued, Mrs. Spafford's first reaction was one of complete despair. Then she heard a voice speak to her, "You were spared for a purpose." And she immediately recalled the words of a friend, "It's easy to be grateful and good when you have so much, but take care that you are not a fair-weather friend to God." Upon hearing the terrible news, Horatio Spafford boarded the next ship out of New York to join his bereaved wife. Bertha Spafford (the fifth daughter of Horatio and Anna born later) explained that during her father's voyage, the captain of the ship had called him to the bridge. "A careful reckoning has been made", he said, "and
I believe we are now passing the place where the de Havre was wrecked. The water is three miles deep." Horatio then returned to his cabin and penned the lyrics of his great hymn.
IT IS WELL WITH MY SOUL.

~Pastor Rhonda Spencer

December 23

Is all well? "It is well with my soul" Part 3

The words which Spafford wrote that day come from 2 Kings 4:26. They echo the response of the Shunammite woman to the sudden death of her only child. Though we are told "her soul is vexed within her", she still maintains that 'It is well." And Spafford's song reveals a man whose trust in the Lord is as unwavering as hers was.

It would be very difficult for any of us to predict how we would react under circumstances similar to those experienced by the Spaffords or the Shunammite woman, but we do know that the God who sustained them would also be with us.

No matter what circumstances overtake us may we be able to say...

When peace like a river, attendeth my way,
When sorrows like sea billows roll;
Whatever my lot, Thou hast taught me to say,
It is well, it is well with my soul.
Though Satan should buffet, though trials should come,
Let this blest assurance control,
That Christ hath regarded my helpless estate,
And hath shed His own blood for my soul!
It is well ... with my soul!
It is well, it is well, with my soul.

~Pastor Rhonda Spencer

December 24

Up on the Rooftop. CLICK, CLICK, CLICK...

I LOVE THAT SONG! Santa is coming to deliver the presents tonight and he arrives with his sleigh and how many reindeer?
I remember as a small child, when we would be made to go to bed on Christmas Eve, trying to stay awake all night long so I could hear the hooves hit the rooftop.
I never did hear them, but I tried.
Whether you believed in Santa or not, that jolly ole mass of a man was going to sneak into our house and leave some gifts under the tree.
TODAY, Jesus will never try to sneak into your life.
He will never come on the rooftop or down the chimney.

Jesus is standing at your front door!
Revelation 3:20 Behold, I stand at the door and knock. If anyone hears My voice and opens the door, I will come in to him and dine with him, and he with Me. Jesus is at your front door knocking for permission to come in and spend time with you.
Some will open it wide enough to get a business card, others will open it enough to let Him stand at the bottom of the stairs. But how many will let Jesus have rule of their lives?

The presents He comes to bring are eternal!
They are awesomely good, and never bad!

THE KNOCK, KNOCK, KNOCK IS BECKONING, BUT JESUS WILL ONLY COME IN AS FAR AS YOU WILL LET HIM.

~Dr Micheal Spencer

December 25

Merry Jesusmas

As the dawn breaks, the children's hearts leap with excitement to see what is under the tree! As a parent, it is so much fun to watch the children open the gifts that surround the Christmas tree. TODAY, LET'S JUST TAKE A MOMENT WITH OUR FAMILIES AND READ THE CHRISTMAS STORY BEFORE THEY RIP APART THEIR GIFTS. It is found in Luke 2:1-20 And it came to pass in those days that a decree went out from Caesar Augustus that all the world should be registered. This census first took place while Quirinius was governing Syria. So all went to be registered, everyone to his own city. Joseph also went up from Galilee, out of the city of Nazareth, into Judea, to the city of David, which is called Bethlehem, because he was of the house and lineage of David, to be registered with Mary, his betrothed [a]wife, who was with child. So it was, that while they were there, the days were completed for her to be delivered. And she brought forth her firstborn Son, and wrapped Him in swaddling cloths, and laid Him in a manger, because there was no room for them in the inn. Now there were in the same country shepherds living out in the fields, keeping watch over their flock by night. And behold, an angel of the Lord stood before them, and the glory of the Lord shone around them, and they were greatly afraid. Then the angel said to them, "Do not be afraid, for behold, I bring you good tidings of great joy which will be to all people. For there is born to you this day in the city of David a Savior, who is Christ the Lord. And this will be the sign to you: You will find a Babe wrapped in swaddling cloths, lying in a manger."And suddenly there was with the angel a multitude of the heavenly host praising God and saying: "Glory to God in the highest, And on earth peace, goodwill toward men!"So it was, when the angels had gone away from them into heaven, that the shepherds said to one another, "Let us now go to Bethlehem and see this thing that has come to pass, which the Lord has made known to us." And they came with haste and found Mary and Joseph, and the Babe lying in a manger. Now when they had seen Him, they made widely known the saying which was told them concerning this Child. And all those who heard it marveled at those things which were told them by the shepherds. But Mary kept all these things and pondered them in her heart. Then the shepherds returned, glorifying and praising God for all the things that they had heard and seen, as it was told them.

GIVE JESUS GLORY TODAY BY MAKING HIM THE PRIORITY THIS MORNING. ENJOY THE DAY WITH YOUR FAMILY AND SHARE JESUS WITH ONE OF THEM TODAY!

~Dr Micheal Spencer

December 26

Salty Lives Part 1

Matthew 5:13 "You are the salt of the earth; but if the salt loses its flavor, how shall it be seasoned? It is then good for nothing but to be thrown out and trampled underfoot by men.

WHAT IS THE CHEMICAL IMPORTANCE OF SALT?
The two elements of salt — sodium and chloride — each play a variety of crucial roles in our bodies. Sodium enables the transmission of nerve impulses around the body and regulates the electrical charges moving in and out of the cells that control taste, smell and tactile processes. It also helps our muscles, including the heart, to contract.
Chloride is the key for the digestion process. It preserves the acid base balance in the body and absorbs potassium. Chloride also helps blood carry carbon dioxide from respiring tissues to the lungs.
When we have insufficient salt, we get muscular weakness and cramps and our bodies cannot perform all its vital functions.

Without salt we will die!
If the church continues to remain salt-less, the town, county, region, state, nation, and world will die spiritually.

Is your life SALTY?

~Dr Micheal Spencer

December 27

Salty Lives Part 2

Salt has a HUGE IMPACT ON OUR WORLD
We cannot live without salt in our diet.
If you go to the hospital and you get an IV, you are usually getting a salt solution to control your metabolism.
We feed our animals salt, we fertilize our plants with salt.
Salt has been used as money. The Roman soldiers were paid their wages, their salary, in salt.
In fact our word salary comes from "salarium" which means payment in salt. You might have even heard the expression, "they are worth their wages in...salt."
Wars all over the world have even been fought because of salt, won or lost because of salt.
We use salt to flavor our food. It seasons the food. It tastes better...right? What would french fries be without salt?

Salt flavored their religious sacrifices as well.
Romans 12:1 tells us "We are to offer ourselves as living sacrifices, holy and pleasing to God." The operative word is "pleasing". That means flavoring.
We're to bring out the God-flavors, the God-values, the God-beliefs in others and ourselves in all we say and do.
Salt is a preserver.
In ancient times there was no refrigeration. So meat was salted to keep it from rotting, from being "corrupt."
The salt would retard the decaying process.
Salt was used to heal.
As a child I remember a cut on my finger getting infected. Mom got out the Epsom Salt and put the salt in water. Then I soaked the infected finger in the salt water and, voila-I was healed!
We! The Church! We are the SALT!
We bring the FLAVOR of Jesus, we are the PRESERVERS of the planet, we are the ones who bring HEALING to the lost (physical & spiritual)!

ARE YOU SALTY?

~Dr Micheal Spencer

December 28

Salty Lives Part 3

2 Corinthians 4:18, “While we do not look at the things which are seen, but at the things which are not seen. For the things which are seen are temporary, but the things which are not seen are eternal.”
Matthew 5.13 MSG “Let me tell you why you are here. You’re here to be the salt seasoning that brings out the God-flavors of this earth.”
Matthew 5:13 NKJV “You are the salt of the earth; but if the salt loses its flavor, how shall it be seasoned? It is then good for nothing but to be thrown out and trampled underfoot by men.”
WHAT DOES SALT DO?
1). Flavors 2). Preserves 3). Heals
WE ARE THE SALT OF THE EARTH
When Jesus said to them, “You are the salt of the earth,” it was huge. It might not seem like much to us.
Salt might not look like much in a little saltshaker, but it is not just needed for health; it also preserves and flavors.
We are the salt of heaven - WE ARE THE SALTSHAKERS
1) Are we creating health in our region as an individual, and as a church?
2) Are we holding back and preserving this region from Satan?
3) Are we bringing healing in the spirits, souls and bodies?
We are their ONLY HOPE – **YOU ARE THEIR ONLY HOPE!**
Salt cannot lose it abilities!
“Wait a minute-you just said salt doesn’t lose it’s saltiness.”
You’re right. Salt doesn’t change and it never really loses its saltiness. So what was Jesus talking about? The people of that time would easily understand this.
Much of the salt at that time, in that area, was taken from the Salt Sea, or the Dead Sea. When the water of the Dead Sea evaporated it left salt, usually mixed with other minerals.
Clutter of life is like the minerals. The salt gets all covered up and has no use.
Today what is cluttering your live that would keep you from being SALTY?

~Dr Micheal Spencer

December 29

SOMETHING IS GOING TO HAPPEN

When you put seed in the ground, something is going to happen.
Hearing and doing: But be doers of the word, and not hearers only, deceiving yourselves. For if anyone is a hearer of the word and not a doer, he is like a man observing his natural face in a mirror; for he observes himself, goes away, and immediately forgets what kind of man he was.
James 1:22-24
"Oh that was a powerful word!"; if we don't DO it,
IT PRODUCES NOTHING and we forget about it.

Faith produces: Hebrews 11
v2 TESTIMONY, v3 UNDERSTANDING,
v4 LEGACY, v6 PLEASES GOD, v7 ACTION,
v8 OBEDIENCE & COURAGE, v9 STABILITY,
v11 STRENGTH, v12 ABUNDANCE,
v15 DETERMINATION, v20 BLESSINGS, v23 SECURITY,
v 26-27 ENDURANCE, v28 PROTECTION, v29 MIRACLES,
v30 BREAKTHROUGH, v31 FAVOR

If you want Testimony, Understanding, Action, Courage, Stability, Strength, Abundance, Determination, Endurance, Protection, Miracles, Breakthrough, Favor,
If you want to please God,
If you want to leave a legacy,
If you want to activate the power of God in your life,
PRACTICE FAITH! HEAR IT (often and always...more and more) AND DO IT!

FAITH COMES BY HEARING THE WORD OF GOD...And hearing the Word of God is like planting seed in your heart and mind and life. WHEN YOU PLANT SEED SOMETHING IS GOING TO HAPPEN!
Now if there is no action put with your faith, NOTHING HAPPENS. (James 2:17)
COME ON AND LET'S GET TO PLANTING THE WORD IN OUR HEARTS AND WATCH FAITH FLOURISH!

~Pastor Rhonda Spencer

December 30

Finish Strong!!!

2 Timothy 4:7-8, I have fought the good fight, I have finished the race, I have kept the faith.

BE A FINISHER. It is so easy to be a starter...
You see something fun and it stimulates your interest –
so you start it
You meet someone you like and want a relationship –
so you start
You want a new job and see one that looks better –
so you start
You have a goal to accomplish losing 20lbs and you see a new exercise machine on TV that looks easy and promises great results –
so you start
You want to accept Jesus and live for Him –
so you start
You see a good church and want your family to know God –
so you start
You see a ministry or class that you want to join –
so you start

Starting something is EASY, the true test –
ARE YOU A FINISHER?

BETWEEN THE BEGINNING & FINISH LINE...
Anything is easy to START, but what lies between the start and finish line is why so many never cross it.
It is not how you START – it is how you FINISH

FINISH STRONG!!!

~Dr Micheal Spencer

December 31

Not Another Resolution!!!

Oh my goodness! Is it time again? Resolution time...... How many years in a row have you made the same resolution, and you look back and nothing has happened? Started off great! Stopped smoking, went to the gym, went to the in-laws with a smile, went to church, but after a month or so, back to NORMAL.
You really meant it, you really attempted, you really desired, but in the end.......no results! WHY?
The reason is called “desired attempt”! We desired, we attempted, we realized it was a pain in the butt, we stopped! Commitment is a lost art in today’s society. We like commitment as long as it doesn’t inconvenience us, or we get something out of it. If we only lose 2 pounds the first month, well, the gym isn’t working for me. We go to church 4 times, and realize, it’s not always easy getting up on Sunday morning. We commit to TAKE 15 minutes in prayer & the Word, but realize, it’s every morning and inconvenient.
DESIRED ATTEMPTS ALWAYS FAIL!
It must be a determined, decision, without the choice of recession. I will accomplish this. It will get done. Quitting is NOT an option. I will only succeed. PERIOD! Starve the flesh, bring it into subjection, this is my resolve, it will be finished and not just started. You can’t change the past!

Philippians 3:13-14 Brethren, I do not count myself to have apprehended; but one thing I do, forgetting those things which are behind and reaching forward to those things which are ahead, I press toward the goal for the prize of the upward call of God in Christ Jesus.

YOU CAN CHANGE YOUR FUTURE!

~Dr Micheal Spencer